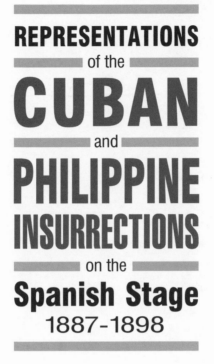

REPRESENTATIONS
of the
CUBAN
and
PHILIPPINE
INSURRECTIONS
on the
Spanish Stage
1887-1898

Bilingual Press/Editorial Bilingüe

General Editor
  Gary D. Keller

Managing Editor
  Karen S. Van Hooft

Associate Editors
  Barbara H. Firoozye
  Thea S. Kuticka

Assistant Editor
  Linda St. George Thurston

Editorial Consultant
  Evelyn Partridge

Address:
  Bilingual Press
  Hispanic Research Center
  Arizona State University
  P.O. Box 872702
  Tempe, Arizona 85287-2702
  (480) 965-3867

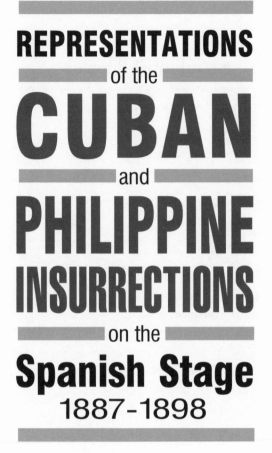

REPRESENTATIONS
of the
CUBAN
and
PHILIPPINE
INSURRECTIONS
on the
Spanish Stage
1887-1898

D. J. O'CONNOR

Bilingual Press/Editorial Bilingüe
TEMPE, ARIZONA

ISBN 0-927534-92-4

Library of Congress Cataloging-in-Publication Data

O'Connor, D. J., 1936-
    Representations of the Cuban and Philippine Insurrections on the Spanish stage, 1887-1898 / D.J. O'Connor.
      p. cm.
    Includes bibliographical references and index.
    ISBN 0-927534-92-4 (alk. paper)
      1. Spanish drama—19th century—History and criticism. 2. Spanish-American War, 1898—Literature and the war. I. Title

PQ6113.O36 2000
862'.509358—dc21   00-037900

PRINTED IN THE UNITED STATES OF AMERICA

Cover and interior design by John Wincek, Aerocraft Charter Art Service

Cover photograph of the Alberto Lezcay monument to Antonio Maceo by Xanthippe Blood-Walker

Acknowledgments

The Bilingual Press gratefully acknowledges the assistance of the Program for Cultural Cooperation Between Spain's Ministry of Culture and United States Universities in making this publication possible.

This book is dedicated to my father,
David E. Walker.

CONTENTS

CHRONOLOGY

Chronology of events in Cuba, Puerto Rico, and the Philippines 1868-1898

PRELIMINARY DATA

Abolishment of the slave trade:

Denmark	1792
England	1807
United States	1808
Sweden	1813
Dutch Empire	1814
Spain	1820
Brazil	1850
End of slave trade to Cuba	1867
(rumored to continue until 1872)	

Abolition of slavery:

Haiti	1793-1794
Argentina	1816
Gran Colombia and Chile	1821
Mexico	1821
Peru, Guatemala, and Uruguay	1828
England	1833
Spain (on the peninsula)	1836
France (colonies)	1848
United States	1863
Dutch Empire	1863
Spain (in Puerto Rico)	1873
(in Cuba)	1886
Brazil	1888

Population:

Cuba in 1899	1,572,797
Puerto Rico in 1899	953,242
Philippines in 1898	7,600,000
Spain in 1900	18,600,000
United States in 1898	76,000,000

CHRONOLOGY

1868 (October)	Cuba: Grito de Yara. Eastern planters rose up against Spain with Carlos Manuel de Céspedes as commander.
1868	Puerto Rico: Grito de Lares led by separatist rebels headed by coffee plantation owners protesting high taxation.
1872	Philippines: Members of the garrison at Cavite mutinied. Execution of the Catholic secular priests, Javier Burgos, Mariano Gómez, and Jacinto Zamora in February.
1873 (22 March)	Puerto Rico: Declaration (by the *cortes*) of the emancipation of slaves.
1878	Cuba: Pact of Zanjón ended the ten-year insurrection. Since the pact did not provide for the liberation of the slaves, Guillermo Moncada, Flor Crombet, and the Maceo brothers refused to sign—the Protest of Baraguá.
1879	Cuba: Guerra chiquita. Defeat in August of the rebels who refused to accept the Pact of Zanjón.
1884	Madrid: Juan Gualberto Gómez conspired with Calixto García in favor of the March 1884 movement headed by Máximo Gómez and Antonio Maceo.
1886 (23 July)	Cuba: "igualdad jurídica de los siervos"—total freedom of slaves.
1892 (6 January)	José Martí founded the Partido Revolucionario Cubano.
1894 (Autumn)	José Martí announced the beginning of Cuban War of Independence.
1895 (24 February)	Cuba: El Grito de Baire; hostilities commenced.
1896 (24 August)	Philippines: El Grito de Balintawak launched the Philippine revolution.

1896 (Spring)	Cánovas rejected la "nota Olney." U.S. intervention now appeared inevitable if Spain did not win in Cuba.
1897 (20 May)	U.S. Senate officially recognized Cuban belligerancy.
(August)	Antonio Cánovas (1828-97), Spanish prime minister, assassinated.
(9 October)	General Weyler relieved of his command in Cuba.
(November)	Moret project: (1) universal suffrage (including blacks) in both Antilles. Universal suffrage meant that men twenty-five years and over who were in full possession of their civil rights and had been resident in a municipality for at least two years could vote; (2) same rights for colonies and metropolis; (3) future autonomous government would have the right to sign treaties and decide on tariffs (no more closed markets).
1898 (19 January)	Filipino leader, Emilio Aguinaldo, signed the Peace of Biac-Na-Bató.
(15 February)	Cuba: The battleship *Maine* exploded in Havana Harbor.
(25 April)	United States declared war against Spain.
(1 May)	Philippines: United States sank the Spanish fleet in Manila Bay (Guam and Wake Island taken next).
(31 May)	The Philippine Revolution resumed.
(12 June)	Filipinos declared their independence.
(3 July)	Cuba: United States sank the Spanish fleet in Santiago Bay.
(7 July)	United States annexed Hawaii.
(17 July)	Cuba: Surrender of Santiago.

(25 July)   Puerto Rico: General Nelson Miles, Indian
                   Wars veteran, landed with his soldiers on
                   Guánica Beach.

(12 August)   Preliminary peace treaty signed. Spain recog-
                   nized loss of Cuba and Puerto Rico.

(14 August)   Manila surrendered.

(10 December)   Treaty of Paris. Spain recognized loss of
                   Philippines also, and accepted $20,000,000
                   indemnification from the United States.

                   Spain collected 25 million marks from Germany
                   for the Carolinas, the Marianas (except for
                   Guam) and the Palaos.

WAR-RELATED LOSSES

Spanish losses in Cuba: Of the 200,000 men sent to the colony, 786 died in battle, 8,627 died of wounds, 13,313 died of yellow fever, 40,127 died of other diseases. Total: 62,853.

Spanish losses in the Philippines: Definitive casualty figures for the 30,000 Spanish troops in the Philippines are not known. According to *El Imparcial* (4 February 1897) there were 255 by February 1897.

Cuban losses: 300,000 (lost in action or as the result of the concentration policy).

Filipino losses during the insurrection against Spain are not known. According to *El Imparcial* (4 February 1897), there were 8,210 by February 1897.

Filipino losses during the Philippine-American War: 16,000-20,000 dead in battle; 250,000 civilian deaths from war-related causes and from disease.

U.S. losses in Cuba: 268 men were killed and wounded in the field and 3,752 died of disease.

U.S. losses in the Philippines: Of the 126,468 soldiers sent, 4,234 were killed and 2,818 wounded.

INTRODUCTION

A serious threat to the integrity of the motherland and its remaining colonies arose when the first insurgent movement in Cuba began in 1868. The Philippines contributed to that threat soon after with a short-lived revolt in Cavite in 1872. The second period of insurgency from 1895 to 1898 furnished an abundance of written material on the rebellious colonies for Spaniards to mull over in the form of pamphlets, newspaper reports, and magazine articles, along with stories and vignettes published in the press. An additional source of information, attitudes, and interpretations on the Cuban and Philippine insurrections is provided by the sixteen plays examined here. Inspired by immediate events and intended as appeals to patriotism, they did not, with few exceptions, go through second editions. As a result, they are largely forgotten, and not readily located. These plays, nonetheless, supplemented by the contemporary press and other written popular literature, broaden our knowledge of what was communicated to the general public about the wars as well as how it was meant to shape public opinion.[1]

I cannot claim that the plays I discuss here constitute an exhaustive list of all the plays that dealt with the Cuban and Philippine insurrections in the late 1880s and early 1890s. The titles of some of them appeared in theater schedules published in the contemporary press. Others I found through reviews or references in memoirs. All of them may be found in one or another of the collections of Spanish theater housed in several libraries in this country. While some plays have doubtless escaped my net, I believe that those presented here attest to the range of ideas represented on stage as grist for the public discourse on the insurrections. The present study adopts the cultural studies framework according to which popular culture is a contested area where different ideologies compete to influence public opinion and organize public consciousness.[2] Consequently, I have emphasized the choice of the issues represented in the plays and the ideologies that inform and shape them. The recurring themes of race, conscription, women's role in war, the meaning of patriotism, and the call for national unity embodied issues that those in power during the last decade of the nineteenth century sought to control.

Any discussion of popular culture in *fin-de-siglo* Spain must take into account the low rate of literacy (35 percent). This circumstance made it a special case in the European context of the time. The middle range of European national literacy levels in 1900 was about 77 percent, with France at 80 percent. Only Portugal in the rest of western Europe had a lower literacy rate than Spain.[3] There was no lack of institutions and individuals launching ideas and programs in the area of popular culture in the hope that they would influence and direct public opinion. But what did popular culture encompass and how extensive was it? The contemporary discussion of public opinion and consciousness included in this study indicates a high level of frustration on the part of would-be opinion makers who did not believe that they were connecting significantly with the public. How could ideas communicated largely through print (newspapers, pamphlets, popular fiction, i.e., fiction published, for the most part, in the high-circulation press) have "meaningful impact" on a population with a rate of illiteracy as high as Spain's? And, considering the question from a different angle, how could meaningful impact be assessed when prior restraint or police repression occasioned by the colonial crisis blocked public responses that might have led to the expression of dissenting views?

Traditionally, the theater has been important as a conduit for ideologies and propaganda because it does not require a literate audience. In effect, the theater was a vibrant part of popular culture; its importance as a place where competing ideas might be aired was not lost on potential molders of opinion during the period from 1895 to 1898. In the 1890s it also served as a sensitive—if frustratingly unspecific—gauge of what could be said or represented in public: officials (civil governors typically) who disapproved of dramatic texts for ideological reasons did not have to file detailed charges since productions could be closed down simply on the grounds that they might lead to public disorder.

In view of the relatively limited number of plays examined here, and in order to contextualize them more effectively, the discussion of issues raised in the theater has been expanded to include material on those same or related issues that appeared in the press and in other forms of expression most likely to have reached the general public. In order to attenuate the illiteracy factor, this study also takes into account visual representations, such as graphics and paintings reproduced in newspapers and magazines, which were related to the principal issues. For the same reason, it reviews attitudes and sentiments occasioned by the well-attended Philippine Exposition in Madrid (1887) and in Barcelona (1888), and the Exposition of Ashante in Madrid (1897). Although there were relatively few popular demonstrations connected to the insurrections, the most important among them have been registered and their representation in the press noted. The activities and propaganda of the Spanish church with regard to the colonial wars also contributed to the formation of popular culture; this, however, requires a separate study, and only occasional references to the church's role are included here.

In a review essay entitled "The Evolution of Social History," Steven C. Hause quotes historian Mary Louise Roberts who argues that our study of the past is directly linked to our understanding of how people in the past viewed their society. Roberts wrote, "My purpose . . . has been to destabilize the notion that 'lived' or empirical reality can be studied apart from how people choose to imagine it."[4] The present study sets out to show primarily how certain issues were represented so as to shape the public's views. While it suggests how Spaniards may have come to choose the ways in which they would imagine the insurrections and their implications for Spanish society, it does not pretend to determine in any definitive way how those choices were made. Nonetheless, by laying out a broad and representative array of material (the words and images to which ordinary Spaniards were exposed) along with a discussion of how that material was packaged, it aims to understand how limits for the choices were set.

• • •

I wish to thank members of the staff at the Hemeroteca Municipal in Madrid, especially Inmaculada Zaragoza of the División de Información, for their help. Dr. Everette E. Larson, head of the reference section of the Hispanic Division at the Library of Congress, generously alerted me to the whereabouts in the United States of several of the plays discussed here. I deeply appreciate the efforts of interlibrary loan librarian Gayle Barclay of the University of New Orleans in locating material for this project. Dennis M. O'Leary at the Philippine Center in New York has taken an interest in my work and has sent me much useful material from the contemporary Manila press. Above all, I am grateful to him for personally introducing me to the works of José Rizal. I am most indebted to Fred Balinong, S. J., who has encouraged me from the outset, kindly providing me on many occasions with journals, articles, and books related to the part of this study that deals with the Philippines. Finally, John T. O'Connor read and criticized the manuscript. The book would not have been written without his expert advice and loyal support.

Notes

[1] The plays are:

Cuba libre by Federico Jaques y Aguado, with music by Manuel Fernández Caballero. First performed at the Teatro de Apolo in Madrid on 11 November 1887.

¡A Cuba y viva España! by Rufino Cortés. First performed in Sevilla in 1895.

Familia y patria by Isidoro Martínez Sanz. First performed at the Teatro de Novedades in Madrid on 7 March 1896.

España en Cuba by Ricardo Caballero y Martínez. First performed at the Teatro Principal in La Coruña on 18 April 1896.

Cuba by Jesús López Gómez and with music by Luis Reig. First performed at the Circo de Parish in Madrid on 11 December 1896.

¡Sacrificios heroicos! by Manuel Núñez de Matute. First performed at the Salón Zorrilla in Madrid on 22 January 1897.

Los dramas de la guerra by Vicente Moreno de la Tejera. First performed at the Teatro Martín in Madrid on 14 February 1897.

Filipinas por España by J.M. Valls. Performed at the Teatro Circo Barcelonés on 6 June 1897.

Muerte de Maceo by M. Dolcet. No performance information available. Published in Barcelona: Tipografía de F. Badía, 1897.

Marta y María o la muerte de Maceo by three anonymous authors. performed in the Teatro de Novedades in Barcelona on 30 December 1897.

Un alcalde en la manigua by Pascual Martínez Moreno. Performed at the Circo de Cartagena in Cartagena on 1 January 1898.

El padre Juanico by Angel Guimerá. First performed in Madrid on 18 March 1898.

Aún hay patria, Veremundo by Eduardo Navarro Gonzalvo and with music by Caballero y Hermoso. First performed at the Teatro de la Zarzuela on 10 May 1898.

El mantón de Manila. Text by Fiacro Yrayzoz and music by Chueca. First performed at the Teatro de Apolo on 11 May 1898.

Gigantes y cabezudos. Text by Miguel Echegaray and music by M. F. Caballero. First performed at the Teatro de la Zarzuela on 29 November 1898.

¡Quince bajas! by Pascual Millán. First performed at the Nuevo Teatro in Madrid on 2 December 1898.

See José-Carlos Mainer, "1998 [sic] en la literatura: las huellas españolas del *desastre*," *Casa de las Américas* 211 (April-June 1998): 46-55. Mainer usefully reviews some examples of literature that do not fall into the category of popular literature and are not, for that reason, discussed here.

[2]For a discussion of the problems involved in identifying, defining, and delimiting popular culture, see Bob Scribner, "Is a History of Popular Culture Possible?" *History of European Ideas* 10 (1989): 175-91. In regard to the theater, Scribner notes that formerly this "cultural product" was thought to provide direct access to the "popular," whereas now we are inclined to believe that it tells us more about its producers than its consumers (p. 176). My study emphasizes the role of the producers, drawing attention to consumers whenever they made their presence known.

[3]See Harvey J. Graff, *The Legacies of Literacy. Continuities and Contradictions in Western Culture and Society* (Bloomington: Indiana University Press, 1987), 294.

[4]See *French Historical Studies* 19 (1996): 1208.

PART I

THE TOPICAL THEATER AND PROPAGANDA IN SPAIN

Throughout the nineteenth century the theater fed on newsworthy events. Whenever extraordinary actions and personalities emerged out of a host of contemporary conflicts and happenings and suggested narratives adaptable to the stage, the theater—like the press—rushed to satisfy the public's curiosity. Thus, in mid-nineteenth-century America when abolitionists focused public attention on the plight of the people aboard the *Amistad*, a slave ship commandeered in Cuba by its African captives, a play about the incident, *The Black Schooner, or the Pirate Slaver Amistad*, appeared at New York's Bowery Theater within a week of the ship's capture off the shore of Long Island. Its timely debut gratified audiences eager for a dramatic interpretation of the ship's mysterious appearance and significance. *The Black Schooner* gratified its impresario as well: the play netted $1,650 in its opening week.[1]

During the last half of the 1890s, the news in Spain was dominated by events connected to the insurgent movements in both the Antilles and the Philippines. The second Cuban insurrection, launched in 1895, and the renewed rebellion in the Philippines, initiated in 1896 by the secret society known as the Katipunan (a Tagalog word translated as "the highest and most respected association of sons of the fatherland"), quickened the Spanish public's interest in the motives behind the desire for independence, the nature of the insurgents, the obligations of patriotism, and the meaning of nationalism for Spaniards in the metropolis as well as for Spanish subjects in the Caribbean and Pacific colonies. As the wars dragged on, Spaniards also became increasingly aware of how the struggle to retain the colonies was affecting political, economic, and social conditions in the Peninsula.

A number of plays whose subject matter was based on current events in Cuba and the Philippines were produced in theaters in Madrid, Barcelona, La Coruña, Seville, Cartagena, and elsewhere in

1

the Peninsula between 1887 and 1898. They dramatized a spectrum of issues including methods of recruitment, the conflict between duty to the family and the demands of patriotism, race, nationalism, and the role of women in wartime—topics also discussed in the press, in pamphlets and books, in public lectures, and at private gatherings *(tertulias)*.[2]

Occasionally, a historical personage appeared as protagonist. The death of the insurgent Cuban mulatto general Antonio Maceo inspired several plays in the Iberian peninsula. Two plays with Maceo as protagonist were written in Spain within weeks of his death in December 1896, though they were not performed in public until early 1898. As for Portugal, the Madrid daily *El Imparcial* notified its readers on 15 March 1897 that performances of *Maceo o el guerrillero cubano* were prohibited in Lisbon.[3]

This study examines how Spanish dramatists interpreted historical participants in the colonial insurrections—a man such as Antonio Maceo, for example, who came to symbolize the treacherous nature of the mulatto—as well as how they represented war-related issues in productions nearly all of which were aimed at a broadly varied public. Since the focus here is on works that were seen by relatively large numbers of people, it does not include the anarchist or the workers' theater. The anarchist movement in Spain did foster public performances of plays whose influence was, however, generally confined to small, local venues and to a largely anarchist readership when such material was later published in cheap editions.[4]

The *Género Chico* as a Vehicle for Propaganda in Spain and the Colonies

Well over half the plays discussed here belong to the *género chico*, defined most commonly as one-act theatrical pieces, with or without music. Historians of the genre usually include, as well, zarzuelas of one and two acts that combine words and music.[5] In contrast to the "serious theater"—plays of more than one act whose weighty themes, frequently decked out in equally ponderous language, were directed to an educated middle- and upper-class audience—the *género chico* typically featured ordinary people and drew its audiences from all classes. The often excellent musical scores of the zarzuelas as well as the "plebeianization" of Spanish culture—a consequence of the upper classes' taste for the dress, language, and amusements of the lower classes, evident since the eighteenth century—help to account for the great appeal this genre held for elite as well as popular audiences.[6]

In times of national crisis popular theatrical genres normally serve as a vehicle for political propaganda. Contemporary Spanish journalist and cultural critic Eduardo Haro Tecglen has reminded audiences and listeners, accustomed to hearing musical excerpts from zarzuelas but not complete texts, that at the time of its greatest popular success (the end of the nineteenth century through the 1920s) the zarzuela constituted an expression of "racial and regional identity" ("una expresión racial y regional"). That aspect of the zarzuela, Haro Tecglen argues, makes it attractive to modern nationalists, nostalgic for a past in which Spain was clearly demarcated from the rest of Europe.[7] The zarzuela's foregrounding of race and region also made it particularly well suited in the 1890s for expressing the sense of racial superiority that supposedly justified dominance over people of color in the colonies and for voicing patriotic, pro-unitary (as opposed to federalist or regional nationalist) government sentiment during the insurrections. Robust expressions of regional affiliation to the central government helped lend credence to the notion that the offshore provinces could similarly retain their identities and at the same time contribute to Spanish national unity.[8]

Theatrical performances in times of crisis as in periods of repression may serve to rally the troops, but they also provide a means—and may also provide a pretext—for the audience to express dissident political opinion. Emilio Gutiérrez Gamero, writing in the early twentieth century, recalled an incident that took place years earlier and involved an opera performance. The incident occurred during the period of Ramón María de Narváez's and Luis González Brabo's mandates (1866-1868) when it was a crime to be a liberal. Police spies were ubiquitous, and deportation to the Philippines was one of several possible and fearful consequences of speaking out against the regime. When the government discovered that as a protest against repression, audiences were fervently applauding a passage lauding fatherland *and* freedom in Bellini's *I Puritani*, it

immediately sent a message to the impresario ordering him to can-
cel all future performances.⁹

During the last quarter of the nineteenth century, Spanish
zarzuelas were performed in the Philippines and in Cuba. But
whereas this genre prospered in both colonies, the viability of the
theater in Cuba was taken for granted while Spanish commentators
who described the theater in the archipelago did not consider its
prospects promising. For example, a short review, representative of
the scorn felt by many Spanish writers for nearly all manifestations
of Filipino life and culture, appeared on 22 November 1892, in the
pro-colonialist journal, *La política de España en Filipinas*.¹⁰ Its author,
Marinduque (a pen name), commented on a zarzuela that had just
appeared in Manila based on Filipino customs and featuring Filipino
performers. Marinduque first informed his Spanish readers that the
theater in Manila was in a sorry state due to a lack of good com-
posers and writers, not to mention appropriate buildings for
performances. Moreover, he claimed that it was not possible to put
on plays that presented Peninsular customs since the indigenous
people could not understand or appreciate them, impervious as they
were to passions they simply did not experience themselves. Nor
could Europeans or *peninsulares* enjoy or value works based on
indigenous customs, which were so inferior to their own. Watching
native productions about natives, he wrote, was equivalent to reading a book of natural history. A dramatist might include references
to indigenous customs in his work in order to provide an element of
contrast, but they should never serve as a basis for the plot.
Marinduque then referred briefly to the zarzuela in question,
observing that it offered little interest to readers indifferent to the
troubles of some Chinaman or other, the potential of various fighting cocks, and the duties of the native bureaucrats.

Antón Chápuli Navarro wrote in the same vein on Filipino inca-
pacity for developing a theater in the European tradition. He
claimed that the traditional *moro-moro* (plays about muslims, introduced to the *indios* by the Spanish missionaries) was all that the
Filipino wanted or was capable of appreciating.¹¹ Vicente Barrantes,
a writer whose work on the indigenous Tagalog theater served main-
ly to discredit it, began publishing material on the subject in *La
Ilustración artística* (Barcelona), then in the *Revista contemporánea*, and

finally, in book form in *El teatro tagalo*.[12] In these works, Barrantes, who had held a high position in the colonial government in Manila, voiced opinions unfavorable to Filipinos and Filipino culture. The Filipino patriot, José Rizal, among others—Filipinos and non-Filipinos alike—publicly contested Barrantes's views. On 15 June 1889, for example, José Rizal wrote a response to Barrantes's study in the newspaper put out by Filipinos and first published in Barcelona, *La Solidaridad*.

In fact, during the 1890s there was Spanish theater, Chinese opera, and Tagalog theater in Manila. In 1883 José Montero y Vidal mentioned the well-known theater located in the Tondo neighborhood of Manila. He wrote that it had become famous for its sui generis productions performed by natives in Tagalog.[13] Montero y Vidal also described the Teatro Español in the neighborhood of Arroceros. Good-sized and tastefully decorated, he wrote, it was a frequently used venue for traveling Italian opera troupes.[14]

In the Philippines the zarzuela developed into the *sarswela*, a form that retained the genre's music and dance, introduced familiar local types, and typically reflected social issues important to Filipinos. After the struggle (between 1898 and 1901) to establish a Philippine republic ended in defeat, authors of *sarswelas* sought to bolster nationalist sentiment through their plays. Eventually, the *sarswelas'* pointed criticism of the American occupation—rendered the more significant because of the genre's great popularity—led the Americans not only to ban them, but also to jail two of their best-known authors.[15] In Cuba, *peninsulares* loyally patronized the Albisu, the so-called temple of the Spanish zarzuela, up to and after the moment of their bitter defeat. Meanwhile, despite censorship and attempts at prohibition, the native *teatro bufo*—a genre that like the zarzuela combined music and words—and the short plays in prose typical of the *género chico*, entertained audiences and, at the same time, assumed a political role by affirming the distinct nature of Cuban culture and, more directly, by advocating the reformist ideology of Cuban autonomists.[16] The highly charged politics that informed the theater scene in Cuba will be discussed further in connection with the play *Cuba libre*.

The *género chico*—whether performed in Spain or in the colonies—was primarily a source of entertainment, but it was also a

potential vehicle for both political and social propaganda. The resul-
tant mix of entertainment (which guaranteed a large and varied
audience) and propaganda makes the plays discussed here significant
sources of information about how issues connected to the two insurrections were represented to Spanish audiences.

Public and Private Theatrical Performances

Although all but one, and possibly two, of the plays examined here
were first performed in public theaters, private domestic performances were not uncommon in the 1880s and 1890s. In the late
1880s, a critic for *Madrid Cómico* (10 September 1887, 3) noted the
numerous performances of "plays in private homes and not only in
the mansions of aristocrats but also in the dwellings of the humblest
of tax collectors" ("comedias caseras, y, no sólo en los palacios aris-
tocráticos, sino en los domicilios de los más modestos recaudadores
de contribuciones"). Referring to his experiences of some twenty
years earlier, José Ferrer de Couto, the Spanish author of an influential study on Africans in their homeland and in the New World
published in 1864, testified in his book to the impact that plays performed in private homes might have on a wider public. He recalled
"a certain play entitled *The Negro of Sensibility* that was very successful, above all in home performances, and that gave me also the first
negative notions concerning the material at hand" ("cierta comedia
titulada *El Negro sensible*, que tuvo gran éxito sobre todo en los
teatros caseros, y que me dio también a mí las primeras nociones
negativas de la materia que ahora trato").[17]

When *Marta y María o la muerte de Maceo* premiered in
Barcelona in January 1898, its three anonymous authors claimed that
the success of private performances in the course of the previous year
had prompted them to present it in public. M. Dolcet's sixteen-page
monologue *Muerte de Maceo* was published in Barcelona in
December 1897 with no indication on the title page—as was cus-
tomary—of the theater in which it had premiered. It is plausible,
though not certain, that it was performed in private. Some years later
(in 1926) Pío Baroja, whose ideas about theater audiences and the
demands they made on dramatists were formed in the 1890s, set up
a theater in the dining room of his Madrid home. José Monleón

describes this venture in his study of the Spanish theater at the turn of the century: "The undertaking was modest and destined to develop in a circle limited for all practical purposes to the family . . . There, don Pío, surrounded by his people, far from the 'ferocious beast,' [the public] must have reflected more than once on how lovely it would be to write and produce plays for a curious, open, and sympathetic audience" ("La empresa era modesta y destinada a vivir en un círculo de carácter prácticamente familiar . . . Allí, don Pío, rodeado de los suyos, lejos de la 'bestia feroz,' [the public] debió pensar más de una vez en lo hermoso que sería escribir y hacer teatro para un público curioso, abierto y con buena uva.").[18] Private performances may well have ensured a sympathetic reception. Whether public or private, topical dramatic productions in nineteenth-century Spain contributed ideas and attitudes to popular culture, difficult as it may be to measure their impact on audiences.

The Theater and Public Opinion

In his 1987 study, *Le Tour du Peuple*, Carlos Serrano alludes to the part the theater played in reflecting divisive social issues during the 1890s. He singles out Ángel Guimerá's *El Padre Juanico* (1898) as one of the first representations on stage of negative attitudes toward a military recruitment policy that permitted the purchase of substitutes and had earlier rewarded those who denounced potential and actual deserters with exemption from service. Serrano recommended study of the theater for further evidence of commentary on the military, especially of dissident views regarding recruitment.[19] In 1997, Sebastian Balfour referred to the theater's part in reflecting views on the insurrections that were at odds with official propaganda. Balfour cited *Gigantes y cabezudos*, the popular zarzuela that premiered in November 1898, as one of the first to suggest— through a letter read aloud from a soldier—how greatly ordinary soldiers suffered in Cuba.[20]

The play's depiction of the chorus of returning soldiers lifting their voices in patriotic homage to Zaragoza when they get their first look at the city from across the Ebro river should also be mentioned in this connection. While the chorus drew enthusiastic applause from the zarzuela's first viewers, these healthy, stalwart men stood, nonetheless, in vivid contrast to the spectacle of ill and maimed soldiers who had begun to arrive in large numbers at several Spanish ports during the previous two months. Although the stage directions specify that the men should all be dressed in Aragonese attire with some article of clothing—such as a soldier's cap—to indicate that they had been soldiers, real-life repatriates were readily identified as such: they typically returned in rags, as poorly clothed as they were fed and cared for.[21] Many members of the audience no doubt registered the painful contrast.

Although both Serrano and Balfour refer to the theater's significance as an occasional reflector of dissident, unorthodox opinion, modern literary historians stress the fact that political, economic, and social realities in the *fin de siglo* determined the theater's role as reflector primarily of middle-class concerns and interests—a role that presumably left little room for dissenting voices.[22] The plays examined here generally bear out the assumption that when politically and socially sensitive issues arose they were handled so as to accord with official propaganda and the class interests of those who supported it. José Monleón, author of the above-mentioned work on the turn-of-the-century theater, notes the divergence between contemporary political reality and its public image on stage without, however, referring to any of the plays on the colonial insurrections discussed in this study.[23] He does stress the need felt by impresarios to please their middle-class audiences: "The theater existed in order to pacify a middle class that increasingly lacked economic resources and was increasingly in need of some compensation for its being out of synchrony with history" ("El teatro existía para tranquilizar a la clase media, cada vez con menos recursos económicos, cada vez más necesitada de una compensación a su asincronía histórica.") These plays unquestionably provide more examples of ideological conformity and indoctrination than of dissident views—a circumstance that makes such views the more arresting when they do emerge.

A modern student of the *género chico*, Nancy J. Membrez, has drawn attention to one of the political satirists of the *fin de siglo* theater and author of a play reviewed here, who frequently did express dissident views. Active in the theater from the 1870s to 1902, Eduardo Navarro Gonzalvo in 1870 authored an early play opposing conscription: *¡Abajo las quintas!* The provisional government that assumed power in 1868 did not fulfill its promise to abolish *la quinta*, a conscription system that all but exempted those well-off from military service.[24] Draft riots resulted and were taking place in 1870 when Navarro Gonzalvo wrote his anti-*quinta* play. Membrez wrote of this playwright: "The Spanish government, particularly the Cánovas administrations, feared him and often prohibited his plays. Political allegory, in which Navarro excelled, was a tactic to persuade and educate the masses to the election fraud of the *turno pacífico* [the artificial alternation in power, starting in 1875, of the two parties, the Liberals and the Liberal-Conservatives]. Navarrito was no Calderón, nor did he claim to be, yet his *revistas políticas* molded the opinions of a generation of Spaniards and his name, however fleetingly, became a household word."[25]

Membrez's claim that Navarro's *revistas políticas* molded the opinions of a generation of Spaniards raises several questions. How were the public and public opinion defined at the time? Was there any discussion or awareness of strategies for "molding" opinion? How can we know—apart from the occasional remarks of letter writers, memoirists, and the like—that dissident voices in the theater were heeded by the mixed, but largely middle-class, audiences who heard them?

Public Opinion, the Theater, the Press, and the Elite

COLUMBUS STONED

A Seville paper has just published
a report from Granada from which we have
taken the following curious news item:

'The night before last at seven-thirty
several women, the mothers of as many
soldiers killed in the Cuban campaign,
took out their anger on the statue
of Christopher Columbus by pelting it
with a barrage of rocks.
Asked by some passers-by why they
were stoning it, they answered by
pointing to the statue and saying:

—Why else except that this **meddling
scoundrel** is the primary cause of our
misfortunes. If he hadn't discovered
those **mulatto dogs**, our sons wouldn't
have gone off to war.

And, momentarily suppressing their
bellicose fury, they all shouted:
—May the Lord **grant** that all those people
who are responsible for our misfortunes
come down with a **fever** hot enough
to **roast** corn from three leagues away!'

COLÓN APEDREADO[26]

Un periódico sevillano publica una
correspondencia de Granada de la que
entresacamos la siguiente curiosa noticia:
'Anteanoche, a las siete y media,
varias mujeres, madres de otros tantos
soldados muertos en la campaña de Cuba,
desahogaron sus iras contra la estatua
de Cristóbal Colón, haciéndole algunas
descargas a pedrada limpia.

Preguntadas por algunas personas que
a la sazón pasaban por aquel sitio por
qué la tiraban, contestaron señalando a
la estatua y diciendo:
—¿Por qué ha de ser, sino porque este
camastrón pata gorda, es el primer
causante de nuestras desdichas? Si no
hubiera descubierto a los **perros
mulatitos,** no hubieran ido nuestros
hijos a la guerra.

Y reprimiendo por un momento sus
furores bélicos, exclamaron todas a un tiempo:
—¡El Señor **premita** que a los
culpables todos de nuestras desgracias,
les dé una **calentura** que con su calor se
puedan **asar** panochas a tres leguas a la redonda!'

El Imparcial, 14 December1898

The phrase "public opinion" appears frequently in the 1890s, but there was not much discussion as to what it meant. It was not clearly defined by those who used the term in press articles and essays. The formation of public opinion was rarely discussed at the time in relation to Spain's 65 percent illiteracy rate, perhaps because awareness of the fact that two out of three Spaniards could not read or write was taken for granted by most commentators on the contemporary state of the Spanish public.[27] When an event occurred that seemed to constitute a genuine expression of public opinion, the question of how it was mediated or represented in the press seldom arose. Despite a frustrating vagueness in most discussions of these matters, the following brief survey of the views of several mainstream figures—men whose ideas and opinions appeared in the high-circulation press and who were perceived as neither far to the left nor to the right—does reveal considerable agreement on the nature of the public and the role of elite groups in forming opinion.

For the most part, those who made pronouncements on the public in the 1890s thought of it as a mass of anonymous individuals who made their existence known in three principal ways. Individuals emerged from the masses by attending or participating in public events such as theater performances, bullfights, expositions, and so on. They also revealed their presence by buying newspapers and, occasionally, by writing letters (or perhaps having them written) to the editors of those papers. The rejection of specific charges, such as compulsory military service, or of circumstances directly affecting individual and familial well-being, such as extreme poverty, might also cast a light on previously invisible members of the masses. Knowledge of how many men had evaded conscription by fleeing the country, or how many men had bought exemption from military service, for example, or awareness of widespread food riots, brought to light the existence of individuals making choices that had a public impact. Some members of the faceless mass formerly characterized by passive conformity were, at the very least, counted.

The contemporary commentators discussed here often implicitly linked the words *public* and *pueblo* (people). Anonymous members of the "public" and anonymous members of the "people" were frequently conflated to the extent that both were conceptualized as largely uneducated and nonprofessional. As a consequence of their lack of professional preparation, they were without a voice. Members of the professional classes and those who were economically or socially privileged, on the other hand, might make use of the voice accorded them by their position so as to make themselves heard. When they spoke or wrote, they were not thought of as individuals emerging from the public. They were separate from it by virtue of their place in the social, political, and economic hierarchy. An individual placed high enough in the hierarchy might be "in the public" temporarily without being part of it. A fishmonger who went to a bullfight was a member of the masses, the public, but a prominent member of the *cortes* (parliament) who attended bullfights was an *aficionado* (fan). Thus the terms *public* and *pueblo* were often for all practical purposes interchangeable, their shared meaning determined largely by class considerations

• • •

Zeda (pseudonym of Francisco F. Villegas), a literary critic whose comments appeared frequently in the press and in journals during the 1890s, wrote an essay, "From the Footlights" ("Desde la batería"), for *El Imparcial* on 27 December 1897, in which he offered a definition of the theater-going public that implicitly affirmed its political significance to molders of opinion. Zeda began by drawing an important distinction between the individual and the theater audience, "that formidable gathering that depending on circumstances is termed audience, mob, masses, public" ("ese conjunto formidable que según los casos se llama auditorio, turba, masa, público"). Zeda believed that the particular public that made up the theater audience expressed itself less hypocritically than people taken singly. He went on to argue that because of its collective transparency the nature of audiences could be studied and described. This, in turn, made it possible to pose and answer questions of interest to government officials: How did audiences understand patriotism, honor, and justice? What were their instincts and preoccupations? Up to what point were the laws of the [Spanish] race fulfilled in them, and which traits bequeathed by their historical character did they preserve? The study of theater audiences, he concluded, would be useful in mapping the national psychology.

For Zeda, transparency was one of the Spanish audience's principal characteristics; mediocrity was the other—mediocrity in the sense
that the level of the Spanish audience's sensitivity and intelligence lay
midway between that of its best and worst members. Modern ideas
and a modern esthetic had not penetrated that shield of mediocrity,
yet Spaniards would not be able to appreciate modern theater or participate in modern life unless it was lifted. How was that to be
accomplished? The tastes and mentality of the public could only be
changed through the vigorous efforts of genius. Zeda approvingly
quoted Friedrich von Schiller's advice to playwrights that they should
give contemporaries what they needed, not what they praised.
Presumably, Zeda believed that audiences would prove receptive and
that mentality, taste, and, no doubt, opinion (stands on issues) would
ultimately be transformed and molded by dramatists' bold and repeated use of innovative techniques and material. Study of the theater
audience's fortunately transparent collective character would help to
guide their efforts. Something resembling national regeneration was
the ultimate goal: the study of theater audiences—a group that Zeda
conflated with the general public—would enable playwrights to
develop strategies for change transcending the theater itself.

Commentators on cultural matters in the 1890s often referred
to theater audiences along with readers of high-circulation newspapers as constitutive of the public—an identification of the public
primarily as a receptor at a time when, aside from the church, the
theater and the press were the two principal conduits for conveying
information, ideas, attitudes, and values to Spaniards.[28] Like Zeda,
most critics claimed that this was a public whose political, social, and
artistic consciousness was unquestionably in need of direction and
control by the more qualified. When the public was not only identified as deficient but was also considered to be the instigator—not
just the recipient—of ideas, attitudes, and values purveyed by the
press, it was often blamed for the press's perceived deficiencies (its
submission to the depraved tastes of the masses by running lurid
crime stories) and for those of the theater (its persistent *efectismo*, its
encouragement of an unexigent audience's preference for light
entertainment with an abundance of musical numbers).[29]

The prevailing conventions regarding theatrical performances
and the fare on offer clearly contributed to whatever preference for

light entertainment may have existed. In 1897 seven of Madrid's twelve theaters offered hourly shows, that is, the price of admission entitled the viewer to an hour's worth of whatever might be onstage: an act taken from a zarzuela, a one-act play, or perhaps a single act of a longer play. A contemporary theater critic remarked that the popularity of this format (the *teatro por horas*) had proven to be as contagious as smallpox.[30]

Leopoldo Alas (pseudonym, Clarín), a powerful arbiter of taste in the 1890s and a critic of Spanish culture whose pronouncements were in the liberal republican tradition, had suggested a decade earlier that the public might be less responsible for the sorry state of affairs (i.e., the demand for frivolous fare on stage) than most people supposed. In his short story, *Avecilla*, Alas portrayed a petit bourgeois family's quest for entertaining uplift through a night at the theater. The affordable amusements available to the family were limited to the carnival-like shows set up near the Retiro Park as part of a trade fair organized by the Madrid municipal government and a zarzuela at the Eslava *(teatro por horas)*. The freak show that the family first attended featured a fat lady in partial undress, while the zarzuela bombarded them with off-color jokes and further glimpses of women's legs. Father, mother, and adolescent daughter returned home profoundly demoralized and unsettled, having exposed themselves unwittingly to the sight of so much unseemly female flesh. The narrator, standing in for the author, implies that the government and the theatrical establishment had failed their comically pathetic and woefully ignorant but nonetheless earnest public as personified by this modest family.[31]

Most critics, however, generally endorsed the notion that what they deplored in the press and the theater was dictated by a public that was thoughtless, frivolous, overly fond of violence, and resistant to innovation. In addition, both before and after the *Desastre* (the term Spaniards applied to their defeat by the United States in 1898), the public was often charged with having ignored serious national problems along with those specifically caused by the colonial wars. Critics bemoaned the fact that Spaniards flocked to the *teatros por horas*, to fireworks displays, and to bullfights, evidently oblivious to widespread rural misery and other grave internal problems or to the suffering of combatants and noncombatants alike in the colonies.

Even a cursory glance at press reports may have lent credence to these charges, and worse. At the end of November 1897, for example, and again in January 1898, 14,000 people in Madrid (population 500,000) filled the bullfight arena to watch a tiger pitted against a bull and later, a bull in mortal combat with an elephant. The Barcelona public was cheated of the same spectacle when the tiger, badly wounded in its Madrid appearance, died before it could take on another bull. The elephant was also soon out of combat, having died of pneumonia (*El Imparcial*, 29 November 1897). Although attendance at those events was unremarkable in terms of numbers— 14,000 out of 500,000 people is not that significant—on 5 September 1897 Eusebio Blasco warned readers of the consequences of similar demonstrations of public frivolity. In an article for *El Imparcial* entitled "Fireworks" ("Fuegos artificiales") the well-known playwright and journalist wrote: "There is great misery in these regions, workers will die of hunger this winter. We, on the other hand, go into ecstasy when we see fireworks displays, and when the socialists hold meetings and criticize men who corner commodities and squander wealth, people call them monsters and enemies. Our children will be looking at missiles of a very different kind!" ("La miseria es grande en estas comarcas, los trabajadores se morirán de hambre este invierno. Nosotros, en cambio, nos extasiamos ante los fuegos artificiales, y cuando los socialistas se reúnan y hablan mal de los que acaparan y derrochan, les llaman monstruos y enemigos. Otros cohetes verán nuestros hijos!").

The assumption that frivolity or indifference characterized the Spanish people during the late 1890s was widespread inside as well as outside Spain. The press did report occasional protest demonstrations connected to the insurrections, but because they were few in number compared to the recent past, commentators tended to attribute the causes of public apathy either to the current inexplicable psychological condition of the masses or to the failure of the elite to prepare them for meaningful participation in events.

Two demonstrations received wide-spread publicity in 1896. On 4 February a Guardia Civil allegedly shot to death a poor fishmonger, Tomás Carrera. The latter was said to have whistled disrespectfully at the ex-military commander in Cuba, General Arsenio Martínez Campos, in the course of a demonstration mounted on the occasion of the latter's homecoming procession in Madrid. Carrera's killing provoked immediate adverse criticism not only in the press, but also in one of Spain's most prestigious legal journals. Ángel Ossorio y Gallardo, a lawyer and the future civil governor of Barcelona, wrote in his weekly "News from the Courts" ("Crónica de Tribunales") that the guardia's excessive reaction to the whistle Carrera allegedly directed at Martínez Campos was completely unjustifiable. How, he asked, could Spaniards call Maceo a barbarian if such an act were not punished.[32] It was not. The military court that tried the case—in the words of the reporter for *El Imparcial* who relayed the results on 1 July 1896—shelved it on grounds of insufficient evidence. The incident thus provided a lesson on police (and government) impunity that was no doubt long remembered.

The second demonstration took place in late July 1896 when a group of women in Zaragoza protested sending the sons of the poor to Cuba. Let the poor and the rich go! their signs read. The press and the authorities represented the women as nothing more than ignorant dupes of Cuban agitators, Protestants, or Freemasons. This incident, and several subsequent demonstrations in Valencia, was reported not only in the Spanish press, but also caught the attention of the press in New York. The *New York Herald* reported that riots took place in Valencia in early August and repeated the Spanish government's claim that the riots had been instigated by Cuban revolutionists. The *New York Times* did not accept the official explanation of the riots, considering them the result of excessive taxation and conscription: "The riots in Spain are a symptom of very serious popular discontent with the course of the government in respect to Cuba."[33]

There were other incidents. Ángel Ossorio y Gallardo, writing in the *Revista de los Tribunales y de Legislación*, protested the jailing of José María de Pantoja, the recorder for the supreme court, on suspicion of aiding Filipino *filibusteros*. The only thing that connected Pantoja to the separatists was the fact (irrelevant from a legal standpoint) that, like them, he was a Freemason. In fact, Pantoja was not found guilty of any crime, but he ended up spending a year in jail.[34] Ossorio wrote that misguided patriotism of this kind recalled the unjust incarceration of the mulatto who was held for nearly a week for the crime of carrying a suitcase, getting off a train when he wished, and preferring not to talk with passers-by.[35] Acts such as these, he concluded, sully the reputation of a country that prides itself on being civilized.

An article in *El Imparcial* of 26 August 1896 offered an explanation for the public's supposed apathy that appeared to take into account police repression of the kind Ossorio detailed. Writing specifically to protest the illegal police round-ups and incarceration of suspects following a recent terrorist attack in Barcelona, the author observed that the least serious of the many grave issues currently confronting the public would formerly have led to impressive mass agitation. But not now: the public spirit was worn down, "flattened" *(aplanado)* by events—a condition the government was well aware of and was using to its advantage. The author argued that when the press did speak out in its capacity as the organ of public opinion, "We are complying with what is for us a duty, but we do it with no hope of any success. To appeal to those in charge of governing with logic, legal considerations, reasons for prudence and foresight is to wish to penetrate the hide of an old elephant with buckshot" ("Cumplimos lo que en nosotros es un deber, pero lo verificamos sin confianza alguna en el éxito. Ir con razonamientos, consideraciones legales, motivos de prudencia y previsiones políticas al espíritu de los que mandan, es querer penetrar con perdigones la piel de un viejo elefante"). In the author's opinion, resignation, even fatalism, were natural reactions on the part of the people—and the press—to being ignored or directly sanctioned.

Later historians have offered explanations for the public apathy contemporaries so often referred to, among them M. Fernández Almagro, who blames the press for failing to inform Spaniards of the seriousness of the insurrections.[36] Elena Hernández Sandoica and María Fernanda Mancebo suggest that the public may have feared government reprisal in view of its swift response to the widespread demonstrations throughout Spain at the news of the 1 May 1898 defeat in Manila Bay. Those demonstrations were followed by an immediate government crackdown: in Madrid the military commander of the region took control and declared a state of war. In general, according to the two authors, the crowded, unsanitary conditions on ships transporting soldiers home provoked most of the uprisings linked to the war.[37]

In a more recent study of different forms of protest in Spain at the turn of the century, Eduardo González Calleja notes that the state adopted strongly repressive measures not only against anarchists, terrorists, and Carlists, but also against the people as a whole. "We must not forget," he writes, "that the period 1895-1902 is one of the longest periods without individual guarantees, along with the 'Cánovas dictatorship' of 1876-1878, the post-World-War I period (1919-1921) and the dictatorship of Primo de Rivera. More than one third [*sic*] of the year 1898 (238 days) was spent with all the national territory under the regimen of a state of war" ("No debemos olvidar que el período 1895-1902 es uno de los períodos más largos sin garantías individuales, junto con la 'dictadura Cánovas' de 1876-1878, el período de la postguerra mundial (1919-1921) y la dictadura de Primo de Rivera. Más de un tercio del año [*sic*] 1898 (238 días) transcurrió con todo el territorio nacional bajo el estado de guerra").[38] Commentaries such as those cited above indicate that the public's alleged apathy masked complex attitudes and reactions to specific circumstances that were rarely probed by its critics.

Contemporary defenders of the public did not deny what they viewed as its inadequacies, including its supposed apathy, but as Leopoldo Alas had done earlier, they largely attributed its state to the failures of elite groups. In 1896, for example, Salvador Canals, a well-known journalist and drama critic, questioned the commonly accepted notion that the press echoed public opinion, calling it no more than an "agreed-upon lie" ("convenida mentira").[39] But he also denied that so-called opinion makers in the press were, at that point, contributing at all to opinion, much less forming it. Nonetheless, like most Spaniards who had emerged from the public in order to address it, he believed that they should.

How did the responsible elite propose to direct public opinion? Canals described the process in connection with the press much as Zeda had done with regard to the theater. He believed that an agent—the playwright or the journalist—must impose change on the public. Canals likened the process to the procreative act. The journalist, drawing on his knowledge and experience, furnishes the concepts or "seed." His macho energy implants it in the public, figured as female. Provided the public is receptive to the "seed," fecundation takes place and "opinion is born of the luminous copulation" ("la opinión nace como fruto de la luminosa cópula").[40]

Canals's explanation is suggestive for a variety of reasons. For one, its choice of metaphor to characterize the journalists' role in creating public opinion casts Spain's women newspaper writers in an odd light. Admittedly, they were few and, except for Emilia Pardo Bazán, did not write for high-circulation papers. During this period, one of the most valiant was Belén Sárraga de Ferrero, editor and contributor to the Valencia weekly *La Conciencia Libre*. Her paper was shut down several times between 1895 and 1898 for voicing ideas considered politically subversive. Antonia Rodríguez de Ureta, who wrote for the principal Catholic papers in Madrid and Barcelona during the 1890s and directed the *Semana Católica* and the *Archivo Católico* in Barcelona, spent nine years in the Philippines and often wrote about events there. In 1885 she published a novel about a young girl—the daughter of Spaniards—whose short life transpired mostly in the Philippines.[41] The best-known female journalist outside of Spain at the end of the century, Eva Canel, was born in Asturias but lived in Havana during the 1890s. She was a novelist, playwright, and correspondent for *El Comercio* and *La Unión Constitucional* through September 1898. Her 1891 play, *La mulata*, is discussed below.[42]

When Canals offered his explanation, he believed that journalists writing for the Madrid press were unable to report what people needed to know because of their inadequate knowledge of political, social, and economic realities not only inside but also outside the capital. (This criticism could not in fairness have been directed against the well-read and well-traveled women journalists mentioned above.) An editorial in *El Imparcial* on 19 December 1896 offered a different explanation and, in addition, referred to a potent source of public opinion seldom mentioned elsewhere.

The editorialist stated that the government was concealing information about Cuba and the Philippines, that the press was not printing all that it knew, while at the same time thousands of letters from the colonies were arriving in the Peninsula with details of events either silenced or merely alluded to in newspapers. The editorial continued: "These thousands of letters are the equivalent of many printed publications as far as their effect upon public opinion is concerned. Public opinion is based on what those letters contain before the newspapers—when they do end up reflecting it—provoke the anger of government ministers. In order for the system put in place by the current state of affairs to yield results, it would be necessary to suppress all mail from Cuba and the Philippines" ("Esos millares de cartas equivalen a muchas publicaciones impresas, por lo que toca a su efecto sobre la opinión. Ésta se forma sobre aquellos hechos antes que los periódicos, al reflejarla, vengan a provocar los enojos ministeriales. Para que el sistema puesto en práctica por la situación actual dé todos sus resultados, habrá que suprimir los correos de Cuba y de Filipinas").

An example of a letter that no doubt undermined readers' trust in the government's treatment of its troops was sent from a soldier, José Garanger, not in this case to a relative, but to *El Imparcial* on 30 December 1896 requesting the paper's help. The soldier had just returned from service in Cuba and now found himself ordered to report to duty in the Philippines. He explained that he had not recovered from his wounds and was, moreover, ill from the *vómito* (yellow fever) that he had contracted in Cuba. He beseeched the paper to intervene with the military on his behalf.

The question of the press's reluctance to print all it knew did not enter into Canals's discussion. But, to his belief that the press was ill equipped to inform the public, Canals added the notion that the public was not receptive. He claimed not to know whether to attribute its lethargic, dreamlike state to sterility or to sickliness: "What I do know is that there is no fruit, there is no offspring, there is no public opinion" ("Lo que sé es que no hay fruto, que no hay hijo, que no hay opinión").[43]

Leopoldo Alas shared Canals's (and Zeda's) view that qualified spokesmen should form public opinion. However, unlike Canals, he believed that there was a body of recognizable public opinion. The problem was that it had been formed improperly in connection with the Cuban and Philippine wars. By the summer of 1898, Alas was convinced that the public had been misled about the insurrections and about the United States by the "ruling classes, to wit, the majority of the politicians, the bellicose and reactionary newspapermen and writers, and also some clergy, unworthy of the church" ("clases directoras, a saber la mayoría de los políticos, los periodistas y escritores belicosos y reaccionarios, y también algunos clérigos, indignos de la iglesia"). He believed that the fault lay squarely upon those charged with directing the people, not with "the unfortunate masses, scarcely responsible for what they do under the influence of those fools" ("esa pobre muchedumbre, apenas responsable de lo que hace sugestionada por esos mentecatos").[44]

A striking letter published in *El Imparcial* a year earlier (10 June 1897) also claimed that there was no informed public opinion regarding the war because the press and politicians had failed to fulfill their obligations. The author, José María Celleruelo, a deputy to parliament from Asturias, claimed that both groups knew in detail what was going on in Cuba but no one—neither politicians nor journalists—would speak about it except in private. The result was demoralization at the top and, among the masses, a patient resignation that was often confused with stupid indifference:

> I sincerely believe that the blame for all this lies with the newspapers and with us deputies. We have not complied with our primordial duty: to be organs of opinion. If we had complied with that duty—at least since the moment when we became convinced that our silence was only serving to generate, both here and there, greater incentives to audacity and cynicism—it would have come out that our soldiers are almost all dying in the hospitals of Cuba, without honor or benefit to the fatherland; that pacification is a lie; a lie, all talk of reforms; a lie, our good relations with the United States and with the rest of America, and a lie, that continuing along such paths will lead anywhere except to our discredit and ruin.

> Creo sinceramente que la culpa de esto tenemos los periódicos, y nosotros los diputados. Hemos fallado a nuestro primordial deber: el de ser órganos de la opinión. Si lo hubiéramos sido, por lo menos desde que pudimos convencernos de que nuestro silencio servía únicamente para comunicar, aquí y allá, mayores alientos a la audacia y a la impudicia, se habría sabido que nuestros soldados mueren casi todos en los hospitales de Cuba, sin honra ni provecho para la patria; que es mentira lo de la pacificación; mentira lo de las reformas; mentira lo de nuestras buenas relaciones con los Estados Unidos y con el resto de América, y mentira que por caminos tales se llegue a punto que no sea el de nuestro descrédito y nuestra ruina.

Celleruelo urged that the truth be conveyed through all the "means and channels by which opinion is made manifest" ("medios y conductos por donde la opinión se manifiesta"). Nevertheless, little more than six months earlier, the press was operating under the threat of official government censure and suppression. On 19 January 1897, *El Imparcial* noted that Sr. Luciano Puga, the attorney charged with representing the government in matters concerning the justice system, had written a report directed to the Supreme Court that favored the jurisdiction of military tribunals over infractions allegedly committed by the press. The report was based on his interpretation of Article 249 of the Code of Military Justice that read: "Anyone who through speech, writing, or any other means *spreads ideas among the troops* that may lead to criticism of military service, or to aversion or slackness in the performance of duty will be punished by a prison sentence" ("Será castigado con la pena de prisión correccional el que de palabra, por escrito, o valiéndose de cualquier otro medio, *vierta entre las tropas* especies que puedan infundir disgusto o tibieza en el servicio o que murmure de él") The proposed change remained no more than a threat for the time being, but the pressure on the press to refrain from criticism of the war's conduct and of the military, in particular, was constant.[45]

A somewhat later *El Imparcial* article, "The Height of Indignity" ("El colmo de la indignidad") published on 30 January 1897, noted that thousands of letters and accounts by soldiers had convinced the newspaper that Spanish soldiers were being iniquitously exploited in Cuba, but that as soon as the newspaper expressed its apprehensions in print rather than conveying them confidentially to the government, the arbitrary threat from the government "broke its pen" so that the paper could not engage in the discussion that the Spanish people most wanted and needed.

Charges analogous to those made against the Spanish press were also made against the U.S. press both during and after the Spanish-American War. Thomas C. Leonard's article "The Uncensored War" reassesses the usual view that the U.S. press was uniformly biased and untrustworthy in its reporting of the 1898 war, especially in comparison to the Gulf War when U.S. news organizations acquiesced to the military's plan for restrictive press pools, and the result was managed news—even, on occasion, what amounted to news blackouts.[46] The *Imparcial* article quoted above, along with those of Pablo de Alzola and Felipe Trigo, referred to below, together with others not specifically cited here, similarly suggests that the mainstream Spanish press was not as consistently and effectively muzzled with regard to criticism of the military and its support systems as has usually been stated. It is evident, moreover, that press criticism of the government's conduct of the war stimulated criticism of the official reasons given for continuing the war. In fact, even a Madrid-based paper such as *El Imparcial*, like the mostly local papers in the United States that Leonard mentions, managed to include reports and vignettes about people affected by government policies perceived as misguided that provided, in Leonard's words, "an unfiltered brand of news" to the public. It is telling, in this connection, that the duque de Tetuán (an ex-minister of state and member of a right-wing group that left Sagasta's ministry of 1885-1890) in reference to the period from 1895 to 1897, asserted that the Spanish press, out of a misguided sense of a professional duty to provide information [!], "constituted itself, in effect, as the official propaganda organ of the *filibusteros*, insurgents and enemies of Spain" ("se constituyó, de hecho, en organismo oficioso y propagandista de los filibusteros, insurrectos y enemigos de España").[47]

Only two months later a nationally known politician approached the question of public opinion and, in particular, of misinformed, misguided public opinion. On 22 March 1897, approximately one year before Leopoldo Alas voiced his disillusionment with those who should have been guiding the country, Antonio Maura spoke on "Public Opinion and the Cuban Problem" ("La opinión pública y el problema de Cuba") before the recently formed (1895) Press Association in Madrid. According to *El Imparcial*, which reported on his presentation the following day, he argued that public opinion demanded total victory in Cuba because it lacked information and what it did have was distorted by divergent political interests. Individuals who, like himself, dissented from a military solution to the Cuban problem could not, he claimed, make themselves heard in the hope of winning support at the very time when their participation in making policy was crucial. (Four years earlier, in 1893, Maura had tried without success to effect administrative reform in Cuba.)[48]

Maura did not address the implicit question raised by his speech: how, in view of the distorting effect of the powerful political interests he referred to (along with the economic interests they cloaked), were elite, minority, dissident views to reach the public? In the end, Maura's assessment of the problem of forming public opinion was in line with that of Zeda, Canals, and Leopoldo Alas: the elite who should be charged with the task were not able to carry it out for a variety of political and social reasons, all of which served to muffle their voices.

The press campaign waged by Pablo de Alzola constituted an apparent exception to Maura's argument. Alzola was not a politician; his expertise lay in trade relations. Because he was appalled by what he perceived as the "jingoismo" of much of the Spanish press and by Antonio Cánovas's pledge to expend the last man and the last peseta on the insurrections, Alzola began to write articles in December 1896 urging an immediate halt to the bloodletting that in his view threatened to destroy the metropolis. His first article was reprinted in a number of national and local papers, leading him to believe that his ideas had not disappeared into a vacuum. A second set of articles elicited a response from the Madrid daily *La Época*. Alzola's views on the errors of the Spanish military, on the shortsightedness and misleading statements put out by the government, on the futility of autonomy in Cuba, and on the deleterious effects of the insurrections on the mainland itself—views expressed in several subsequent articles—did circulate and did provide an alternative to the national press fare that Alzola deplored.[49]

The future historian Rafael Altamira, who in 1897 was only thirty-one years old, offered still another explanation for the failure to communicate effectively with the public. Within a week (March 29) of Maura's talk at the press association, Altamira wrote an essay, "In Praise of Fanaticism" ("Elogio del fanatismo") for *El Imparcial* in which he accused people who congratulated themselves on representing the country's intellectual life of a failing even more fundamental than not knowing how to reach the people. Those individuals who profess to have ideas, he wrote, lack the will to fight for ideals that, in fact, they do not have. His explanation emphasized the effects of what he saw as a mood of prevailing cynicism. Altamira, however, essentially agreed with the critics referred to earlier in holding the press and other elite groups more responsible for the failure to form intelligent opinion than the public itself because he also saw the latter's role as relatively passive—that of an accommodating receptacle for ideas and attitudes. In the end, all of the critics cast the public in the role of an infantilized, or feminized, relatively homogeneous multitude in a scenario that featured individuals (mostly males) from elite groups as the tragically ineffective actors and directors.

It was common during the 1890s to find the public described as not only passive but somnolent and, as such, it became the target of further criticism. One example among many: an editorial in *El Imparcial* on 12 September 1896 entitled "A Sad Truth" ("Una triste verdad"), decried public apathy in connection with the Cánovas administration's prolonged and unjust detention of the director of *La Justicia* who had angered the military with his remarks about volunteer recruits: "The general conscience is so sound asleep that the loudest shouts are not enough to awaken it. Let us wait until the sleep comes to an end and then we'll talk" ("La conciencia general está tan dormida que los gritos más fuertes no son bastante a despertarla. Esperemos a que el sueño termine y entonces hablaremos"). Such a characterization of the largely uninformed and illiterate public anticipates the intensified charges of somnolence and apathy attributed to the masses just before, as well as immediately after, the Disaster.

In an article "No Pulse" ("Sin pulso") published in *El Tiempo* in July 1898, the conservative party chief, Francisco Silvela, claimed that "the country seems to lack a pulse" ("el país parece estar sin pulso").[50] This charge, leveled by a number of intellectuals, served as an explanation—perhaps as exoneration—for their own inability to influence the public. Emilia Pardo Bazán's reply in 1902 to Joaquín Costa's query as to why Spain was lagging behind other nations comes to mind. She wrote that the intellectual deficiencies and somnolence of the masses were to blame. As soon as the masses woke up, she averred, the task of nation building could begin, with intellectuals leading the way.[51]

Economic factors were often omitted from discussion about who the public was that emitted "public opinion" and whether public opinion echoed the press or, on the contrary, determined what was printed. A. Sánchez Pérez, an unjustly forgotten novelist, drama critic, and journalist, tried to correct this omission. Sánchez Pérez was not, to be sure, a mainstream critic. He spoke out during the 1890s on behalf of academic freedom in the Odón de Buen case and favored independence for Cuba, among other controversial issues. (Odón de

Buen was a professor at the University of Barcelona whose textbooks on geology and zoology were placed on the Index in 1895 and ordered withdrawn from circulation: Odón was commanded to submit to the authority of the church.) During this period Sánchez Pérez wrote regularly for the federalist Francisco Pi y Margall's low-circulation weekly *El Nuevo Régimen*—a newspaper that reflected its director's pro-independence stance for the colonies. On 28 February 1898, Sánchez Pérez penned an article for the popular *Ilustración Española y Americana* in order to contest D. Daniel Collado's view that the press shaped public opinion. The *Maine* had blown up two weeks earlier in Havana harbor and the relationship between what appeared in the press and public opinion was taking on more immediate relevance.[52]

Sánchez Pérez argued that the commercial press's sole preoccupation was to increase circulation and that newspapers accomplished that goal not by guiding the public, but by serving it; by pleasing it, not by directing it. Success depended on flattering the majority of the readers. Sánchez Pérez clearly implied that the motives and obligations of the elite, the condition of the masses, and the relationship between the two had long since become moot questions, passed over and discarded in the drive to make profits.

The consensus that emerges from this brief survey of views on public opinion in the 1890s amounts to the following: Mainstream critics agreed that the public (conceived of as a rather homogeneous multitude in possession of scant information and a low level of sophistication and critical acumen) required instruction and guidance in order to understand and express itself on changing political realities such as the inevitable loss of the colonies, and on modern developments in general, including thematic and technical innovations taking place in the theater. But while many members of elite groups, such as Zeda, Canals, Leopoldo Alas, Maura or Altamira recognized the need for meaningful communication between innovators and the public, they had no clear sense of how to reach and organize public consciousness.

Regeneration through the Theater

The question of who was to form and perhaps control public opinion specifically through the theater—a subject Zeda touched on in the 1897 essay discussed above—attracted brief attention in the press precisely when the Disaster was imminent. On 16 June 1898, Wilhelm II, emperor of Germany, addressed members of the Royal Theater in Berlin. His remarks sparked discussion not only in Spain but throughout Europe.[53] The theater, he told the actors, should form the people's spirit and character and ennoble their moral sense. The theater should be primarily dedicated to inculcating idealism and, like the school and the university, should serve the sovereign as an instrument designed to conserve the intellectual treasures of the German fatherland.

Ten days after the emperor's speech Ricardo Becerro de Bengoa wrote an article for the *Ilustración Española y Americana* in which he dismissed the idea that the theater could regenerate the human spirit, especially in Spain where, he claimed, a debased theater reflected the diminished ideals of the people. About two weeks later, in a piece entitled "The Theater and Public Power" ("El Teatro y el poder público") published on 11 July 1898 in *El Imparcial*, Valentín Gómez wrote that the emperor's words served as a timely lesson to men in power in "these latitudes of the Latin world" ("estas latitudes del mundo latino") who care about material well-being for themselves and their hangers-on, but not at all about the theater as a means of combatting "the general depression of the public spirit" ("la depresión general del espíritu público") with "ideas of morality, of the fatherland, of heroism, of abnegation; and it [the theater] should remind the public, by means of the plastic and poetic reproduction of its [Spain's] glorious seals of nobility, of the duty to keep its title of nobility clean and to continue weaving into its national life the golden thread of its historic virtues" ("ideas de moralidad, de patria, de heroísmo, de abnegación, y a recordarle, con la reproducción plástica y poética de sus gloriosos timbres de nobleza, el deber de conservar limpia su ejecutoria y de seguir tegiendo [*sic*] su vida nacional con el hilo de oro de sus históricas virtudes").

Evidently—assuming that he knew at least some of the plays discussed here—Gómez did not believe that the ideas they conveyed concerning morality, patriotism, heroism, and self-sacrifice, not to mention their frequent references to Spain's glorious history, had been successfully communicated to audiences. Gómez undoubtedly discounted some of the plays on the grounds that they belonged to the *género chico* and not to the *teatro serio*.[54] Yet for that very reason the public's access to these plays could not have been an issue: there is no doubt that the messages of the plays discussed here, however characterized, reached a relatively large and varied audience. As mentioned above, impresarios in the provinces contracted to produce a number of them following successful premieres in Madrid or Barcelona.

By the summer of 1898 newspaper articles furnished evidence of generalized dismay at the press as well as the theater for having failed to persuade and direct the public. Press critics reviewing plays on Cuba and the Philippines complained that they exemplified not patriotism but *patrioterismo de charanga* ("military band patriotism"), and were, considering the circumstances (of certain defeat), in bad taste. As such, it was argued, they only increased the public's demoralization.

Censorship and the Theater as a Site for Public Affirmation or Protest

Contemporary speculation as to how public opinion was or should be formed and how it was expressed is a significant part of the history of theatrical representations of the colonial wars. Most significant of all is the reception of dissident ideas. One way of gauging the impact of the few unorthodox ideas that surfaced between 1887 and 1898 is to review instances of censorship.[55] Faced with the vagaries of government and ecclesiastical censors, impresarios made their calculations and, when the times seemed propitious, risked staging plays that injected ideas and attitudes customarily left unspoken into the public discourse on the colonial insurrections. The consequences of miscalculations ranged from revisions of a text to the closing of a play—a penalty that could result in considerable financial loss to the impresario. Only two of the plays reviewed here, *Quince bajas* (1898) and *L'Héroe* (1903), were closed, by order, respectively, of the civil governors of Madrid and Barcelona. Several, however, were revised on the spot at the request of disgruntled members of the audience.

Another way of gauging the reactions of different elements of the public to theatrical productions is to note the frequency and success of benefit performances that featured patriotic material—on Cuba in particular. On 23 August 1896, for example, *El Imparcial* reported that the Teatro Martín was presenting a benefit performance of four one-act plays, one of which featured the premiere of *Un voluntario a Cuba.* On 6 February 1897 the same paper reported that a benefit performance would take place in the Salón Cervantes. Performances included *Juan José*, the monologue *¡Pobre María!*, the poem "Cuba" by ten-year-old Josefina Mauri, and two *juguetes* in one act, *Ciertos son los toros* and *Vivir para ver.* Several months later, on 14 November 1897, soldiers who had fought in Cuba and were currently lodged in the Madrid hospice funded by *El Imparcial* were invited to the benefit performance of the pantomime *Episodios de Cuba* in the Circo de Colón. According to *El Imparcial* the pantomime was well executed and produced great enthusiasm in the large audience.

A different contingent of the public saw performances of patriotic plays as an opportunity for staging political protests. In 1896 protesters identified as *laborantes* and *filibusteros* (political agitators and instigators of insurrection) threatened or did, in fact, succeed in disrupting performances of plays with Cuban themes in Madrid and Barcelona. Those actions, described below in the discussions of *Cuba* and *Familia y patria*, apparently raised an alarm, in part because no one knew for certain how many people approved of them, nor who those sympathizers might be.

Press reports on demonstrations in theaters just before and after the United States declared war on Spain (25 April 1898) indicate that readers fully registered the significance of public expressions of opinion in those locales. Two such demonstrations occurred in Madrid on 10 April 1898. During a performance at the Princesa Theater during the evening, a patriotic cry uttered by a gentleman (identified as such because he was sitting in the section of expensive seats) roused members of the audience to great enthusiasm. They demanded that the sextet on stage play the "Marcha de Cádiz," a request that, once complied with, led to even greater frenzy. Also, there were loud demonstrations in the Circo de Parish that night as well when a performer sang a patriotic verse of the *jota* from "La Dolores." The intentions behind these outbursts of patriotism were not apparent according to the *El Imparcial* report of 11 April. That report included the incidents in the theaters in describing the events that took place during an afternoon and evening of public demonstrations in and around Madrid's Puerta del Sol—demonstrations that ended in police intervention.

The demonstrators in the streets, like the patriots in the theaters, shouted "¡Viva España!" "Long live Spain and the army" ("¡Viva España y el ejército!") rang out in the streets where at one point a man waving a Spanish flag had it snatched from him by a person in authority who ripped it to pieces. At 1:30 in the morning the civil governor of Madrid declared that what had happened was not an expression of patriotism at all, but rather demonstrations prepared in advance by elements that sought to disrupt public order.

While the authorities implied that Carlists were responsible, the demonstrators' shouts, as reported in *El Imparcial*, protested government actions, e.g., ("Down with the armistice!") ("¡Abajo el armisticio!"). A young man holding aloft a Spanish flag shouted out, "Long live Spain with honor!" ("¡Viva España con honor!"), clearly intimating that the government had forfeited honor in its recent accommodations to U.S. demands. There were shouts of "Death to the government" ("muera el gobierno"), followed by the breaking up by force of the various groups. Some of the protestors, in response to the detentions of those around them by Civil Guards and police, cried out: "What kind of country is this where shouting 'Long live Spain!' is a crime? Do they want us to shout 'Long live the United States?' " ("¡Vaya un país donde gritar 'viva España' constituye delito! ¿Querrán que gritemos '¡Vivan los Estados Unidos!'?"). It is possible that some demonstrators, perhaps including those in the theaters, intended their patriotic cries to mean the opposite of what they said, or that they used them to partially mask criticisms directed at government policies. Whatever the motives of individual demonstrators may have been on 10 April, the authorities clearly feared any situation in which public expressions of opinion might serve to channel protests against the government

On 23 May, less than a month after the Madrid demonstrations, Domingo Blanco, the correspondent for *El Imparcial* in Havana, reported on patriotic displays in that city among loyal Spaniards and their sympathizers. There, he wrote, as adherents to the Spanish cause waited anxiously for the arrival of Admiral Cervera's fleet and speculated about an imminent U.S. bombardment, theater audiences enthusiastically applauded patriotic plays. In the course of his remarks on the state of public opinion in Havana, Blanco referred to the success of a play entitled *El Vizcaya* that debuted on 23 May at the Albisu Theater.[56] The house was packed, he wrote, and the work itself was the best he had seen of that difficult genre in which playwrights use the flag as a cover for their artistic deficiencies. *El Vizcaya* brought the audience to its feet with cries of "¡Viva España!" and other threatening cries directed at the United States. Then Blanco remarked that only eight days earlier (15 May), when the outbreak of hostilities was already inevitable, a Spaniard attending the debut of another patriotic play had uttered a cry of "Death to the Yankees" and had promptly been carted off to jail. In all parts of the empire, theaters were venues in which expressions of opinion on stage, as well as those issuing from the audience, were closely monitored.

Notes

[1] See Donald Dale Jackson's "Mutiny on the Amistad," in the *Smithsonian* (December 1997): 118. See also Eric Foner's review of *The Amistad Slave Revolt and American Abolition* by Karen Zeinert, in the *New York Times Book Review* (31 August 1997): 13.

[2] Emilio Gutiérrez Gamero suggested the extent of the impact on a wider public of conversations held by key political figures in their *tertulias* in his memoirs dealing with the 1890s. He recalled passing on remarks made at the *tertulia* of the Liberal Unionist, Romero Robledo, as if they constituted a kind of news release. See E. Gutiérrez Gamero, *Mis primeros ochenta años* (Madrid: Crisol, 1962), 119. Similarly (p. 123), the memoirist remembered Liberal Party chief Práxedes Sagasta's evening *tertulias* as occasions when important issues were discussed—and opinions on them swiftly disseminated to others not in attendance.

[3] I have not been able to locate a published copy of this play.

[4] For the anarchist and workers' theater at the end of the nineteenth century see Lily Litvak's chapter on the anarchist theater in *Musa libertaria* (Barcelona: Antoni Bosch, 1981), 213-52, her "Naturalismo y teatro social en Cataluña," *Comparative Literature Studies* V (1968): 279-302, and Carlos Serrano, "Notas sobre teatro obrero a finales del siglo XIX." *El teatro menor en España a partir del siglo XVI* (Madrid:CSIC, 1983), 263-77.

[5]On the *género chico* see Marciano Zurita, *Historia del género chico* (Madrid: Prensa Popular, 1920); Matilde Muñoz, *Historia de la zarzuela y el género chico* (Madrid: Editorial Tesoro, 1946); and José Deleito y Piñuela, *Origen y apogeo del género chico* (Madrid: Revista del Occidente, 1949). The three volumes that constitute Nancy J. Membrez's Ph.D. dissertation, "The Teatro por Horas: History, Dynamics and Comprehensive Bibliography of a Madrid Industry, 1867-1922 (*Género Chico, Género Ínfimo*, and Early Cinema)" (University of California, Santa Barbara, 1986) provide an indispensable mine of information on the *género chico*.

[6]In support of the idea of "plebeianization," Spanish historians have pointed to the popularity among aristocratic buyers of Goya's cartoons featuring common people at their diversions, to the upper classes' attendance at dances or other popular festivities, masquerading in the eighteenth century as *majos* (young and attractive lower-class men and women of Madrid, distinguished by their flair for dress and language), in the late eighteenth and early nineteenth centuries as *manolos*, and later in the nineteenth century as *chulos* (the post-ancien régime version of *majos* and *manolos*), and to their imitation of lower-class pronunciation and vocabulary. See, for example, Eva M. Kahiluoto Rudat, "The View from Spain: Rococo Finesse and Esprit Versus Plebeian Manners," in *French Women and the Age of Enlightenment*, ed. Samia I. Spencer (Bloomington: Indiana University Press, 1984), 395-406. Rudat ascribes "plebeianization" initially to "a 'patriotic' reaction to the *afrancesamiento* (Frenchified customs)" in vogue since the late seventeenth century in Spain. The phenomenon persisted long after Frenchified ways ceased to pose a threat to genuinely Spanish social customs. See also pages 125-34, in particular, of Steven Suppan's essay, "Managing Culture: *Manolo* and the Majo's Good Taste," in *The Institutionalization of Literature in Spain*, ed. Wlad Godzich and Nicholas Spadaccini (Minneapolis: The Prisma Institute, Inc., 1987), 125-68.

[7]"Internacionalización de la zarzuela," in the International edition of *El País*, 17 October 1985.

[8]Serge Salaün in "El 'género chico' o los mecanismos de un pacto cultural," in *El teatro menor en España a partir del siglo XVI* (Madrid: CSIC, 1983), 257, comments on another aspect of the zarzuela, i.e., the genre's advocacy of a "nacionalismo patriotero," a "my country right or wrong" version of nationalism, noting that, "thus it has been possible to accuse the Zarzuela—and not without reason—of having contributed to maintaining public opinion in favor of the war in Cuba" ("así se ha podido acusar—no sin razón—a la Zarzuela de haber contribuido a mantener una opinión favorable a la guerra en Cuba").

[9]Emilio Gutiérrez Gamero, *Mis primeros ochenta años (Memorias)* (Madrid: Aguilar, 1962), 254. Foreign operas were immensely popular in nineteenth-century Spain; native music dramas, at first in the form of the

long three-act zarzuela, began to supplement them by mid-century. For the popularity of opera in nineteenth-century Spain, see Adolfo Salazar, *La música de España. Desde el siglo XVI a Manuel de Falla* (Madrid: Espasa Calpe, 1953), 154-56; see also Antonio Peña y Goñi, *España desde la ópera a la zarzuela* (Madrid: Alianza, 1967), 40-46.

[10]*La Política de España en Filipinas* 2, no. 47: 301-2. This journal reached a minuscule number of actual subscribers (3,200 copies in 1891, 2,300 for the Philippines, and 1,000 for the Peninsula and elsewhere), but its writers were indefatigable in their efforts to influence Spaniards' view of the Philippines through articles published in other journals and newspapers, lectures, and advice to the colonial bureaucracy.

[11]See "El teatro filipino . . . del porvenir," in *Siluetas y matices: galería filipina*. Prologue by Javier Gómez de la Serna (Madrid: La Viuda de Minuesa de los Ríos, 1894), 155-72.

[12]*El teatro tagalo* (Madrid: M. G. Hernández, 1889).

[13]See the author's *Cuentos filipinos* (Madrid: Tipografía del Asilo de Huérfanos del Sagrado Corazón de Jesús, 1883), 15. José Rizal described it on page 162 of *Noli me tangere* [First published in 1887]. Prólogo Leopoldo Zea (Biblioteca Ayacucho, 1982.) In chapter 21 of his 1891 novel, *El filibusterismo* (Manila: Instituto Nacional de Historia, 1990), Rizal described the reception of a French operetta troupe in the Teatro de Variedades in Manila.

[14]Montero y Vidal, *Cuentos filipinos*, 15-16. In 1887, a Dominican, José María Ruiz, and a Jesuit, Francisco Sánchez, together collaborated on a *Memoria complementaria de la sección 2a del programa pobladores aborígenes, razas existentes y sus variedades. Religión, usos y costumbres de los habitantes de Filipinas.* Published in Manila by the Imprenta del Colegio de Sto. Tomás, this volume was meant to furnish supplementary material for those attending the Philippine Exposition of that same year in Madrid. On p. 306 the two authors note that Spanish zarzuelas are replacing the *moro-moros* but that the *indios* listen to them with little interest. *Sainetes* or *entremeses* (short plays usually in prose) written in Tagalog and featuring local customs in which native types were satirized were more popular. The coauthors wrote that these plays deserved to be translated into Spanish and studied for their historical interest. They further noted the excellence of the characterization and the fine acting, concluding with the observation that the *indio* was by no means to be excluded from the realm of art and literature. Their sympathetic assessment of developments in the Tagalog theater was uncommon among Spaniards.

[15]Catherine Diamond, "Quest for the Elusive Self. The Role of Contemporary Philippine Theatre in the Formation of Cultural Identity," in *The Drama Review* 40, no. 1 (Spring 1996): 143. See also Arthur Stanley Riggs, *The Philippine Drama* (Manila, 1905); Isagani R. Cruz, *A Short*

History of Theater in the Philippines (Manila: De La Salle University Press, 1971); Amelia-Lapena Bonifacio, *The "Seditious" Tagalog Playwrights: Early American Occupation* (Manila: Zarzuela Foundation of the Philippines, 1972); Thomas C. Hernández, "The Emergence of Modern Drama in the Philippines (1898-1912) and Its Social, Political, Cultural, Dramatic and Theatrical Background." Ph.D. diss. University of Hawaii, 1975.

[16]See pp. 298-301 and 389-93 of *Perfil histórico de las letras cubanas desde los orígenes hasta 1898*. (La Habana: Letras Cubanas, 1983) for a succinct account of the history and political implications of the *teatro bufo*.

[17]José Ferrer de Couto, *Los negros en sus diversos estados y condiciones; tales como son, como se supone que son, y como deben ser*. (New York: Imprenta de Hallet, 1864), 62, note 2. Luciano Francisco Comella's popular melodrama, *El negro sensible*, was first performed in Madrid in 1798. See Alva Ebersole, *La obra teatral de Luciano Francisco Comella* (Valencia: Albatros, 1985), 51-52.

[18]José Monleón, *El teatro del 98 frente a la sociedad española* (Madrid: Cátedra, 1975), 199.

[19]Carlos Serrano, *Le tour du peuple. Crise nationale, mouvements populaires et populisme en Espagne (1890-1910)* (Madrid: Bibliothèque de la Casa de Velázquez, 1987), 13.

[20]Sebastian Balfour, *The End of the Spanish Empire 1898-1923* (Oxford: Clarendon Press, 1997), 99.

[21]See Miguel Echegaray y Manuel Fernández Caballero, *Gigantes y cabezudos* (Madrid: R. Velasco, 1914), 27.

[22]For a representative formulation of the theater's role vis-à-vis the middle class during this period, see pp. 52 and 182-84 of Leonardo Romero's introduction and appendixes to his edition of Leopoldo Alas's *Teresa, Avecilla, El hombre de los estrenos* (Madrid: Castalia, 1975).

[23]Romero, *Teresa*, 146-47.

[24]Article 3 of the Constitution stipulated that every Spaniard was obliged to defend the fatherland with arms when called upon by the law to do so. A lottery determined who was to be called up. In regard to recruitment, the laws of 11 July 1885 and 21 August 1896 allowed a man to avoid service in the Peninsula through payment of 1,200 pesetas; to avoid service outside the Peninsula the payment was increased to 2,000 pesetas. The cost of "purchasing" a substitute to serve in one's place typically ranged from 500 to 1,250 pesetas. See Elena Hernández Sandoica and María Fernanda Mancebo, "Higiene y sociedad en la guerra de Cuba (1895-1898). Notas sobre soldados y proletarios," *Estudios de Historia Social*, no. 5-6 (1978): 364.

[25]Nancy J. Membrez. "Eduardo Navarro Gonzalvo and the *revista política*," *Letras Peninsulares* 1, no. (1988): 326. See also Raymond Carr,

Spain 1808-1939 (Oxford:Clarendon, 1966), 309; 325 for the failure to abolish the *quintas*.

[26]The words in bold were used in the newspaper to indicate words and phrases used by the women that were colloquialisms or incorrect.

[27]For literacy statistics see Mercedes Vilanova Riba and Xavier Moreno Juliá, *Atlas de la evolución del analfabetismo en España de 1887 a 1981* (Madrid: Centro de Publicaciones del Ministerio de Educación y Ciencia, CIDE, 1992).

[28]For the history of church organizations during this period and for the role of the church in Spanish society, see Domingo Benavides Gómez, *Democracia y cristianismo en la España de la Restauración (1875-1931)* (Madrid: Editora Nacional, 1978); Frances Lannon, *Privilege, Persecution and Prophecy: The Catholic Church in Spain, 1875-1975* (Oxford, New York: Clarendon Press, 1987); and Francisco Martí Gilabert, *Política religiosa de la Restauración 1875-1931* (Madrid: Rialp, 1991). In 1884 Félix Sardá y Salvany published his influential, much reprinted tract *El liberalismo es pecado*, a work that casts light on how Catholics were urged to put politicized religion into practice at the time. For the church's role in opposing independence for the colonies, see Carlos Serrano, *Fin del imperio: España 1895-1898* (Madrid: Siglo XXI, 1984), 64-74; and Sebastian Balfour, *The End of the Spanish Empire 1898-1923* (Oxford: Clarendon Press, 1997), 28. See also Cristóbal Robles Múñoz, "1898: la batalla por la paz. La mediación de Leon XIII entre España y Estados Unidos," *Revista de Indias*, 46, no. 177 (1986): 247-89.

[29]For elitist characterizations of readers of the press, see D.J. O'Connor, *Crime at El Escorial: The 1892 Child Murder, the Press, and the Jury* (San Francisco-London: International Scholars Press, 1995), 21-24. The drama critic and historian José Yxart, in *El arte escénico en España*, vol. 1 (Barcelona: La Vanguardia, 1894-1896): 356-367, remarked on and regretted Spanish audiences' persistent taste for theatrical effects and violence.

[30]Dionisio de Las Heras, *Madrid en la escena: crítica teatral* (Madrid: Samper, 1897), 73.

[31]*Avecilla*, written in 1882, appeared four years later in a collection of Alas's short stories, *Pipá* (Madrid: Fernando Fe, 1886). My reading of this complex story isn't meant to be comprehensive, it merely aims to represent fairly Alas's depiction of the family's frustrating theater experience and its external causes.

[32]See *Revista de los Tribunales y de Legislación Universal* 30 (8 February 1896): 88-90.

[33]*The New York Times*, 7 August 1896. Quoted in Joseph E. Wisan, *The Cuban Crisis as Reflected in the New York Press (1895-1898)* (New York: Octagon Books, 1965), 215.

[34]Vol. 30 (29 August and 10 October 1896): 551, 656. E. Caballero de Puga, like Pantoja, a member of the Gran Oriente Nacional de España, was detained at the same time as his fellow mason. He was also later exonerated. See Pere Sánchez Ferré, "La masonería española y el conflicto colonial filipino," in *La masonería en el siglo XIX*, 491-92.

[35]I have found no other reference to this mulatto. Mulattoes and blacks were sufficiently novel in 1890s Spain as to attract stares and suspicion.

[36]See Fernández Almagro's *Historia política de la España contemporánea*. Vol. 2 (Madrid: Alianza, 1969), 275 ff.

[37]See the two authors' "Higiene y sociedad en la guerra de Cuba (1895-1898): notas sobre soldados y proletarios," *Estudios de Historia Social* (1978): 376-80.

[38]See Gonzalez Calleja's essay, "Las 'tormentas del 98': viejas y nuevas formas de conflictividad en el cambio de siglo," in *Revista de Occidente* (Marzo 1998): 109-10. For a discussion of current interpretations of the political culture of the Spanish people in the 1890s, see Carlos Dardé, "La vida política: elecciones y partidos," in *Vísperas del 98: orígenes y antecedentes de la crisis del 98*, ed. J. P. Fusi and A. Niño (Madrid: Biblioteca Nueva, 1997): 65-74. Dardé notes that for historians who believe in the importance of repression as a primary factor in determining that culture: "there existed a public opinion that was systematically repressed by the ruling elite, a public opinion that manifested itself openly only when the elite showed themselves to be somewhat tolerant" ("existió una opinión pública que fue sistemáticamente reprimida por las elites gobernantes, opinión que se manifestó abiertamente siempre que las elites se mostraron algo tolerantes"), 69.

[39]*El año teatral: crónicas y documentos. 1895-1896* (Madrid: Establecimiento Tipográfico El Nacional, 1896), 132.

[40]Canals, *El año teatral*, 132-33.

[41]See *Pacita, o la virtuosa filipina; novela recreativa de costumbres orientales* (Barcelona:Impresor de Jaime Jepus, 1885; 2d ed. Herederos de la Viuda Pla, 1892).

[42]For two brief overviews of Canel's life and work, see María del Carmen Simón Palmer, "Biografía de Eva Canel (1857-1932," *Estudios sobre escritoras hispánicas en honor de Georgina Sabat-Rivers* (Madrid: Castalia, 1992), 294-304; and Jean Kenmogne, "Una escritora asturiana en América: Eva Canel," *Cuadernos-Hispanoamericanos* 546 (1995): 45-61.

[43]Canals, *El año teatral*, 135.

[44]See Yvan Lissorgues, "España ante la guerra colonial de 1895 a 1898: Leopoldo Alas (Clarín), periodista, y el problema cubano," in *Cuba: Les*

Étapes d'une libération (Toulouse: Université de Toulouse-Le Mirail, Centre d'Études Cubaines, 1979), 65.

[45]See Rafael Núñez Florencio, "Las raíces de la ley de Jurisdicciones: los conflictos de competencia entre los tribunales civiles y militares en los años 90," in *Antes del "Desastre": orígenes y antecedentes de la crisis del 98*, ed. Juan Pablo Fusi and Antonio Niño (Madrid: Universidad Complutense de Madrid, 1996), 195-96.

[46]Leonard's article appeared in *Culturefront* 7, no. 1(spring 1998): 59-62. Two years into the Cuban war General Weyler went to even greater lengths than his U.S. counterparts during the Gulf War in his attempts to control the press. Hugh Thomas notes in *Cuba. The Pursuit of Freedom* (New York: Harper & Row, 1971), 340, that "from February 1897 Weyler had prohibited reporters from accompanying troops." For an account of media coverage of the Gulf War, see John J. Fialka, *Hotel Warriors. Covering the Gulf War* (Washington, DC: Woodrow Wilson Center Press, 1991).

[47]Quoted in M. Fernández Almagro, *Historia política de la España contemporánea 1885-1897*, vol. 2 (Madrid: Alianza, 1969), 441.

[48]For Maura's proposed reforms in Cuba and the Philippines, see M. Fernández Almagro, *Historia política*, 191-202; James Durnerin, *Maura et Cuba: Politique coloniale d'un ministre liberal* (Besançon: Les Belles Lettres, 1978); Sebastian Balfour, *The End of the Spanish Empire 1898-1923* (Oxford:Clarendon Press, 1997), 189; and on Maura's life and career in general, Javier Tusell, *Antonio Maura: una biografía política* (Madrid: 1994).

[49]Pablo de Alzola y Minondo, *El problema cubano* (Bilbao: Andrés P.-Cardenal, 1898). This volume contains Alzola's press and journal articles, his commentaries on their reception, and his final reflections on the reasons for the Disaster. On 29 August 1898, Alzola wrote: "In a country still locked into an absolutist mold, only two factors have counted: the direction taken by the press and the path followed by certain military men" ("En un país constituido todavía con moldes absolutistas, sólo se cotizan dos factores: la corriente de prensa y la tendencia de ciertos militares.") The press and the military, he continued, usurped the role of the men of state who, for their part, showed no civic valor or foresight (p. 189.)

[50]See M. Fernández Almagro's essay on Francisco Silvela with a discussion of the "Sin pulso" article (37-48) in the former's *En torno al 98: política y literatura* (Madrid: Ediciones Jordan, 1948).

[51]Joaquín Costa, *Oligarquía y casticismo como la forma actual de gobierno en España*. Vol. 2, *Informes o testimonios* (Madrid: Ediciones de la Revista de Trabajo, 1975), 296, 298.

[52]For recent studies on the *Maine* explosion, see Louis A. Pérez, "The Meaning of the *Maine:* Causation and the Historiography of the Spanish-American War, *Pacific Historical Review* 58 (1989): 293-322; Tom Miller, "Remember the *Maine*," *Smithsonian* (February 1998): 46-57; Hugh Thomas, "Remember the *Maine?*," *New York Review of Books* (23 April 1998):10-12; and Louis A. Pérez, *The War of 1898: The United States and Cuba in History and Historiography* (Chapel Hill: University of North Carolina Press, 1998).

[53]See Thomas A. Kohut, *Wilhelm II and the Germans. A Study in Leadership.* (New York: Oxford University Press, 1991), 241.

[54]In her article "Yanquis, filibusteros y patriotas: prensa y teatro en la España del 98," *Cincinnati Romance Review* 10 (1991): 135-36, Nancy Membrez cites a response to Gómez's essay. Felipe Pérez y González, author of the zarzuela, *La gran vía*, wrote a piece in *El Liberal* 20 July 1898 with the same title Gómez had used, "El teatro y el poder público." Pérez y González charged that Gómez wanted to minimize responsibility for failed government policies, administration, and administrators by shifting blame to the writers for the popular theater. Gómez's scorn and dislike for the *género chico*, Pérez continued, led him to excoriate dramatists, who instead of writing old-style dramas and tragedies to be presented "on one consecutive night," on which occasion no one—not even Valentín Gómez—would go to see them, write works that fill the theaters for a hundred nights and produce fat revenues for the entrepreneurs. This harsh criticism aside, it is indeed likely that Gómez preferred a more "elevated" dramatic genre to convey nationalistic uplift.

[55]Pp. 503-7, vol. 1, of Nancy J. Membrez's 1987 Ph.D. dissertation, "The *Teatro por horas:* History, Dynamics and Comprehensive Bibliography of a Madrid Industry, 1867-1922 (*Género chico, Género ínfimo*, and Early Cinema), deal with censorship from 1881 to 1898. Membrez recommends Santiago Arimón and Alejo García Góngora, *El código del teatro* (Madrid: Centro de Publicaciones Jurídicas, 1912) for texts of all government decrees while acknowledging that the authors do not name the authorities responsible for legislating the decrees in question.

[56]The Albisu frequently showed Spanish zarzuelas and was, with the Tacón, the theater most patronized by Spaniards. The Tacón was built in 1838 and in 1959 became the Teatro García Lorca. Other Havana theaters that offered this fare were the Pairet and the Alhambra or Irijoa built in 1884. In 1899 the Irijoa changed its name to Eden Garden and later to José Martí. Josep Conangla, *Memorias de mi juventud en Cuba: Un soldado en la guerra separatista (1895-1898).* Edited and introduction by Joaquín Roy (Barcelona: Ediciones Península, 1998), 185.

"Juegos de Igorrotes," from *Exposición de Filipinas: colección de artículos publicados en El Globo diario ilustrado, político, científico y literario* (Madrid: Establecimiento Tipográfico de *El Globo*, a cargo de J. Salgado de Trigo, 1887), 133.

Portrait of José Rizal by Félix Resurrección Hidalgo, frontispiece in *Epistolario Rizaliano*
(Documentos de la Biblioteca Nacional de Filipinas compilados y publicados bajo la
dirección de T. M. Kalaw) (Manila: Bureau of Printing, 1930-1938), vol. 1.

Left "El fantasma del separatismo,"
El Imparcial (30 December 1895)

Below "Los ocios de Maceo," *Los
Lunes del Imparcial* (2 March 1896)

LOS OCIOS DE MACEO

41

"Adiós," Picolo, *La Ilustración Española y Americana* (1898)

"¡De la guerra!",
Alberto Pla y Rubio,
*La Ilustración
Española y Americana*
(30 July 1897)

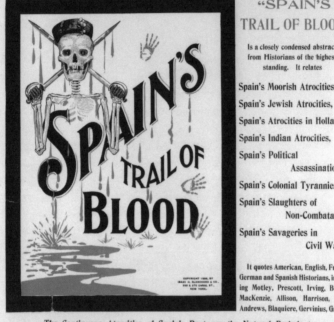

WHY ARE WE AT WAR?

Every Patriotic American Wishes to Answer That Question Fairly. He Cannot Unless He Knows Spain's Character, as Revealed by Four Centuries of Crimes Against Humanity....

"SPAIN'S TRAIL OF BLOOD"

Is a closely condensed abstract from Historians of the highest standing. It relates

Spain's Moorish Atrocities,

Spain's Jewish Atrocities,

Spain's Atrocities in Holland,

Spain's Indian Atrocities,

Spain's Political Assassinations,

Spain's Colonial Tyrannies,

Spain's Slaughters of Non-Combatants,

Spain's Savageries in Civil War.

It quotes American, English, French, German and Spanish Historians, including Motley, Prescott, Irving, Buckle, MacKenzie, Allison, Harrison, Dyer, Andrews, Blaquiere, Gervinius, Grosse.

The Continuous Atrocities of Spain's Past are the Natural Prelude to

THE STARVING OF THE RECONCENTRADOS.

k in detail. The Story of Spain's Latest Atrocities in Cuba told in this boo

IT CONTAINS:

s Consuls in Cuba.
atement.
n's Statement.

General Weyler's Orders.
President McKinley's Cuban Message.
Reports of Eye Witnesses.

Reports of the United State
Senator Proctor's St
Senator Thurste

WITH ILLUSTRATIONS FROM PHOTOGRAPHS.

R SALE HERE. PRICE 10 CENTS. FO

"Why Are We at War? Spain's Trail of Blood," poster by Isaac Blanchard (1898), negative number 73171, from the collection of The New-York Historical Society

THE PLAYS

Cuba libre

Cuba libre, a *sainete lírico y casi histórico* in two acts, premiered at the Teatro Apolo in Madrid on 11 November 1887. Federico Jaques y Aguado wrote the text—in verse—and Manuel Fernández Caballero composed the music. The play's opening stage directions allowed for certain changes when the play was performed in Cuba. Although the changes were all ideologically insignificant, the fact that Spanish plays were performed in the colony raises the question of what was permissible (and profitable) on the Cuban stage in the late 1880s.

Theater censorship ended in Spain in 1881; nonetheless, provincial laws regarding censorship on stage might be and were enacted, and individual authorities often moved against plays that alluded unfavorably to political figures, policies, or government institutions. In an article on political plays written for *La Ilustración Española y Americana* (30 September 1885: 179-82), the conservative theater critic Manuel Cañete described what happened after Navarro Gonzalvo's *El puesto de las castañas*, set to music by Rubio and Espino, premiered in September 1885. The civil governor of Madrid, offended by the work's political satire, announced that in order to effect further compliance of Article 25 of the Provincial Law, no work would be tolerated in the future that attacked institutions, that besmirched the good repute of any corporate body such as the army or the navy, or that held up political figures to ridicule.

Unsurprisingly, given the prevailing climate opposing criticism of state policy, there were no plays in Spain or in the offshore provinces advocating independence between 1881 and the early 1890s. *Cuba libre*, a play that ridicules the idea of independence for the colony, would clearly have appealed to the Spanish and Creole supporters of continued colonial rule who were, moreover, numerous enough in Havana to make the play's presentation financially

45

feasible. An indigenous *género chico* did promote autonomy on the Cuban stage, but it must be emphasized that there was much ambivalence as to what constituted "autonomy."

This ambivalence has led to disagreement among some modern scholars as to how autonomy was conceptualized in the Cuban theater. For the anonymous author of the entry on the theater in the *Diccionario de la literatura cubana*, for example, "autonomist ideology [had prevailed] to the point that the theater had become a tribunal for the castigation of colonial rule."[1] Rine Leal, another historian of nineteenth-century Cuban theater, acknowledges the dominance of autonomist thought in the theater, but he views its agenda as virtually the same as that of promotors of assimilation. Referring to the period between 1886 and 1890, he writes: "The popular savor, the ardent nationalism of Sarachaga [the popular playwright, Ignacio Sarachaga, who wrote for the *teatro bufo*] are substituted by an idyllic, reformist vision cloaked beneath the deceptive mantle of assimilation as the antithesis of full independence. Concord, work and liberty are its principles: they seem like liberal mottoes of the neo-colony" ("La savia popular, el ardiente nacionalismo de Sarachaga son sustituidos por una idílica visión reformista bajo el manto falaz de la asimilación como antítesis de la plena independencia. Concordia, trabajo y libertad son sus principios: parecen lemas liberales de la neocolonia").[2] The interpretations of these two literary historians underscore the difficulty in delimiting the range of meaning of *assimilation* and *autonomy*, terms that were closely associated in colonialist discourse. Advocates of assimilation normally meant the term to refer to the integration of Cuba into Spain with the same rights as those enjoyed by the provinces in the peninsula. Yet the term was often used to denote a necessary precondition for autonomy, and occasionally it was used to mean nearly the same thing as autonomy.

Despite their differing interpretations—autonomist ideology as meaningful criticism of colonial rule, or as what amounted essentially to the continuation of a kind of neocolonial status—each of the two authors cited above underlines the Cuban theater's relevance to social history. Indeed, the author of the dictionary entry quoted above writes that in order to understand the "historia íntima" that extends from Zanjón to Baire (i.e., from the peace of

Zanjón in 1878 to the outbreak of a new insurgency in 1895), it is necessary to analyze the theater because it reflects, as nothing else can, the death throes of the colony, the death rattle of a sick society.[3] Placed within this context, the themes developed in *Cuba libre* contribute meaningfully to the ideological struggles carried out on the Cuban stage.

Its appeal in Cuba may be explicable, but why did *Cuba libre* appear in Spain in 1887, nearly ten years after the end of the first Cuban insurrection and eight years before the second? Several events, along with a number of significant ideas advanced between 1878 and 1887, help to account for its timeliness. Three years earlier (in 1884) Spaniards had learned about a renewed movement for independence launched by Máximo Gómez and Antonio Maceo—the two men who in 1895 would lead the insurgent military forces. Then, in 1885 Juan Gualberto Gómez, the pro-independence Cuban mulatto in exile in Madrid, published a series of articles in the Madrid newspaper *El Progreso*. (Founded in 1881, it was the organ, first of Republicanism and later of the Progressive Democratic party.) Entitled "La cuestión de Cuba," Gómez's articles posed the question of Cuba's fitness for independence from Spain. In interested circles his ideas provoked discussion that may, to some extent, have filtered through to the general newspaper-reading public.

Historian Aline Helg notes that in 1887, Gómez and others "organized already existing all-black clubs and societies into a federation, led by the Directorio Central de las Sociedades de la Raza de Color (Central Directorate of the Societies of People of Color) that successfully coordinated antidiscriminatory actions across the island and challenged Spanish authority."[4] Actions such as these would surely have attracted the attention of readers of the press. Furthermore, one year before *Cuba libre* appeared, Cuban slaves finally won total freedom. Their emancipation and the campaign for autonomy at its height in Cuba only a year earlier (1885), combined with frequent rumors of preparations for a new insurrection, undoubtedly fueled apprehension about the colony's future, including speculation about the possibility of losing it. While no single event accounts for the play's arrival on stage in March 1887, the threat of renewed military action alone justified a patriotic display, which would be especially appropriate for audiences in Cuba. All the better was a patriotic play enhanced (for the sake of commercial success, in Spain especially) by humor and the exoticism guaranteed by the presence of blacks and mulattoes.

The action takes place in the days immediately preceding the end of the first Cuban Insurrection in 1878. A couple long resident in Cuba is returning to that country after a visit to their native Spain. They plan to join the insurgents, the husband as a *comandante* and his wife as the leader of a troop of *amazonas* (mounted female fighters). A nephew whose pro-Spanish stance has led them to deny him their daughter's hand in marriage is also returning to Cuba to join in the battle. Once there, in the depths of the *manigua* and surrounded by the blacks and mulattoes they command, the parents are confronted by a mulatto soldier who also demands the daughter's hand in marriage. The parents refuse, but were it not for the nephew's timely intervention, the mulatto would have abducted the young woman. At this juncture, news of the truce arrives. Cuba and Spain are reunited and, on a personal level, the grateful parents forget past enmity and accept the nephew as their son-in-law.

All of the themes touched on in subsequent plays regarding the insurrections are present in *Cuba libre*, beginning with the issue of recruitment. On board the ship sailing for Havana is a Spanish recruitment agent who describes how he enlists men to sign up as substitutes *(sustitutos)* for service in Cuba or Puerto Rico. He offers them the lowest payment possible, then sells them to the government for a set price. The recruiter is transporting 400 "little lambs" *(borregos)*, i.e., simpletons, to whom he has paid about 20 pesetas per head. He has already sold each one for 1,500 pesetas. If the Minister keeps requesting replacements, he exults, he'll soon be a rich man. In a Catalan accent (it was commonly assumed that Catalans, heavy investors in Cuba, were making the most of wartime conditions to turn a profit), he hands out this advice: "If you want to get rich fast, get a job in Havana either as a man who can see with the lottery or as a blind man with customs, or land a contract like mine that lets me do with whites what I wouldn't be allowed to do with blacks" ("Quien quiera ser pronto rico / que logre un empleo en la Habana, / o de vista en loterías, / o de ciego en Aduanas. / O pesque cualquier contrata / cual la que he pescado yo, / que me deja hacer con blancos / lo que con negros no").[5]

The recruiter's monologue is sung, making it difficult to inter-
pret in the absence of the music that set its tone and of any
indication of how it was performed. Nevertheless, its satiric bite—
perhaps more accurately, its cynicism—is apparent and may have
provoked complicitous laughter from its 1887 audiences.

When the ship lands in Havana harbor, a group of black female
vendors (negras vendedoras) advertise their wares—sweets—in song.
Mulatto sweets, they croon, are delicious: white sweets have no fla-
vor. The knowing allusion to the physical charms of black and
mulatto women as sweets or exotic fruit is a commonplace in these
plays. In the course of Cuba libre, the black and mulatto women
engage in relatively uninhibited sexual repartee—a source of amusement for the audience that also helps to define a contrasting ideal of
the white woman whose sense of decorum would not countenance
such innuendo.

The mulatto soldier's lust for a white woman (the Spanish turncoats' daughter) is at the root of one of the commonest recurring
ideas associated with racial stereotyping in this period: mixed blood
leads to inappropriate, perverse desire, to betrayal and disorder.
When the mulatto demands the daughter in marriage, and her mother—fighting, it should be recalled, on behalf of the insurgents—cries
out, "What an outrage! A mulatto marry Cachita!" ("¡Qué atrosidad
[sic]! / ¡Con Cachita / casarse un mulato!"), the mulatto answers, "And
why not! In free Cuba there are no colors" (¿Y por qué no? / En Cuba
libre / no hay colores"). The mother then cries, "What dishonor! We
shall never consent to it! Nor will she!" (¡Qué deshonra! / ¡Jamás lo
consentiremos! / Ni ella tampoco"). Here, as in several subsequent
plays, it is the presumption of equality on the part of blacks and
mulattoes and their determination to win it by force and by separation from Spain that makes it imperative that Cuba not become free.

Except for the passive, innocuous Spanish daughter, the women
are cast in an unfavorable light. The black and mulatto women are
licentious, and female combatants are portrayed as unnatural. Not
only is the Spanish mother a turncoat fighting for Cuban independence, but she also wears the pants in the family: she has reduced her
hen-pecked husband to a cipher.

The review of the play that appeared the day after its premiere
(12 November 1887) in the high-circulation paper, El Imparcial, did

not comment on the themes discussed here. The unsigned review concentrated on the expensive sets and costumes, on a comical speech delivered by a widow lamenting her lot, and on a few musical numbers, including the song of the sweets-vendors and a song and dance performed by the female insurgents. The reviewer also commented on the attractiveness of the women, noting that some looked like authentic *mulatas*.

Were there black or mulatto actors on stage in Spain at this time? In connection with the private, home stage there is an intriguing reference to a black woman who took a role alongside whites. In 1887, the society chronicler for *El Imparcial* described a soirée at the home of the Señora de Rute—in effect, a rehearsal of a program to be given the following day at the Teatro Roma. Among the performers, who included the celebrated novelist Emilia Pardo Bazán and the French actress, Mme. Henri, was "a little negress with a slender figure and shining eyes, with the beauty appropriate to women of her race, [who] suddenly assumed the role of Marion, earning much applause, including that of the Sra. de Rute and the Baroness of Lasdaing" ("una negrita de esbelto talle y ojos brillantes, con la belleza propia de su raza, [la cual] se encargó repentinamente del papel de *Marion*, recogiendo gran cosecha de aplausos, que compartieron la señora de Rute y la baronesa de Lasdaing"). While photographs of black or mulatto players have not been found in the contemporary works on the theater consulted by the author of this study, some may emerge from the collection of nearly 10,000 photographs taken between 1887 and 1895 and held in the Fundación Juan March in Madrid.[6]

Cuba libre's reviewer further noted the audience's amusement at the antics of two boastful Spanish soldiers. However, he did not mention an exchange in which one soldier showed the other traces of insurrectionist blood on his sword, averring that it was black not red since all the insurgents were blacks and mulattoes. This representation of the enemy as predominantly colored was common in all the plays on Cuba. It reinforced the portrayal of the insurrection that a number of vocal politicians promoted, i.e., that it was at bottom a race war. The same charge was made in 1895 at which time it was estimated that over half of the soldiers in the Liberation Army were black or mulatto.[7] As for the general population of Cuba, at the end of the war in 1899, out of a total of 1,572,797 people, 66.9 percent were white, 14.9 percent black, 17.2 percent mulatto, and 0.9 percent Asiatic.[8]

Unfortunately, the reviewer of *Cuba libre* did not describe or comment on the final scene, an "Alegoría de la paz" in which the only stage directions have the nephew first and then everyone else shouting "¡Viva España y Cuba!" This scene may have been rather modest compared to those staged in later plays that were designed to bring the audience to its feet in a frenzy of patriotic fervor. Nonetheless, a note in the published version does identify the set designers by name and attributes the production's success "in great part" to their contributions.

The reviewer spelled out the moral: "We're left, at the end, with the thought that the peace and prosperity of Cuba is incompatible with a Free Cuba" ("Quedamos al final, en que la paz y la prosperidad de Cuba y Cuba libre son incompatibles"). The play, he wrote, was the hit of the season. Indeed, the Teatro Apolo later added shows at 8:30 and 10:30 P.M. on Saturdays and Sundays in order to accommodate public demand. Another contemporary critic, Manuel Cañete, the conservative reviewer for *La Ilustración Española y Americana* who did not usually comment on zarzuelas, praised *Cuba libre* as an agreeable spectacle that "did not attack institutions" ("que no atacaba a las instituciones").[9] The historian of the *género chico*, Deleito y Piñuela, noted that *Cuba libre* earned 15,000 *duros* (75,000 pesetas) for the impresario in little more than one month.[10]

Neither the contemporary commentators nor Deleito y Piñuela, writing in the late 1940s, suggest that audiences reacted to anything but the comic aspects of the show. Deleito y Piñuela particularly emphasized the popularity of the scene with the Spanish *guerrilleros*. The two actors who created the roles made the scene their own through nightly improvisations that drew people back into the theater again and again: "Since the shows at the Apolo were 'by hours,' or by acts, it always turned out that the second act of *Cuba libre*, with the famous scene of the guerrillas, was much better attended than the first one. All the night owls in Madrid went to see it" ("Como las funciones en Apolo eran 'por horas,' o por actos, ocurría siempre que el acto segundo de *Cuba libre*, donde estaba la famosa escena de los guerrilleros, tenía más concurrencia que el anterior. Todo el Madrid noctámbulo acudía allí").[11]

Public reaction to this production, in Deleito y Piñuela's view, was determined by timing:

> It mustn't be forgotten that it was 1887. Eleven years before the colonial catastrophe. Spanish public opinion—unaware of the reality of the situation until after the blow had been struck—didn't glimpse the vaguest possibility of independence, or even autonomy, for Cuba. Of course, the play upheld the thesis that Cuba would always be Spanish, and that its prosperity was at odds with its emancipation from Spanish rule. That was the moral suited to the general admission audience, and in this matter, almost the entire country constituted "the general admission audience".
>
> Flattering commonly-held sentiments contributed to its success; but, in addition, the zarzuela was well made and its musical numbers were repeated every day.

> No se olvide que era el año de 1887. Faltaban once para la catástrofe colonial. Y ni remotamente se vislumbraba aún por la opinión española (no enterada de la realidad hasta después de recibir el golpe) que fueran posibles ni la independencia, ni siquiera la autonomía de Cuba. Naturalmente, la obra sustentaba la tesis de que Cuba sería siempre española, y que su prosperidad estaba reñida con su emancipación. Era la moraleja acomodada a la galería, y "galería" era entonces en eso casi todo nuestro país.
>
> El halago de los sentimientos generales contribuyó al éxito; pero además, la zarzuela estaba bien hecha y sus números musicales se repetían a diario. [*Origen y apogeo*, 164]

• • •

Of the several themes dramatized in *Cuba libre* that recur in the other plays discussed here, the racial theme is one of the two (the other is the method of conscription) that received most attention from the press. Both the plays and the press coverage advanced the official Spanish government position regarding the role of people of color in insurrectionary Cuba and in a Cuba separated—if the worst came to pass—from the mother country. An editorial in *El Imparcial* of 1 April 1896 conveys one of the ideas essential to the official message. White insurrectionists, it stated, must recognize "the savage character, entirely African in origin, that people of color imprint on the struggle. Such barbarism clearly announces what will finally be in store for them on the day when the soldier from the Peninsula will no longer be there to contain those savages" ("el carácter de salvajismo enteramente africano que la gente de color da a la contienda. Ese carácter les anuncia cuál sería a la postre su porvenir el día en que para contener a esos salvajes no estuviese en Cuba el soldado peninsular").

Aline Helg has pointed out that the "Spanish-imposed concept" of people of color, which she traces back to the time of the alleged conspiracy of La Escalera in 1844, created a racial system that denied upward mobility to mulattoes—a system that had "no parallel in Latin America and the Caribbean at that time." Afro-Cuban leaders such as Juan Gualberto Gómez took this system—devised in part to cause hostility between blacks and mulattoes—and used it instead to foster racial pride by uniting the two within one large group.[12] Press coverage and the plays under consideration here clearly support Helg's argument by showing that throughout the 1895-1898 insurrection, Spanish propaganda was aimed at separating Cuban people of color into blacks and mulattoes and setting them against each other, a policy clearly designed not only to create divisiveness and sow suspicion in Cuba, but also to convince Spaniards that their dominance was essential if order was to be maintained.[13]

Newspaper characterizations of Cuban mulattoes normally asserted that they manipulated purportedly less capable blacks and assured readers that if mulattoes gained power they would use it to oppress blacks. Yet, at the same time, press graphics often equated the two. Drawings in the press sometimes converted Antonio Maceo, for example, from the light-skinned mulatto he was in reality, to a full-blooded black. A memorable cartoon, published in *El Imparcial*, represents Maceo in his double role as dominant mulatto and barbaric man of color. He is seated at a camp table in the *manigua* feasting on human flesh. Blacks who are noticeably darker than he are barbecueing fallen Spanish soldiers and serving them up to their chief. Both the press and the plays occasionally alluded to the alleged practice of cannibalism among Maceo's predominantly black troops. Among the many Spanish publications that carried cartoons, nearly all of which presented a derogatory view of insurgent

Cubans and Filipinos, three Spanish weeklies may be singled out in particular: *El Cardo: Semanario Literario, Artístico y de Sport* (Madrid); *Gedeón: Semanario Satírico* (Madrid); and *Blanco y Negro: Revista ilustrada* (Madrid).[14]

Historical figures such as Maceo and Juan Gualberto Gómez, the mulatto separatist, along with the black and mulatto fictional characters in the plays, were represented in the press and in fiction through the prism of race. What did Spaniards understand by this term? At times—as will be noted in the discussion of perceptions of Filipinos—the press and the popular fiction of the 1870s, 1880s, and 1890s used the word "race" to refer to what was conceived of as a biologically distinct group of people. Thus, for example, Francisco de Paulo Cañamaque in an 1880 study of the Philippine Archipelago claimed that Filipinos shared certain "organic deficiencies" of the Malay "race."[15] The negro race was similarly characterized as having deficiencies, usually intellectual, determined by biological inheritance.

Spaniards perceived themselves as members of the white race when considered in relation to people of color such as Filipinos and blacks. In relation to Europeans, some Spaniards thought of themselves as Latin or Mediterranean. The Spanish anthropologist Manuel Antón discussed the state of scholarship on the question of the races inhabiting Europe in a talk before a university audience in 1895. He warned against definitive statements on these questions, noting that there was evidence of much racial mixing. He opposed Gobineau's belief in the superiority of pure blood, but he unhesitatingly attributed certain traits to racial inheritance. For example, he contended that laziness and superstition were injected into the Egyptian character by the admixture of black blood from the South. Most Spaniards, in his view, belonged to the larger of the two groups that formed an inclusive Mediterranean ethnic group, that is, the frank and resolute *libio-ibéricos*. The other group he believed to be formed by the Semitic race.[16]

The term "race," as applied to Spaniards in the plays under consideration here, normally referred to a group of people defined by selected memories of their common history, by a common religion and language (Castilian), by reverence for the family, and by exaltation of the Spanish woman for her beauty and love of country.

Likewise, people of color were defined according to the same categories. No historical memory was in evidence among people of color (blacks and the indigenous inhabitants of the Philippines), an absence that made it the more plausible to consider them less-evolved human beings, or even to liken them to animals. Typically, there is little or no reference to the original languages of indigenous Filipinos or blacks in the press or in the plays, but there are abundant examples of their inability to speak Castilian properly. The Spanish press often printed bogus manifestoes and declamations pronounced by *mambises* (Cuban independence fighters) expressed in garbled Castilian. Filipinos' efforts to speak Castilian were similarly mocked. Neither are there references to pre-Christian religious beliefs in the two colonies. As for African religions practiced in Cuba, there are vague allusions to religious elements in the rituals of the poorly understood *ñáñigos* who were represented in the press primarily as criminals.

During the war years the Spanish government confined hundreds of *ñáñigos* in the African penal establishments of Ceuta and Fernando Po. Originally they were members of all-male mutual aid societies formed by slaves from the region of Calabar, and their ritual reproduced scenes and personages from the myths that accounted for their appearance in Africa. The correspondent in Cuba for *El Imparcial*, Domingo Blanco, wrote a long article on the *ñáñigos* on 20 November 1896. He noted their imitation of certain Masonic rites and gave as an example of the desecration of which they were capable the use of the colors of the Spanish flag for the curtains in their *fambá*, or temple.[17]

Surprisingly, though there were many references to them in the press, *ñáñigos* did not appear on the Spanish stage in plays set in Cuba. In the article for *El Imparcial* noted above, Domingo Blanco did mention their appearance on the Cuban stage. He explained that the *ñáñigos* initiated the tradition in Havana of mounting processions through the streets as part of the celebration of the arrival of the Three Magi. The *ñáñigos*, in African attire, carried lanterns and halted their procession's progress periodically in order to execute their dances. Blanco saw this spectacle, adapted for the stage, at the Irijoa Theater in Havana. He wrote that it produced a delirium of excitement in both whites and blacks, although it was a "piece of foolishness" ("una majadería") and agreeable only to low-class people.

In the plays dealing with Cuba there are several "good" black servant women who pray to Christian saints and observe the rites of the Church. Black males are not linked to religious practices. Furthermore, they are usually represented as loners, men living outside families.

Black ability is reduced to a talent for singing and dancing. Finally, the infantile and thoughtless nature of black men is reinforced in fiction by frequent references to their two favorite pastimes, eating and sex. Fictional Spaniards unfailingly praise the physical and spiritual beauty of Spanish women in marked contrast to the tastes of fictional black males whose expectations of women are less rigorous.

Male mulattoes and mestizos (relevant to the Philippines) in fiction and in nonfictional works published in Spain were typically represented as an ambiguous (i.e., mixed) race of men. One of the most detailed expositions of accepted attitudes and beliefs about blacks and mulattoes in nineteenth-century Spain may be found in Emilio Castelar's novel *Historia de un corazón* (1874) and its sequel, *Ricardo* (1878). Castelar, a liberal politician who served as the last president of the First Republic, dealt in his first novel with the doomed love between the white wife of a Louisiana plantation owner and a mulatto slave born in Cuba. His second novel centers on her son by her husband, the son's departure from Louisiana to live in Spain, and his fateful encounter with his mulatta half-sister, the offspring of his mother's adulterous union with the mulatto slave. As a statesman, Castelar was an eloquent spokesman for the emancipation of slaves. As a novelist, he drew upon the romantic protagonists of early nineteenth-century fiction when he fashioned the character of his mulatto slave.[18]

Unlike mulattoes who, as in Castelar's version of the type, might appear as romantic figures partially modelled on Othello or Cain, mulattas were usually confined to the passive role of sexually desirable creatures. Because Eva Canel's play *La mulata* (1891) does not deal with the Cuban insurrection, it is not included in this study. It deserves mention, however, because unlike the plays examined here, it presents a mulatta who does not conform to the stereotype.

Abandoned in Venezuela by the Catalan who has seduced her and fathered her child, she eventually makes her way back to Cataluña to reclaim the son he took away with him. The play's forcefulness derives from the contrast between the moral superiority of the mulatta and the moral bankruptcy of the Catalan who exploited her sexually and financially. Although it is true that Canel's mulatta metamorphoses into another stereotype—the white Spanish mother figure—the play nonetheless provides a rare example of the mulatta seen from a perspective other than that of the predatory white male Spaniard.[19]

The ambiguous, divided nature of the mulatto (or the mestizo in the Philippines) had specific consequences. The mulattoes' (and Spanish mestizos') white ancestry presumably explained their ability to speak correct Castilian. It certainly accounted for their audacity in pursuing white women and for the conviction that their passion merited reciprocity. Most importantly—in connection with armed insurrections—mulattoes and mestizos inherited the white man's thirst for power along with sufficient wit to attain their ends by treachery. The African ancestry of the mulatto, on the other hand, explained the savagery of his nature—the blood lust that welled up on occasion, leading to unspeakable atrocities. The equivalent atavistic trait believed to manifest itself in the indigenous and mestizo inhabitants of the Philippines was called *hamok*. This state of uncontrollable fury is discussed below in connection with the Filipino separatist Juan Luna.

The mulatto male thus emerges in two basic guises in nineteenth-century Hispanic literature: as a refashioned romantic protagonist, a tragic lover whose racial ancestry alone prevents his union with a white woman; and as a marginalized figure bent on seizing power. Despite propaganda-inspired contrasts drawn between mulattoes and blacks, in the end they were all people of color and potential enemies of Spain. Rafael Gasset's reaction to a scene he viewed in Cuba in 1895 typifies the fundamental racial message of the plays discussed here that deal with black and mulatto insurgents. Gasset was the editor of *El Imparcial* and the first Spanish journalist to go to Cuba to cover the insurrection. He arrived in Havana on 20 October 1895. On 2 December 1895, he turned down a chance to interview Antonio Maceo despite the offer of a safe-conduct pass, claiming that he would not take advantage of that admittedly important journalistic opportunity because of Maceo's dynamiting of passenger trains—a tactic that especially outraged Spaniards. On 22 December although he had not met Maceo, he described him as a mulatto who was almost black, a man of gross manners, crude behavior and no education. Gasset unfailingly described blacks for his Spanish readers as savages barely removed from the jungles of Africa.

A month earlier (on 24 November) Gasset wrote that he and his companions passed through Las Lajas, a spread-out village of rude huts, which had furnished a contingent of five hundred men and two chieftains to the insurrectionary forces—including the mayor, who was one of the first to pass over to the rebel camp. Gasset continued:

> Standing in the doors of the houses you saw only women and children, most of them members of Maceo's race. They were certainly charming, those big negresses with cigars in their mouths. They would make excellent bogeymen to frighten crying babies, and I think they might even have the same effect on adults. If the Cid had come across an enormous, exceedingly ugly negro woman blowing out mouthfuls of black smoke—like exhalations of her own breath—I wonder whether he wouldn't have abandoned all the striving of his great soul.

> Realmente en las puertas de las casas sólo se veían mujeres y chiquillos en su mayoría pertenecientes a la raza de Maceo. Por cierto que estaban encantadoras aquellas negrazas con su puro en la boca. Eran valiosísimos ejemplares para imponer silencio a los niños que lloran, y aun estoy por decir que servirían de *coco* para los adultos. Si el Cid se hubiera tropezado con una enorme y feísima mujer negra echando bocanadas de humo oscuro que parece su aliento, no sé yo si hubiera dado al traste con todo el esfuerzo de su ánimo bizarro.

The thought may be rather murky, but the juxtaposition of images—a fat, ugly negro woman puffing on a cigar and the gallant Cid—could not be more expressive of the almost visceral abomination one side was encouraged to feel for the other. [20]

In his 1901 novel, *Finis: últimos días de España en Cuba*, the Spanish journalist and writer resident in Cuba, Waldo Insúa, summed up the meaning of defeat for those Spaniards in Cuba and in the Peninsula whose sentiments regarding race as an impediment to independence accorded with Gasset's intimate sense of revulsion.[21] At the novel's end, in early 1899, Insúa's two exquisitely refined protagonists of European descent, the Marqués de Santa Fe, one of whose forebears had been governor-general of Cuba, and his lover, Julia, are about to leave Havana for Europe:

> When they got to St. Lazaro's, they saw a cordon of Spanish troops. Near by, negroes and mulattoes, whites and Chinese, the sexes intermingled, formed a colossal African *cabildo*. Raising Cuban flags by now badly dirtied in the dust, they were singing with Senegambian frenzy and shouting out from time to time:
>
> "Long live Cuba! Long live Free Cuba!"
>
> A half-caste lifted up a dead parrot on the end of a long pole; and then the drunken rabble, dancing and jumping in epileptic spasms around him, sang out:
>
> > "Suck the grape,
> > put down the cane,
> > pick up your suitcase
> > and head for Spain."
>
> Then with feline fury he pummeled the wretched little bird that no longer felt anything, and which an unfortunate chain of events had condemned to serve as a symbol of Spain
>
> Santa Fe turned the coach around. He felt as though he were dying.
>
> Julia saw what he was going through and cried out in exasperation:
>
> "And this is what they call Free Cuba? No; this is Free Africa."

> Al llegar frente a San Lázaro, vio un cordón de tropas españoles. Cerca de él, negros y mulatos, blancos y chinos entremezclados los sexos, formando un *cabildo africano* colosal, enarbolando banderas cubanas que el polvo había manchado ya horriblemente, cantaban con frenesí senegámbico, voceando de tiempo en tiempo:
>
> "¡Viva Cuba! ¡Viva Cuba libre!"
>
> Un chusco levantaba en alto un *guacamayo* muerto, que izaba en la punta de un palo largo; y entonces la turba beoda, bailando y saltando con epilépticos espasmos a su alrededor, cantaba:

"Chupa la uva,
deja la caña,
coge la maleta
y vete pa España."

Y aporreaba con ira felina a la triste avecilla que ya nada sentía, y que una ocurrencia malhadada condenara a simbolizar a España.

Santa Fe hizo dar a la vuelta a su coche. Sentíase morir.

Notólo Julia y exasperada gritó:

—¿Y esto es Cuba libre? No; esto es África libre.

¡A Cuba y viva España!

Eight years passed between performances of *Cuba libre* and *¡A Cuba y viva España!* The latter, a play by Rufino Cortés, was performed in Sevilla in 1895. The slight plot serves only to move some Spaniards to Cuba where they have no difficulty prevailing in skirmishes with the insurgents. Racial denigration through humor is the point of the play, its main spokesman a stage Andalusian whose regional speech lends color to his characteristic boastfulness and scorn for people of color: "I, all by myself, am going to kill *so* many mulattoes" ("¡Voy a matar yo sólo más mulatos!"). Later, the same character, Melitón, denies that the insurgents could ever inspire fear in his breast: "Well, a brave little . . . pansy I'd be if I were afraid of those rascals! *Lookit* here, *lootenant*, they throw me, one by one, three or four dozen of those mulattoes *over my way*, and with this here thing and *nothing but* (he takes out a razor and gestures as if he were cutting throats) I cook 'em up a stew" ("¡Pues valiente . . . lila estaría yo si le tuviera miedo a esos sinvergüenzas! Yo, *mirusté*, mi *tiniente*, uno a uno, me echan *pa cá* tres o cuatro docenas de mulatos de esos y con esto *na* más *[saca una navaja de afeitar y hace ademán de cortar cuellos]* les hago un guisao." In this play the insurgents, quite predictably, are cowards, the Spaniards fight like lions.

Familia y patria

Familia y patria appeared on 7 March 1896 at the Teatro Novedades in Barcelona. It was a rewrite of *¡Viva Cuba española!* (1871) by the playwright's father of the same name, Isidoro Martínez Sanz. As would happen later with *Cuba*, a play that opened in December 1896, the premiere of *Familia y patria* served as a pretext for demonstrations. Carlos Serrano has suggested the connivance of agents hired by a proindependent Cuba agent in Paris as an explanation for the cries of "¡Viva Cuba libre!" that repeatedly interrupted the performance.[22]

The agent to whom Serrano refers was Dr. Ramón Emeterio Betances, a leader of the Puerto Rican independence movement and a Cuban sympathizer who provided money so that agents in Spain could put up *pasquinades* and mount demonstrations. In the Spanish press he was at first debunked as a foolish progagandist whom no one believed. *El Imparcial* (12 July 1896) wrote that it was unnecessary to inform readers that Betances was one of the greatest prevaricators in the service of *filibusterismo*. Resident in Paris, the paper went on, he spends his time inventing news, collecting money for his bilingual paper, *Republique Cubaine*, and giving himself airs as the "ambassador without portfolio" ("embajador extraordinario y fuera de abono") of Generalísimo Gómez and of the honorable Maceo. It was he who told the *Intransigent* that Havana was going to be bombed by two destroyers bought by Estrada; he who said that Martínez Campos had committed suicide in Coliseo, along with other equally fraudulent claims. "A fine person!" ("¡Buena persona!").[23] The commercial press typically expressed ridicule and scorn for *filibusteros* and their activities, a tactic that may have increased apprehension instead of quelling it.

It cannot be said with assurance that the content of *Familia y Patria* in any way fueled the demonstrations. Of its two principal themes—the patriotic duty of Spaniards to fight wherever the fatherland sends them and the baseness of the black and mulatto insurgents in Cuba—the first might possibly have constituted a provocation because of increasing unrest over the injustices of the conscription. It is more likely that *any* production centering on the insurrection could have served as a pretext for a demonstration.

Although this play is one of several discussed here whose plots hinge on dramatic complications arising from conscription and volunteer recruitment, its title clearly indicates from the outset how the dramatist wished to frame his material—as a reconciliation of family interests and concerns with the legitimate demands of the fatherland. *Familia y patria* begins by focusing on a mother. At the end of the first *cuadro*, Ricardo's mother reads a letter from her son. In the archaizing and exalted language of newspaper feuilletons and of much contemporary popular fiction, he writes that patriotic fervor has led him to enlist. He has left for Cuba to fight and to search for his father whom Ricardo believes to have been killed in action:

> "My adored Mother: forgive me if the pure affection I profess for you has not permitted me, in your state of grief, to moisten your breast with my weeping, and to seal with a kiss the sorrow that such a bitter parting caused me . . . It was impossible, Mother dear, to appear in your presence: your tears would have drowned the patriotic sentiment and the desire for vengeance on behalf of an affectionate father that animates me. For, although they tell me that he is only wounded, I retain the fear that he may lie in the sepulchre of glory reserved by the fatherland for its heroic martyrs."

> "Mi adorada madre: dispensadme si el acendrado cariño que os profeso, no me ha permitido, en su pesadumbre, humedecer vuestro pecho con mi llanto y sellar con un beso el dolor que me causara tan amarga despedida . . . Imposible me era, madre mía, el verme ante su presencia: vuestras lágrimas hubieran ahogado el sentimiento patrio que me anima y el de venganza, hacia un padre cariñoso, que si bien sólo me anuncian se halla herido, yo abrigo el temor de que yace en el sepulcro de gloria, donde guarda la patria a sus heroicos mártires."

Nearly fainting at the realization that she is now quite alone, she cries, "What is to become of me?" and collapses in an armchair. The pathos of the mother's concern, even if it appears to be directed exclusively at herself, is evident and amounts clearly to concern not for economic survival but apprehension at being left in solitude. Her family is patriotic, not poor: the father and son cannot do other than fight for Spain whether war takes them to Africa, Cuba, or the Philippines. The atypicality of the case—sons of comfortable families did not normally go to war—is significant. In real life, the poverty of the typical conscript's mother would have made her economic survival an important issue.

The contrast between the way in which Ricardo's mother reacts to losing a husband and a son to the war effort and in the next scene the sentiments of a father who has just learned that his son too is leaving for Cuba is also significant. At first, the father rebels against his son's decision, reflecting that paternal devotion is as important as patriotism, and that after anxious years spent raising his son he deserves to see him grow into manhood—not swept off to war. "Damn this war," he cries, "a punishing whiplash on the country's back" ("Maldita sea esa lucha/ azote de nuestro pueblo"). In the midst of this lament, the father's grandson approaches and tells him how he along with other boys staged a mock battle, inspired to do so by a story heard at school about a boy in Cuba who single-handedly defended a sugar mill *(ingenio)* against insurgents. The father's wrath and disappointment fade away: bellicosity, after all, is manly.

There was no need in this or in other patriotic plays to insist on the notion that violence and its expression in war signalled a healthy virility in men, in nations, and in the "race." Years before Max Nordau's *Degeneration* (first translated in Spain in 1901, but much discussed in the press in the early 1890s) brought troubling questions about degeneracy and decadence to public attention, and long before Lord Salisbury's "Dying Nation" speech on 2 May 1898, thoughtful Spaniards reflected on the purported decadence of the Latin race. (Though Salisbury did not specifically name Spain, most people took it to be the "dying nation.") Some Spaniards believed that their countrymen's penchant for violence gave the lie to charges of absolute decline. The critic and novelist Armando Palacio Valdés, for example, had already written in 1881:

> No one who closely observes the Spanish genius and the literature derived from it can doubt that our people love blood in accord with an intimate impulse—I dare not say of the spirit—but rather of temperament. Tragedy, like a heart, pulsates in the depths of the national character. We crave bloody spectacles; crime stories fascinate us, and even in the theater we demand sanguinary dramas. This is a proof of virility and it clearly demonstrates that if there is decadence in the Spanish people, there is no sign of the inner, fatal degradation that makes other nations deserving of scorn.

> No ofrece duda para cualquiera que observa con alguna atención el genio español y la literatura que de él se deriva, que nuestro pueblo ama por un íntimo impulso, no me atrevo a decir del espíritu, sino del temperamento, la sangre. La tragedia late en el fondo del carác-

ter nacional. Apetecemos los espectáculos cruentos; nos seducen las relaciones de los crímenes, y hasta en el teatro pedimos dramas sangrientos. Esta es una prueba de virilidad, y demuestra claramente que, si hay decadencia en el pueblo español, no existe la degradación interior y mortal que hace despreciable a otras naciones.[24]

The father in the second scene and the mother in the first conform to the criteria for the conduct of the two sexes implicit in all but one of these patriotic plays. Fathers take pride in sons who fight in the colonial wars; mothers weep, but in the end willingly send them off to war. All mothers, except for the turncoat mother in *Cuba libre*, are presented in a sympathetic light.

The role of sorrowing wife and mother was not the only role for women that won approval in plays, popular prose fiction, the press, or other sources of propaganda between 1895 and 1898. Women had, in a sense, come a long way. Only thirty-six years earlier, at the time of the African war, Emilio Castelar had spelled out the role of women—and children—in wartime: "weak womankind [should] make bandages and salves to heal the wounds of our martyrs, innocent children should lisp the inspiring names of our heroes of old."[25]

In 1895 women were more actively and publicly engaged. Sisters of Charity, whose selfless activities as nurses and teachers in the colonies had always been praised, earned further admiration for serving in Cuba, impervious to discomfort or danger. Many Spanish women, not previously enlisted in their number, became Sisters of Charity for patriotic reasons. An article sent to *El Imparcial* from Havana and published on 18 December 1896, described the consequences of doña María Luisa Raya y Villaroel's decision to accompany her husband José Pando Alcázar to Cuba with the Wad-Ras batallion from Madrid. Once in Cuba she remained with the batallion as a Sister of Charity sharing their hardships and bearing up bravely under gunfire from the *mambises*. "Piña americana," a story by José Múñiz de Quevedo, published in *El Imparcial* on 29 March 1897, exalted a young creole loyalist's dedication to nursing as a Sister of Charity following a disappointment in love. Her sorrow was more than compensated for by the gratitude she earned for her irreplaceable ministrations to Spanish soldiers: "All the wounded were lodged and cared for with maternal love by those good angels called Hermanas de la Caridad, whose humanitarian mission can never be carried out by male nurses" ("Todos los heridos fueron aposentados y cuidados con maternal amor por aquellos ángeles buenos que se llaman Hermanas de la Caridad, cuya misión humanitaria no habrá jamás enfermeros que sepan suplir"). [26]

For the Exposición de Bellas Artes of 1897 in Madrid, the Valencian painter Cecilio Pla submitted a canvas entitled *Heroínas* that depicted Sisters of Charity departing for the battlefields. The influential art critic and novelist Jacinto Octavio Picón praised the turn toward subject matter that reflected contemporary reality in several of the paintings exhibited in Madrid in 1897. In an essay on the exposition, published in *El Imparcial* on 7 May of that year, he rejected propaganda paintings, but approved of works inspired by dramatic scenes or events that painters could experience personally. He specifically approved of compositions that depicted the consequences of war.

Meanwhile, there was much contemporary interest in female combatants in Cuba and the Philippines. In 1897 E. Reverter Delmas informed Spaniards that Josephine Bracken, the widow of the executed Filipino patriot José Rizal, along with Rizal's two sisters had joined the insurgent forces. In the United States, the North American journalist Nathan Green devoted a chapter of his 1896 book on the Cuban insurrection to the subject "How Women Fight in Cuba." He also recorded the comments General Weyler made on female fighters—most of them said to be mulattoes—to Green's fellow correspondent, Kate Masterson.[27] Drawings or photographs of armed Cuban women occasionally appeared in the Spanish press. Fictional Spanish women engaged in actual battle figure in *Cuba libre* and in *Cuba*. But in real life, although the Spanish press informed the public that, in the great tradition of doña Catalina de Erauso, Manuela Sancho, and Agustina Aragón, some of its women sought to serve Spain directly on the field of battle, it produced no reports on Spanish women combatants in Cuba or in the Philippines. (Catalina de Erauso, also known as the Monja Alférez, fought, dressed as a man, against the *indios* in America for which deeds she was awarded a pension by Philip IV; Manuela Sancho in the first siege and Agustina Aragón in the second actively defended Zaragoza against the French in the War of Independence, and both received pensions as a reward.)

Most often, women followed fiancés or husbands to Cuba with no explicit intention of joining in the actual fighting. Typically, they settled in Havana to await the end of their husbands' tour of duty. Occasionally, young Spanish women were discovered en route to Cuba disguised as men and wearing a uniform, but this dress was perhaps nothing more than a stratagem to secure free passage. Early on in the Cuban insurrection, *El Imparcial* (29 February 1896) reported that a young and beautiful girl from Málaga was discovered on board the steamer *Buenos Aires* after five days at sea, disguised as a man; she meant to accompany her fiancé to Cuba. On 31 August 1896 the same paper revealed that officials removed a girl outfitted in the striped uniform of a soldier from the train taking her and her soldier husband to Barcelona for embarkation to Cuba. The report's author, Mariano de Cavia, pitched the story as a commentary on the failure of a colonial policy enacted by a government formed by men: "Many times in our history female heroism has had to make up for the faults of masculine misgovernment" ("Hartas veces se ha dado el caso en nuestra historia de tener que suplir el heroismo femenil culpas del desgobierno masculino"). The author's sarcastic implication was that the woman from Zaragoza should have been allowed to go to Cuba since the deteriorating situation there was such that before long women recruits would be needed to fight alongside men.

Women were often depicted as guardians of the moral virility that men had somehow forfeited. For example, on 15 May 1896, an editorial in *El Imparcial* praised the gallant cheerfulness Spanish women displayed while doing their duty compared to the unmanly and unpatriotic conduct of Italian males: "While in Milan men were going to the station to prevent the departure of a train carrying troops to Eritrea, here women went to cheer up the expeditionary batallion with their smiles and hurrahs" ("Mientras en Milán los hombres iban a la estación del ferrocarril a impedir que saliera un tren que llevaba tropas a Eritrea, aquí iban las mujeres a animar con sus sonrisas y con sus vítores al batallón expedicionario").

War, as Jean Bethke Elshtain has argued, cannot be conducted without the cooperation of women.[28] Spanish women were clearly expected to cooperate in the war effort by expressing solidarity with government policy through public demonstrations of support.

Anything less could provoke criticism. On 26 April 1896 Rafael Gasset wrote an editorial for *El Imparcial* assuring readers that Spanish newspapers were read in Cuba. If they were to include reports on the tears shed in public by Spanish mothers distraught at sending their sons off to war, on the financial problems occasioned by the war, and on the exhaustion and lukewarm public spirit evinced toward the war, it would surely give comfort to the enemy who might then resist peace overtures: "That's why it would be doing Spain grave damage to go about snivelling for peace" ("He aquí por donde se puede hacer un grave daño a España lloriqueando la paz."). (An editorial of 19 January 1897 in *El Imparcial* claimed that it was regularly sending two or three hundred copies to Cuba; other Madrid papers, it stated, like *El Imparcial*, arrived only from time to time due to communications difficulties in Cuba.)

Patriotic plays, no less than the press, celebrated women who cooperated. The basis for acceptable roles for women in wartime, as the plays make evident, was active or passive self-sacrifice. It is useful to compare this attitude to the position taken by the Filipino patriot José Rizal in his pamphlet *A Letter to the Young Women of Malalos*. He urged the young women of Malalos to continue to think for themselves, to put an end to their subservience to men, and to assert themselves. Like progressive Spaniards, Rizal wanted to sever the bonds between women and priests.[29] The dangers to liberalism implicit in that relationship are inadvertently suggested by an editor's note in *Filipinas: problema fundamental por un español de larga residencia en aquellas islas*, which referred to the separatist conspiracies in the Philippines and continued: "Almost all of them have been uncovered and denounced [to priests] by indigenous women very devoted to Spain" ("Casi todas las han descubierto y denunciado mujeres indias, muy adictas a España . . ."[30]

The second and third acts of *Familia y patria* take place in Cuba. An insurgent camp is the setting for songs and dances performed by blacks and mulattoes. As in *Cuba libre*, when Spaniards are on stage with the *mambises* there is some discussion about the reasons for the insurrection, but these interchanges always end with the Spaniards' denial of any justification at all.[31] Other topics of conversation revolve around the charms of dark-skinned women compared to white women, the beauty of the Cuban landscape, the bounty of its fruit. (In the mouths of blacks, the word "fruit" always has the double meaning alluded to earlier.)

Once again a mulatto, Waldo, figures in the plot. Waldo is the leader of the black insurgents. When Ricardo's sister, María, comes to Cuba to search for him and for their father, Waldo manages to seize her. He then tries to seduce her. She responds or, rather, declaims angrily: "Like a new Judas you betray your sworn faith for an infamous passion sprung from an impure soul" ("Nuevo Judas / por una pasión infame / nacida en un alma impura, / vendéis vuestra fe jurada"), thus underlining the essentially treacherous nature of the mulatto. The mulatto's defeat at the hands of a virtuous woman happens in the same way here as in *Cuba*, performed some eight months later. Rather than yield, the Spanish woman presents her breast to be stabbed by the would-be seducer, but the mulatto—restrained perhaps by his Spanish blood—declines to do the deed. In the end, Ricardo and María find each other and confidently await a Spanish victory.

España en Cuba

España en Cuba premiered in La Coruña on 18 April 1896. Written by the "distinguished" naval accountant Ricardo Caballero y Martínez, it fully deserved the praise it garnered in the Galician capital according to the drama critic who reviewed it at its premiere in Madrid on 5 July 1896. The critic remarked on the play's simple but well-prepared situations. Its plot is, indeed, of negligible interest: essentially, this play is a variation on a theme also found in *Familia y patria* and *Cuba* in which Spaniards in the *manigua* are contrasted to blacks whose ignorance and naiveté are at the forefront. Humorous effects depend upon the latters' inability to speak correct Castilian. The opening dialogue illustrates these notions and sums up the substance of the author's comments throughout the play in regard to Cuban blacks. A black man has just told a black woman what the insurgents have done in a neighboring *ingenio*. When she asks why they did so much damage, he responds in his flawed Castilian:

> Ta give us
> an idea of how guud
> independence is gwinna be
> in a Free Cuba.

Pa danos
una idea de lo güeno
que ha de ser la independensia
de Cuba libre.

She cries,

Big bullies!
Gawd protek us from doze peeple:
thank Gawd they didn't pass by here.

¡Sopencos!
Guádenos Dió de esa jente:
glasia que acá no vinieron.

As rebels, the audience gathers, blacks are wantonly destructive. And away from their leaders, who are usually mulattoes, they reveal their gullibility.

Un voluntario a Cuba

A play entitled *Un voluntario a Cuba* was advertised in *El Imparcial* for 23 August 1896 at the Teatro Martín. One of several works to be performed at a benefit performance, neither the play nor a review (if, in fact, it was performed) have been located.

Cuba

On 9 November 1896, *El Imparcial* ran an article entitled "Masked Political Agitators" ("Laborantes con careta"). Noting that the rumor he was about to retail had appeared in several other papers, the author proceeded to relate the following story. A dramatist had submitted a "patriotic work" *(obra patriótica)* entitled *Cuba*, in which "the *mambises* came out badly" ("los mambises salían mal parados") to the Teatro-Circo de Parish. The impresario accepted it and was preparing its production when it was learned that a group of Cuban *laborantes* (political agitators) who met regularly in a Madrid café meant at any cost to prevent performances of the play. A delegate from the district of Buenavista, Sr. Puga, investigated the matter and concluded that the threats were real. He approached the soprano Srta. Pretel, whom the Cubans had purportedly asked to withdraw from the production, but she claimed ignorance of the entire affair. When Puga talked to the Cubans, "those men, who at the outset were energetic and disposed to cause an uproar and shed their generous blood in defense of the *mambises*, declared that they were so many innocent doves, not involved in any separatist demonstration or bellicose undertaking" ("los que al principio se mostraban enérgicos y en disposición de armar un escándalo y de verter su sangre generosa en defensa de los *mambises*, declararon que eran unos palomos inocentes, agenos [*sic*] a toda manifestación separatista y a todo proyecto belicoso"). The reporter concluded that it seemed that the show would go on if the impresario chose to stage it. But, he added, there will always remain this terrible doubt: "Are there disguised agitators among us? Is it true that they hold meetings? Are we safe?" ("¿Existen entre nosotros laborantes disfrazados? ¿Es cierto que celebran reuniones? ¿Estaremos seguros?")

Cuba, the play in question, with music by Maestro Luis Reig and book by Jesús López Gómez, was intended, in part, to extol the Madrid garrison. Its dedication stated that the play was inspired by the holy love for the fatherland that the valiant sons of Spain manning the garrison honored and defended on all occasions. *Cuba* premiered on 11 December 1896 at the Parish. All the seats in the house were taken—the gay note of military uniforms predominant, according to the reviewer for *El Imparcial*—with an audience eager to applaud effusions of the purest *españolismo*. The audience did applaud the play's patriotic effusions, but found it difficult—again according to the reviewer—to conceal its laughter at the melodramatic plot.

The play opens as Roberto, a mulatto plantation owner, has taken advantage of the wartime chaos to abduct the white wife of a Cuban landowner, Don Santiago. A somewhat similar situation develops with two black men vying for possession of a black woman. Neither Roberto nor the black abductor succeeds in forcing the woman he desires. At the play's end, the rebels are on the run while Spanish reinforcements arrive in a scene mounted in spectacular (and expensive) fashion. It is morning, the sun is rising. The Spaniards and the blacks loyal to them are kneeling on stage waving Spanish flags. Beyond the tree tops the audience spies a Spanish vessel slowly moving toward shore. Cries of "¡Viva España¡" ring out, accompanied by military music.

The use of the Spanish flag on stage in several of these plays clearly constituted an especially potent appeal to patriotism, yet, as Carolyn P. Boyd notes in her recent study *Historia Patria*, the flag's significance was problematical in the nineteenth century. It was not depicted in nineteenth-century textbooks since it was, for many, "a partisan and, thus, divisive symbol." Boyd notes further that the flag, devised in 1785, was "declared the emblem of the Spanish monarchy and extended to the army by the Moderados only in 1843 and was not flown over public buildings until 1908."[32]

Judging by audiences' reaction as reported by theater reviewers, the flags raised and waved on stage effectively conjured up the strong sentiments experienced by the troops when flags were unfurled in Cuba and the Philippines after successful battles. On 28 March 1897, for example, *El Imparcial* carried an account of the Spanish flag being raised on top of the church at Imus following the 24 March defeat of the Tagalos in that town, seat of the insurgent government. In less than a dozen lines, the correspondent evoked the unity—symbolized by the flag—constituted by the throne, the military, and the church. The brief scene opened as the triumphant General Arizón gathered all his troops in the plaza before the church:

> It was a moment of genuine and most beautiful emotion. While a soldier raised the flag on the cupola of the church, the band played the Royal March, and the soldiers all gave frenetic *vivas* to Generals Polavieja, Lachambre and Marina.
>
> Around those troops which formed a column of honor, the ruins of the settlement were smoking, for everything had been burned—all but the church.
>
> Fue aquel un momento de verdadera y hermosísima emoción. En tanto que un soldado izaba la bandera en la cúpula de la iglesia, la música entonaba la Marcha Real, y los soldados todos daban vivas frenéticos a los generales Polavieja, Lachambre y Marina.
>
> En torno de aquellas tropas formadas en columna de honor, humeaban las ruinas del caserío, que estaba todo incendiado, excepto la iglesia.

Only two months earlier (on 31 January) Domingo Blanco described for *El Imparcial* a sight on board the steamer *San Augustín* designed to evoke the emotive power of the flag in combination with religious imagery. On board the ship were 480 soldiers, all of them ill and in the process of being repatriated from Cuba. With a cabin partition as background, the Sisters of Charity had arranged the Spanish flag to serve as a kind of throne for a picture representing the Virgen del Carmen. Blanco commented, "The positioning of their cots places those unfortunate soldiers face to face with the holy and glorious display and thus, in the midst of their bitterness, they have the consolation of seeing the precious image and the flag of the fatherland" ("La posición de las literas hace que aquellos infelices soldados estén de frente al santo y glorioso pabellón, y así tienen en medio de sus amarguras el consuelo de ver a la preciosa imagen y a la bandera de la patria").

Long after the defeat of the Spanish flotilla in Manila Bay on 1 May and the surrender of Manila on 14 August 1898, Spaniards learned about the heroic stand taken at Baler on Luzón by soldiers who did not know that Spain had surrendered to the United States. The Spanish captain, Enrique de Las Morenas, held out against the Tagalos until 2 June 1899. Here again, the flag became an important symbol of Spanish loyalty and fidelity: "when the wind and the elements tore [the flag] to pieces they patched it up with sacristans' red surplices and with yellow mosquito netting."[33] Like the rousing strains of the "Marcha de Cádiz," which for a time became a national anthem, the flag's appearance on stage in patriotic plays was clearly a powerful rallying cry to Spanish unity in the face of the enemy from 1895 to 1898.

The *mambises*, as the Cuban *laborantes* feared, are depicted as cowards and turncoats in *Cuba*. Further, the author has represented blacks and mulattoes as the most numerous groups within the insurgent camp. In doing so he has reiterated two of the key ideas presented in *Cuba libre:* most of the insurrectionists were blacks or mulattoes; their uneasy alliance with each other and with whites must crumble eventually; and independence would certainly lead to a race war. The author drew on the stereotypical notions that distinguished mulattoes from blacks and opposed them to each other: mulattoes believed themselves to be superior to blacks and always sought mastery over them. Furthermore, mulattoes were not grateful for the white blood coursing through their veins that should unite them to Spain. Thus the mulatto Roberto is guilty, above all, of ingratitude to the fatherland that gave him Spanish blood. In order to underline these essential features of the mulatto—ingratitude, treachery, and betrayal—the author likens Roberto to the dark-skinned execution-ers of Christ, to Cain ("What devouring thirst for extermination is this that consumes and burns me?" ["¿Qué devoradora sed es ésta de exterminio que me consume y abrasa?"], Roberto cries out at one point) and to a vampire sucking the blood of Spain.

While the mulatto's mixture of black and white blood obscures his true allegiances and makes his treachery—so deceitfully con-cealed—especially heinous, the majority of blacks in this play are "good negroes". Good in the sense that they are less problematical and less dangerous. They are good because they are "white" inside: they have internalized a rudimentary ethics based on the Catholic religion and the Spanish code of honor. Trinidad, the white wife's black maid, resolves to save her mistress from Roberto's clutches even at the cost of her own life. She explains her decision thus, "I have a black face but my heart is lily white" ("Yo tengo la cara more-na; pero el corasón mu banco" [sic]).

Although calls for Christian assimilation of blacks into the Spanish "family" are infrequent, a sketch by Miguel Ramos Carrión appeared in El Imparcial on 4 January 1897 whose moral pointed to the brotherhood in Christ of men of all colors. "El prójimo negro" tells the story of a white Spanish soldier who saves the life of a black infant, taking him along as he seeks a safe place to hide from the mambises. That night the soldier has a dream about the nativity scene traditionally mounted in his church back in Aragón. To his aston-ishment the Christ child in his dream is black. When he awakens, several black rebels surprise him in his hiding place and threaten to kill him. However, they pause long enough to listen to his explana-tion of how he has come to have the baby, and having heard it, let him go. As they leave, they call out that he should remember that he owes his life to a black. He calls out in turn that the black baby owes his life to a white. In short, we are all one, mutually dependent and interchangeable in the eyes of the Christian God.

Good blacks in Cuba are ridiculous when they try to be white on the outside by powdering their faces and wearing white garb, but at bottom they are viewed favorably because of their gratitude and loy-alty to their benefactors. Scene twelve sets out the fundamental attitudes and sentiments attributed to good blacks by their black spokesman, Caracolillo: they have been told and often recall that it was Spain that freed them from slavery; they believe in the notion that if Cuba were independent it would fail for the same reason that Haiti and Santo Domingo failed; only as Spanish subjects can blacks prosper; mulattoes like Roberto in an independent Cuba would try to lord it over them rather than elevate them to positions of power and prestige. Finally, in an emotional outburst of pro-Spanish sentiment, the black spokesman cries out: "Down with separatism forever! Come, Pancha, my girl; you all, come too, for though you are black, blood freed by Spanishness flows through your veins. We are the true masters; the insurgents and *mambises* from this day on are our servile slaves!" ("¡Abajo para siempre el filibusterismo! Anda, Pancha amiga, andad vosotros también, que aunque negos [*sic*], circula por vuestras venas sangre libertada por el españolismo. Somos los verdaderos señores; los insurrectos y mambises quedan desde hoy nuestros esclavos serviles.")

In this play, unlike *Cuba libre*, the femininity of the white wife is not impugned even though she fights alongside male soldiers. Indeed, a Spanish soldier refers to her as "The heroic Amazon who is to lead us to victory" ("La heroica amazona que ha de conducirnos a la victoria"). When her husband shows surprise at seeing her in pursuit of the enemy, she herself explains: "Women become virile when they see their men lying dead" ("Son mujeres varoniles al ver al que adoran muertos"). The author of this play evidently finds the issue of women fighting—for Spain—unproblematical. He shows more interest in contrasting the ways in which black and white women express love and in how they represent different ideals of female beauty. The playwright characterizes the white woman's love in terms of loyalty, while the black woman's love is represented as sensual and passionate. Black men and women perform a song and dance in the middle of the play that captures many of the images associated with black love in the tropics: heat, passion, scents of flowers and fruits, palm fronds waving in the breeze.

An Andalusian soldier sums up the physical differences between black and white women as he tells his comrades why he did not succumb to the blandishments of a black woman one night in Baire:

Since I've been in Cuba I've finished off at least fifty-seven *mambises*, black, white, and yellow. One night, over in Baire, I came upon a girl from the country—blacker than coal but smooth as a kid glove—pretending to be asleep. That negress tried to make love to me. Make love to me? A guy who left a girl back in Triana with more spice in her than in all the Spice Islands combined. I said to that little cupcake, What was it ruined your looks, black girl? Back in my country, there on my dear mother's breast, lies a woman who's pining for me, a woman whiter than ermine, with big, blue eyes and red lips who, when she wraps her body in a Manila shawl, with the air she stirs up, could bleach all you negroes, mulattoes or creoles who are blackened, from your feet to the tops of your heads.

Ende que estoy en Cuba llevo finiquitaos lo menos sincuenta y siete mambises entre negos, blancos y amarillos. Una noche, allá en el Baire, me encontré, fingiéndose la dormida, a una joven guajira más nega que el azabache, pero fina como guante de cabritilla. La nega pretendía camelarme. ¿Camelarme a mí? A mí, que dejé en Triana una niña con más sal que los mares arrastran entre sus arenillas. Yo dije a aquella chinita: ¿Qué te desfiguraste, negrita? En mi patria, allá arriba, en el seno de mi mare querida, pena por este chaval una jembra más blanca que el mesmo armiño, de ojos grandes, azules y labios de purpurina, que cuando envuelve su cuerpo en el mantón de Manila, con el aire que ella arrebuja a su vera cuando camina, puede desteñiros a cuantos negos, mulatos o criollos estáis embetunados, dende los pies hasta la coroniya.[34]

The main theme of this play is the same as that of *Cuba libre:* the civilizing mission of Spain has made Cuba what it is and without continued guidance the country will descend into chaos. What is new here is a greater emphasis on racial difference. This is perhaps, in part, a response to Spaniards' interest and fascination with Antonio Maceo throughout 1895 and up to and even beyond his death at the end of 1896.

¡Sacrificios heroicos!

—What do the soldiers say? . . .
—And the young people? . . .
—And the old people? . . .
—And the mothers?
—The mothers have no more tears; they
have wept so many their souls are

dry, and they only feel anger. The
tide is rising; their patience is exhausted; something
tremendous is crystallizing in the public
consciousness. What is going to happen? Will the
government act
in unison with this sentiment?

—¿Qué dicen los soldados? . . .
—¿Y los jóvenes? . . .
—¿Y los viejos? . . .
—¿Y las madres?
—Ya no tienen lágrimas; han
derramado tantas que tienen seca
el alma, y sólo sienten ira. La
ola sube; la paciencia está
agotada; se va cristalizando algo
grande en la conciencia pública.
¿Qué va a suceder? ¿Estará el
Gobierno al unísono con ese sentimiento?

José Fernández Bremón, *La Ilustración Española y Americana*,
8 April 1898

In early August 1896, four months before *Cuba* appeared in
Madrid, a much-publicized event took place in Zaragoza. Readers of
the press were informed that a group of mothers demonstrated in
protest against sending another convoy of poor conscripts to Cuba.
They reportedly marched through the streets carrying placards that
read "Let the poor and the rich go!" Government officials and the
commercial press tried to discredit the women as misguided dupes
of Protestants, Masons, or *filibusteros*. On 22 August 1896, the prime
minister, Antonio Cánovas, commented in *El Imparcial* on the
Zaragoza demonstration as well as on similar demonstrations
reported in other parts of Spain. He related them to the recent dis-
covery of a conspiratorial group in the Philippines: "That
conspiracy, like the demonstrations in Zaragoza, Valencia and elsewhere, has been promoted by Cuban *filibusteros* in order to distract
Spain's attention and thus prevent all our efforts and all means at our
disposal from being directed to the sole purpose of putting an end to

the Cuban insurrection" ("Esa conjura, al igual de las manifestaciones de Zaragoza, Valencia y otros puntos, ha sido promovido por los filibusteros cubanos con el propósito de dividir la atención de España para evitar que todos nuestros esfuerzos se encaminen al sólo fin de aumentar los medios de acabar con la insurrección cubana"). In the same article, Cánovas blamed similar demonstrations in Barcelona on republican agitators: "They have tried to maintain unrest in Barcelona by shouting 'Let the poor and the rich go to Cuba.' This cry, which would not be seditious in normal situations, is at this time because it is being used to draw attention to the inevitable inequalities implicit in military service and to provoke rebellions and mutinies. That is what the republicans wanted in Barcelona and we have prevented it" ("En Barcelona se ha pretendido mantener la agitación por medio del grito: '¡Que vayan a Cuba pobres y ricos!' Esto, que no sería sedicioso en situaciones normales, lo es actualmente porque con él se pretende poner en relieve las desigualdades inevitables ante el servicio militar y provocar deserciones y motines. Era lo que deseaban los republicanos de Barcelona y nosotros lo hemos impedido").

Whatever Spaniards may have thought about the women's motives for protesting, most of them acknowledged the injustices of the conscription system.[35] The precarious position of the poor mothers of the *quintos* was widely acknowledged. Magazine graphics from 1895 to 1898, for example, often depict scenes in which an indigent mother bids a pathetic farewell at the docks or at the train station to her sole source of support, a son bound for Cuba or the Philippines.

The August demonstration in Zaragoza was nearly unique throughout Spain in opposing the current system of conscription though there were, in fact, a number of less well publicized women's demonstrations in August 1896 in several small towns near Valencia and in Valencia proper. Yet, despite evidence of isolated expressions of opposition to the *quinta*, nothing in Spain between 1895 and 1898 approached the 1863 draft riots in New York City in terms of numbers of participants or the level of violence.[36]

An account of the Zaragoza demonstration in *El Globo* of 25 August 1896 noted that soldiers in that area were approached by *ganchos filibusteros* (filibustering "hooks") who gave them clothes and money so that they could desert. Desertion was obviously a more prudent option than rioting, especially for those men who lived in relatively close proximity to the sea or to land frontiers.[37]

The publicity given the Zaragoza demonstration may have helped make it possible for playwrights to broach the issue of conscription on the stage in wartime to the admittedly limited extent that they did. Playwrights may also have been less reluctant to present material on the *quinta* since it was known that even before the summer of 1896 a number of people—including representatives of the military—had raised objections to its injustices.[38] Criticism of the conscription system was, in fact, broadly diffused throughout Spain between 1895 and 1898. Furthermore, editorial writers for the press did not skirt explicit reference to class, driving home the inequities of the system again and again between 1887 and 1898 in publications ranging from the low-circulation weekly *El Socialista* to the high-circulation daily *El Imparcial*.

A class focus appeared in two stories published respectively in *El Imparcial* on 24 February 1896—Leopoldo Alas's bitter sketch "El rana"—and in *El Socialista* on 15 October 1897—Emilia Pardo Bazan's story "Poema humilde." Alas's story dealt with the heartless treatment accorded volunteers from the lower class who signed up for duty in Cuba out of abject poverty. The story is particularly noteworthy for its explicit criticism of the church's indifference to the departing volunteers. The church is represented as viewing them as nothing more than scraps of humanity to be swept away by the Cuban war in what amounted to a welcome house cleaning. It may be noted here that there are no references to the church's role in the war in the plays discussed here. However, according to its author, a scene satirizing mass in *Un alcalde en la manigua* was protested by some members of the public on opening night and was suppressed in subsequent performances—evidence that audiences made their views known and, at times, demanded changes.

Pardo Bazán's story describes the plight of a humble rural couple separated by the war. The young man, whose father failed to have him exempted from service with a bribe, leaves for Cuba. He returns wounded and dies on the dock as soon as he lands.

The official, patriotic line on how to view the inequities of recruitment policy was expressed in an editorial in *El Imparcial* written by J. Ortega Munilla on 31 August 1896, less than a month after the Zaragoza demonstration. Ortega marvelled at the fact that despite the errors of ministers and generals, and despite the efforts of *filibusteros*, recruits were still filling the trains taking them to the steamships of the Transatlántica on which they embarked for Cuba and the Philippines. That miracle of patriotism, he wrote, was being enacted by the very men who benefited least from Spain's social and economic organization, by men who only registered the existence of the State when the tax collector appeared or a sergeant arrived to fill the *quinta*:

> Perhaps history registers nothing like it. The scoffing at eternal principles that has demoralized the middle class and the upper classes has not been able to destroy the people's heart of gold, which wholly belongs to Spain.
>
> Once again the brave soldier lad sets out, a bit confused with the emotion of the leave-taking, certain that when he sacrifices his life he will be complying with the most glorious of duties.
>
> He expects no compensations; he neither desires nor does he need them. He does what he does because his conscience orders him to, in a confused and poorly understood voice, but one so energetic that it leaves no room for doubt. He is going to fight as his father fought, as his grandfather fought in this eternal Spanish war to which we seem condemned without remission.

> Acaso no registre la historia ejemplo semejante. La burla de los eternos principios que ha desmoralizado a la clase media y a las clases superiores, no ha podido destruir el corazón de oro de la plebe, que es todo entero para España.
>
> Allá va otra vez el soldadito, un poco aturdido con las emociones de la despedida, lleno de entusiasmo, seguro de que al sacrificar su vida cumple el más glorioso de los deberes.
>
> No espera recompensas, ni las desea, ni las necesita. Lo que hace lo hace porque se lo manda su conciencia con voz confusa y mal entendida, pero tan enérgicamente, que no le deja lugar a duda. Va a pelear como peleó su padre, como peleó su abuelo en esta perdurable guerra española a que parecemos condenados sin remisión posible.

The socialists, who had been consistently vocal in opposition to a recruitment system that permitted the well-off to evade service with a cash payment, ran an editorial on 4 September 1896 in *El*

Socialista, a few days after that of Ortega Munilla: "While the sons of the people go off to shed their blood for the Mamma Land, the offspring of the aristocracy employ their leisure by holding amateur bullfights in which they take part as matadors . . ." ("Mientras los hijos del pueblo van a dar su sangre por mamá patria, los chicos de la aristocracia distraen sus ocios celebrando becerradas en las que toman parte como lidiadores . . ." On 19 September 1896 the socialist newspaper in Bilbao, *La Lucha de clases*, called upon Spanish mothers to persevere in opposing the war, and on 25 September 1896, an editorial in *El Socialista* stated the following:

> The only ones who up to now have suffered the hazards of war are the poor. More than 200,000 have gone to Cuba. Who knows how many more are yet to go, and how many will be needed to confront other conflicts?
>
> We send the soldiers off with music, speeches, vivas, bishops' blessings and . . . tears; when they return wounded, sick or disabled, they're welcomed back by lowbred swindlers if they have any money, or, if they don't, they're forced to beg . . .
>
> The people are asked for more and more men. No protests are tolerated, not even the request that there be no special privileges. It has come to the point that men who evade service by emigrating are defamed while others continue to evade it with money.

> Los únicos que hasta ahora han sufrido los azares de la guerra son los pobres. A Cuba han ido más de 200,000, ¿quién sabe los que habrán de ir aun y los que serán necesarios para afrontar los demás conflictos?
>
> Se despide a los soldados con músicas, discursos, vivas, bendiciones episcopales y . . . lágrimas; se los recibe cuando regresan heridos, enfermos o inútiles, por timadores de baja estofa, si traen dinero, o han de pedir limosna si de él carecen . . .
>
> Al pueblo se le piden hombres y más hombres, sin tolerar protestar ni aun pedir que no haya privilegios. Se llega hasta infamar los que eluden el servicio de las armas con la emigración como otros le eluden con el dinero.

The socialists continued their campaign against the inequities of the *quinta* on the national level from mid-1897 on, increasing the number of their meetings and broadening distribution of propaganda.[39] There were, admittedly, few readers for the weekly *El Socialista*, but in 1897 the high-circulation daily, *El Imparcial* (at that, only about 100,000 readers out of Spain's population of 17,000,000), was running frequent pieces with titles such as "Mothers without Sons" ("Madres sin hijos") in which the plight of poor families whose sons were called up was presented in summary form, normally allotting one paragraph to each case.

On 26 October 1897, the newspaper printed a column entitled "To the War Minister: Well-Founded Complaints" ("Al Ministerio de la Guerra: quejas fundadas"), which pinpointed twelve instances of unjust recruitment practice. One typical case described a mother's desperate situation:

> Dolores Cabezas, a resident of Constantina, has her husband incapacitated for work due to physical disability, according to certification executed in accord with the appropriate medical examination, in spite of which, her only son, Manuel, has been called to active service and will be sent to the army in Cuba.

> Dolores Cabezas, vecina de Constantina, tiene a su marido inútil para el trabajo por impedimento físico según certificación expedida en virtud del oportuno reconocimiento facultativo, a pesar de lo cual, su único hijo, Manuel, ha sido incorporado a filas y será conducido al ejército de operaciones en la isla de Cuba.

Another case, reported in *El Imparcial* on 22 May 1898, detailed the precarious situation of Petra Múñiz de la Osa, a widow with three sons. One served in Cuba where he was wounded three times and was finally discharged for disabilty. The second was serving in Cuba. The third had then been called up even though he was the only son left to support his impoverished mother. The report remarked that to deprive Petra of the son who was attending to her needs was to condemn her to death by starvation. It ended by asking, "Will the Minister of War give his consent to such an iniquitous action?" ("¿Consentirá el señor ministro de la Guerra tamaña iniquidad?").

Familia y patria, performed about five months before the Zaragoza demonstration, did not refer to class in connection with military service. The focus was on the merely apparent conflict between the demands of patriotism and family. The audience was first invited to contrast the traditional obligations and responsibilities assigned to parents according to sex, and then to observe which ones best supported the goals of the war. In effect, it was women, normally charged with holding the family together, who had to be convinced that abstract notions—the integrity of the fatherland, honor, race—demanded their allegiance before concrete familial concerns.

Five months after the events in Zaragoza, on 22 January 1897, ¡Sacrificios heroicos!, a one-act play in verse, debuted in Madrid. Here again, the dramatist has avoided class references. Miguel, the protagonist, explains to his wife, Luisa, why he must leave her and their son to fight in Cuba. Mother Spain, he cries, must combat the ferocious hordes, the black mobs bent on destruction in the colony, even if it means draining the last drop of blood from her veins. Cuba is Spanish, he continues, and the blood circulating in its veins [i.e., in the veins of the white Creoles] bears the vital germ of the Spanish race. As a simple soldier he takes pride in being among the first to go and spill his blood.

When his wife protests his going on the grounds that he has a family, he replies that many other soldiers have families. However, her observation that even the rebels have families provokes an energetic denial: Those cowards have all emerged from a wild beast's den, her husband cries, apparently referring only to the blacks among the insurgents. How could ferocious murderers have families? To say so is to prostitute the very name of family. Miguel then takes a different tack, asking her what value a family, a wife, or a son could have in any case, compared to the integrity of the Spanish race and soil. "Race" in this passage, despite the implicit contrast of black Cubans with white Spaniards, refers—as it does in the discussion that follows—more properly to ethnicity: in Louis S. Gerteïs's words, to the "cultural cohesion shaped by consent, in contrast to the biological determinism of racial descent."[40]

The same argument, privileging the survival of the race over the particular demands of family ties, inspired a story by Fernando Soldevilla, "Heart of a Patriot" ("Corazón de patriota"), that had appeared in El Imparcial some four months earlier (14 September 1896). The patriot of the title is a Spaniard who has made his fortune in Cuba where he lives with his Creole wife and two sons. At the time of the first insurrection in 1868, the patriot puts himself and his fortune at the disposition of the Spanish authorities: "He was what Spaniards who live in Cuba ought to be, because the man who is born in Spain and does not defend it and does not glorify it; the man who seeks to lower its prestige or makes compromises regarding it—that man is neither a Spaniard nor an honorable man" ("Era como deben de ser los españoles que viven en Cuba, porque aquel que nació en España y no la defiende y no la ensalza, aquel que procura el desprestigio de su patria o transige con él, ése ni es español, ni es hombre honrado"). Soon after, to his great dismay, he learns that his wife has persuaded his oldest son to join the insurgents and means to influence the youngest son to fight against Spain as well. The patriot hesitates only so long as to experience the full measure of disillusion and grief at his wife's betrayal. Then, having secured to himself all his funds, and despite her pleas for mercy, he leaves his wife and youngest son quite literally in the street. He returns to Spain,

> . . . pensive, melancholy, for affections long rooted in the heart are not torn out all at once; but proud and tranquil, nonetheless, like a man who has complied with the greatest duty we have on this earth—that of sacrificing everything, honors, fortune, position and happiness as an offering to the fatherland.

> . . . meditabundo, sombrío, que no se arrancan de una vez los afectos que llevan muchos años arraigados en el corazón; pero orgulloso y tranquilo, como aquel que ha cumplido con el deber más grande que los hombres tienen sobre la tierra, el de sacrificar todo, honores, fortuna, posición y dicha en holocausto de la patria.

Through the sacrifice of family bonds, patriotism has undoubtedly triumphed. The protagonist of this story did not, in the event, see the need to sacrifice his honor, position, or his fortune, which went back to Spain with him.

The protagonist of *¡Sacrificios heroicos!* addresses his wife with such passion that he ends by eliciting sentiments of patriotism in her as well. She cries out that his words have inflamed her. She is, after all, a woman before she is a mother and a Spaniard before she is Aragonese:

> I am a woman, and a woman who is Aragonese;
> the land of honor and heroism!
> And your wife, who before she is Aragonese is Spanish,
> says to you now in a transport of enthusiasm:
> Go to the war, Miguel, and if you don't return,

my breast will tenderly and lovingly preserve
the memory of the hero whose name
will be the pride and the glory of our son!

Soy mujer, y mujer aragonesa;
la tierra del honor y el heroismo!
Y antes que aragonesa es española
tu esposa, que hoy te dice en su delirio:
¡Ve a la guerra, Miguel, y si no vuelves,
mi pecho guardará tierno y rendido,
la memoria del héroe, cuyo nombre
será orgullo y blasón de nuestro hijo!

The appeal to Spanish women to preserve racial values (i.e., cultural values considered inherent in the Spanish "race"), at least in this case, proved persuasive in subordinating the family, one of the institutions traditionally most cherished by the Spanish race, to the interests of an abstract nationalism.[41]

In the plays discussed here, women's roles in the crisis brought on by the colonial insurrections have included accompanying, even fighting alongside, their men in battle or, more typically, cheerfully sending husbands or sons off to the colonial wars. There was an additional option that had long been available in real life. In 1897, the same year in which *Sacrificios* appeared, Tesifonte Gallego, a former secretary to General Salamanca (captain-general) in Cuba, published *La insurrección cubana*. In his book, Gallego discussed Salamanca's family colonization project designed to "whiten" Cuba. The general, Gallego wrote, was convinced of the usefulness of sending "the genuinely Spanish woman, with her fervent love for the national cause" ("la mujer genuinamente española, con su amor ferviente a la causa nacional").[42]

Did significant numbers of Spanish women, including wives and mothers, participate in any such project? Hugh Thomas, in his history of Cuba, writes that a flood of immigrants took advantage of the Spanish government's offer in 1886 to pay the passage of workers willing to spend one year in Cuba. Thomas further notes that according to official statistics, "224,000 arrived in Cuba from Spain between 1882 and 1894 (excluding 1888) of whom only 142,000 ever returned."[43] Unfortunately, these statistics are not broken down by sex or civil state.

In any event, Spanish women were given the opportunity to express their patriotism by leaving their homeland and emigrating to Cuba. In this way, they were told, they could participate in "whitening" Cuba, thereby helping to avoid a racial imbalance that might lead to a race war. Christopher Schmidt-Nowara has further examined the implications of schemes for "whitening" Cuba: "Even advocates of 'whitening' still imagined racial differences between workers and elites at the end of that process because they projected miscegenation for the working, not the ruling class. In other words, their fellow colonial subjects would always be the 'other' by which Antillean elites knew themselves as 'Cubans,' 'Puerto Ricans,' or 'Latins.' "[44] It seems quite safe to assume that only women from the poorest families would have availed themselves of this opportunity to make even more sacrifices for the fatherland.

Los dramas de la guerra

Less than one month after *¡Sacrificios heroicos!* exalted a patriotism largely rooted in racial pride, a play appeared in Madrid that presented the Cuban war in quite a different light. Vicente Moreno de la Tejera was the author of *Los dramas de la guerra* which premiered on 14 February 1897. The play is in verse, but its language is far removed from the artificial language so reminiscent of the feuilleton that characterizes *Sacrificios*. More importantly, for the first time since the outbreak of war in 1895, conscription is clearly represented on the Spanish stage in terms of class. The lives of the poor protagonist and his fiancée are profoundly disrupted solely because of their inability to pay a fee that would exempt a relative from the *quinta*.

The protagonist, Felipe, enlists as a volunteer because his fiancée has rejected him in order to marry a man rich enough to redeem her brother from service. While his fiancée's father views Felipe's enlistment as a deliberate, desperate courting of death, his own daughter's sacrifice of personal happiness is represented as being as natural for a woman in her position as it is laudable. On one end of the balance is a young man's life, sure to be lost in the unhealthy miasmas of the *manigua*; on the other, the marriage plans of two people who will not, after all, be condemned to death, if those plans are frustrated.

Felipe goes off to war. There is no question here of justifying to parents the sacrifice of a son through an abstract appeal to a patriotism based on a notion of racial or ethnic superiority or on any concept of national integrity. The emphasis from the outset is on the suffering of men at the front and on the social and economic injustices brought to light by the war. Felipe's father, Don Ramón, who had accompanied General Juan Prim to Africa in 1860, delivers a monologue in act two in which he imagines what his son is undergoing in Cuba:

> . . . to fight with traitors
> in the dense *manigua*
> and to fight against that climate
> that poisons a man's body
> is to fight against impossible odds.
> Felipe! My son!
> Where are you now?
> Perhaps in a hospital.
> Amidst horror and suffering,
> perhaps dead and buried
> in that accursed land,
> without a cross on your grave,
> perhaps with no grave at all.

> . . . luchar con traidores
> entre la manigua espesa
> y luchar con aquel clima
> que el organismo envenena,
> es tener en contra suya
> mil probabilidades ciertas.
> ¡Mi Felipe! ¡El hijo mío!
> ¿Dónde a estas horas se encuentra?
> Tal vez en un hospital.
> Entre horrores y entre penas,
> tal vez muerto y enterrado
> en esa maldita tierra,
> sin una cruz en su tumba.
> tal vez sin tumba siquiera.

Don Ramón reflects on the different treatment meted out to officers and common soldiers:

I confess that it is inhuman . . .
The soldier is forgotton
as if he were a drop lost
in the middle of the ocean.
A commander-in-chief dies, an officer,
and since it's a serious matter,
the cable tells us at once
that it is officer so and so.
And then with uncertain data
as if it were of no concern,
the dispatch ends thus:
—and so many dead among the troops—
the number, nothing more.
The soldiers' names!
Let their parents find out the rest.

Confieso que es inhumano . . .
Al soldado se le olvida
como a una gota perdida
en medio del Océano.
Muere un jefe, un oficial,
y por ser grave el asunto,
el cable nos dice al punto
es don Fulano de Tal.
Y con datos siempre inciertos
como caso baladí,
el parte concluye así:
—y de tropas tantos muertos.—
El número nada más.
¡Los nombres de los soldados!
Los padres interesados
que averigüen lo demás.

Convinced that his son has died, don Ramón resolves to write to *El Heraldo de Madrid* in search of information. In fact, that newspaper did attempt to release publicly and in timely fashion the names of ordinary soldiers who had died in Cuba. While he awaits news of his son, don Ramón meditates on (and exaggerates) the role he played in his son's decision to join up. Felipe, as the audience knows, desperate and crazy with grief, went to Cuba expressly to get himself killed. Nonetheless, his father, quite unlike the grandfather in *Familia y patria* who congratulated himself on the successful transmission of a tradition of male bellicosity, blames himself:

> I, in my crazy insistence on
> the joy a soldier feels,
> so exalted his imagination
> that I sent him to his death.
> It was I, it was I, O God!
> Why should it seem strange that
> my life should succumb at last
> to so much grief,
> if I lack even the consolation
> of crying over his grave?

> Yo, que en mi loca porfía
> de ponderar la alegría
> del soldado, con tal fe,
> exalté su fantasía
> y a la muerte le impulsé.
> Yo fui, yo fui, ¡santo cielo!
> ¿Qué extraño que al fin sucumba
> mi existencia a tanto duelo,
> si no tengo ni el consuelo
> de llorar sobre su tumba?

Nonetheless, Felipe does not perish in Cuba. On his return, he reveals that the anger and rage that impelled him to leave cooled when he found himself at sea, and cooled yet more "upon leaving that land, whose beauty—what there is of it—is poisoned." Cuba, in the end, has become a poisoned land, not worth the sacrifice of the poor sent there to keep it Spanish. Thus, with no waving of flags or playing of the "Marcha de Cádiz," ended this most class-conscious play of all those reviewed through January of 1897.

Filipinas por España

> It would be exceedingly interesting to review all the stupidities and nonsense that we who belong to the white or Caucasian race have invented in order to justify our pretension to an innate superiority

over the other races. Everything from Biblical to pseudo-Darwinian fantasies enters into it—without forgetting the business of the blonde dolichocephalic and other similarly ridiculous notions. Any trait that distinguishes us is a privilege or an advantage; whatever we lack is a defect. And when we come up against something like the recent victory of Japan, we don't know how to account for it.

Sería curiosísimo hacer una revista de todas las tonterías y todos los desatinos que hemos inventado los hombres de la raza blanca o caucásica para fundamentar nuestra pretensión a la superioridad nativa y originaria sobre las demás razas. Aquí entrarían desde fantasías bíblicas hasta fantasías pseudo-darwinianas, sin olvidar lo del dólico-rubio y otras ridiculeces análogas. Cualidad que nos distingue es un privilegio o una ventaja, aquella de que carecemos es un defecto. Y cuando nos encontramos con un caso como el reciente del Japón, no sabemos por dónde salir.

Miguel de Unamuno, from his epilogue to W. E. Retana's *Vida y escritos del Dr. Rizal* (1907)

On 6 June 1897, *Filipinas por España* premiered at the Teatro Circo Barcelonés. Written by J. M. Valls, this prose drama in five acts was, apparently, the first Spanish play to focus on the 1896-1898 insurrection in the Philippines. Both before and during the period of the colonial wars, press commentators stated that Spaniards seemed less interested in their Pacific colony than in Cuba. The Philippines were more remote, to begin with, simply in terms of distance. A young Spaniard, D. M. Walls y Merino, wrote an absorbing account of his voyage from Madrid to Manila in the early 1880s: he sailed from Spain in early December 1881 and arrived in Manila on 17 February 1882—a total of seventy-six days en route.[45] By the mid-1890s it normally took one month to get to Manila, while the voyage to Cuba lasted only half as long. Aside from distance, fewer works—whether fiction or nonfiction—concerning the Pacific colony were directed to the general public in comparison to those on Cuba.

Spaniards' awareness of the Philippines received a boost with the Philippine Exposition in Madrid's Retiro Park in 1887. Some of the display items were later moved to Barcelona where they formed part of the Universal Exposition of Barcelona. In less than a month after its opening on 1 July, 87,000 people had visited the Madrid

Exposition: many Spaniards unable to pay the one-peseta fee were able to attend because of a free admission policy on specified days. A number of studies on the Philippines that appeared in conjunction with the exposition conveyed up-to-date information about the islands, including material about the different "races" that inhabited the archipelago and their characteristics. While few Spaniards would have read the scholarly tomes containing these essays, newspapers—including *El Globo*—published articles about the exposition and related topics.

Several Spaniards, together with some Filipinos resident in Spain, wrote articles claiming that it was an affront to human dignity to put Filipinos on display in the exposition as planned. The Spanish author of an editorial in *El Imparcial* of 30 May 1887 noted that the exposition catalog listed "Number 207: a carabou" and directly below it, "Number 208: a Filipino straw weaver." The editorialist commented that such a listing did not provide a very elevated view of how Spaniards understood the concept of respect for human beings. Before the exposition opened, the Filipino reformer Evaristo Aguirre wrote to his friend José Rizal that Filipinos displayed in the exposition will "come to be the object of the mocking, stupid, and rude curiosity of this truly savage people [i.e., Spaniards]."[46]

Graciano López Jaena, a Filipino journalist who had gone to Barcelona in 1875 and was a member of progressive pro-Filipino independence organizations, delivered a speech in 1889 on the expositions held previously in Madrid and Barcelona. Speaking before members of the Barcelona Ateneo, he charged that those in power had deliberately tried to mislead public opinion by exhibiting evidence of the backwardness of the Filipino people with no reference to the progress made during the last twenty years thanks to foreign capital and individual initiative.[47]

When several members of the Ashante people were put on exhibit in Madrid ten years later (September 1897) the adverse criticism voiced by a few individuals was equally pointed. Mariano de Cavia wrote in *El Imparcial* (15 September 1897) that no one really believed in the educational value of those so-called ethnological spectacles, that they only served to give people the brief illusion that they lived in the best of all possible civilizations and in the best-ordered of all possible societies. A report in the 29 October *El Imparcial* appeared to confirm that observation. Readers learned that a group of Ashante were taken to the theater to see a play, *El gran Galeoto*, by the highly esteemed Spanish playwright José Echegaray. The chief of the tribe and several of its members lay on the floor or put their feet up, all of which was said to have struck the audience as more amusing than the play.

During the 1887 exposition, everyone agreed that the twenty-four or so Filipinos on exhibit did, in fact, constitute the principal attraction for viewers. Not long after the exposition opened it was decided that the men housed in the Igorot village would perform dances on a daily basis in order to maintain high attendance levels. An editorial in *El Imparcial* (8 July) regretted that the first, stated purpose of the exposition—to stimulate commerce—had been abandoned and that what remained amounted to a sideshow. According to the press, cockfights and Igorot dances and celebrations in which pigs or chickens were slaughtered and prepared for feasting proved to be popular. Benito Legarda Jr. in an article on Filipinos on display at the St. Louis Exposition of 1904, discusses the impact the Igorots (some of whom had also been on exhibit in Madrid) had on the U.S. public. Legarda quotes a fair goer, James H. Blount: "The Tagalogs, the Visayans, etc., being ordinary Filipinos, did not prove money-makers. But it was great sport to watch the Igorrotes preparing their morning dog. So it was the 'non-Christian' tribes that paid. It was they that were most advertised. It was the recollection of them that lingered longest with the visitor to the exposition, and there was always in his mind thereafter an association of ideas between the Igorrotes and Filipino capacity for self-government generally."[48]

Of all the indigenous peoples of the Philippines, the Igorots apparently struck Spanish observers as the most savage and curious. Located in the mountainous regions of northern Luzon, theirs was the largest grouping of tribal minorities in the archipelago. In 1890 a Spaniard resident in the Philippines, Ángel Pérez, took General Valeriano Weyler on a tour through districts inhabited by Igorots. At one point they passed by several of them scantily clad in ragged cast-off European clothing, at which sight the general laughed in amusement. Later, Pérez writes: "The general rode along silent and pensive, no doubt reflecting on the pitiful state of these people when, shortly after, he said: 'And yet our senators will say that the civil code is applicable to these savages; surely if they could see these little brutes, they would not apply those laws to them.'" ("Caminaba el general silencioso y pensativo, sin duda reflexionando sobre el lastimoso estado de estos habitantes cuando, a los pocos momentos, dijo: 'Y luego dirán los señores Senadores, que el código civil es aplicable a estos salvajes; de seguro que si ellos vieran a estas fierecitas, no les aplicarían esas leyes").[49] Weyler, and others removed from the Philippines, considered self-government unthinkable for people for whom the civil code obtained from the peninsula was not believed to be applicable as yet.

Igorot dances and eating habits, and the inferences that might be drawn from them, figured prominently in Juan Pérez Zúñiga's not entirely tongue-in-cheek report in *Madrid Cómico* (17 September 1887) on what Spaniards could see at the exposition:

> Among the curious sights at the Exposition these days, we might mention those offered by the intrepid Igorots. Go today to see how several Cupids without blindfolds or wings wield their bows and arrows. On another day you can enjoy yourselves by observing the Indian dances, persuasive and elegant as only they can be, authentic imitations of the ones they perform when they go through the jungle, when they wend their way through the jungle on their way to snack on some poor missionary cooked with potatoes or roasted on a grill.

> Entre los espectáculos curiosos de estos días pueden citarse los que en la Exposición de Filipinas nos ofrecen los intrépidos igorrotes. Vayan VV. hoy a ver cómo manejan la flecha varios Cupidos sin venda y sin alas. Otro día pueden VV. divertirse observando las danzas de los indios, persuasivas y elegantes como ellas solas, fiel remedo de las que usan para andar por la selva, fiel remedo de las que usan para andar por la selva cuando van a merendarse algún pobre misionero con patatas o asado a la parrilla.

In 1889, Taga-Ilog (pseudonym of the Filipino writer, journalist, and future commander of the revolutionary army Antonio Luna) alluded to this aspect of the exposition's legacy in *La Solidaridad*, the Barcelona (later Madrid) publication of Filipinos residing in Spain.[50] He also noted that Filipinos in the Spanish theater served a function blacks used to perform:

Clearly, now that the dictionary has been depleted of Cuban resources so far as *tangos, negos, neguitas* and *mulatos* go, it's necessary to look to the Philippines for material to make people laugh. The gratuitous exposition of our Igorots was good for something.

Decididamente, agotado el diccionario de recursos cubanos, en la cuestión de *tangos, negos, neguitas y mulatos*, las corrientes para *hacer reír* se dirigen, al parecer, a Filipinas. De algo sirvió la exposición gratuita de nuestros igorrotes.

Despite wide-spread negative racial stereotyping, several Filipinos were perceived as distinguished in the Spain of the 80s and early 90s. Among them were two Filipino artists, Félix Resurrección Hidalgo and Juan Luna Novicio (Antonio Luna's brother), both of whom won prizes for their work in Spain and earned frequent favorable notices in the press. In April 1897, nearly a year after the insurrection began in the Philippines, Resurrección Hidalgo was still in the good graces of Spaniards. Along with other Spanish painters, he sent a portrait to the Paris Salon. Nevertheless, several months earlier, on 25 October 1896, Juan Luna's separatism had earned him a bitter profile in *El Imparcial*. The author of the essay, Francisco Alcántara, reviewed the painter's career noting that, at first, as an *indio* raised up out of barbarism, he seemed to Spaniards to demonstrate the validity of Christ's claim that all men are equal in the sight of God. The most eminent Spaniards, Alcántara continued, found in the very inferiority of Luna's race added reason to praise the merit of the artist who painted the *Spoliarium* and *The Battle of Lepanto*. Luna returned to the Philippines, ostensibly to visit his family, and there joined the Katipunan, the underground insurrectionist movement. Spain had rescued him from tribal languages and from a society in which men went about in loincloths; it had adopted him as a son, given him a glorious language, and—what ought to have counted most of all for him as an artist—given him the magic palette of its great painters. Even the savages in the Philippines, Alcántara concluded, must reject a monster capable of such black ingratitude.

Ironically, as recently as 18 February 1893, the monster struck at least one Spanish commentator as a model of Spanish honor: when Juan Luna was acquitted of murdering his wife and mother-in-law in Paris, Kasabal (pseudonym of José Gutiérrez Abascal), the popular columnist for *El Imparcial*, wrote: "No one could see a criminal in the man who, overwhelmed by passion, kills his wife whom he adores because she has made a mockery of his love and dragged his honor in the dirt" ("Nadie podrá ver un criminal en el hombre que arrastrado por la pasión mata a la mujer a quien adora porque se ha burlado de su amor y arrastrado por el suelo su honra").

In fact, Luna's trial was highly significant to contemporaries who were arguing issues of race. The not-guilty verdict handed down in the Paris court provided implicit legitimacy to the penal code in effect in the Philippines, which treated Filipinos differently from *peninsulares*. Article 11 of the code stipulated that the condition of being indigenous, mestizo, or Chinese be taken into account by judges and tribunals in order to lessen or increase the penalty in accord with the accused individual's level of education, the nature of the deed, and the circumstances of the person offended.[51] The Penal Code of 1879 in effect in Cuba also treated people of color differently. Article 10 stipulated that race constituted an aggravating circumstance that necessarily increased criminal responsibility in all instances in which criminal acts were perpetrated against whites by nonwhites.[52]

Both the defense and the prosecution had argued that Luna must be judged differently from Europeans because of his race. In support of this argument, a medical doctor familiar with the inhabitants of the Philippines testified that Juan Luna had committed the murders while under the influence of *hamok* (English, *amok*). *Hamok*, said to be a crisis often suffered by Filipinos, was described as a rush of hot blood that flowed to the brain, overwhelmed reason, and reduced a man to the instinctual level of a wild beast. The articles on the Luna trial published in the procolonialist *La política de España en Filipinas*, made it clear to readers that race should be viewed as the principal issue in the trial, and proceeded to argue that the verdict vindicated the penal code in use in the Philippines.[53]

The Filipino best known to Spaniards in the 1890s was the physician and patriot José Rizal. Rizal studied in Madrid during the early 1880s where he mingled with figures sympathetic to Filipino autonomist aspirations, such as Francisco Pi y Margall, editor of the weekly newspaper *El Nuevo Régimen*, and Miguel Morayta, a controversial professor of history at the University of Madrid and president of the Asociación Hispano-Filipina. Rizal achieved some notoriety in Spain in 1887 with the publication of his first novel, *Noli me tan-*

gere. In 1892, his second novel, *El filibusterismo*, continued to argue the issues of reform, autonomy, and independence in the Philippines. Like the *Noli*, it was generally condemned in the peninsula. Rizal was tried four years later for conspiracy in the 1896 uprisings against Spain. He was found guilty and executed in Manila in late December of 1896.[54]

Although the trial and execution were covered extensively in the Spanish press, his death—unlike the death of Antonio Maceo—apparently did not inspire a single play. Yet Rizal was perceived in Spain as the most significant *indio* (by lineage he was, in fact, a Chinese mestizo) civilian leader of the Filipinos, just as Maceo was viewed as the most significant mulatto military leader of the Cuban insurgents.[55] It may have seemed too daunting a task to fit the highly educated, talented, and sophisticated Rizal into the stereotyped version of an *indio* that audiences would recognize and accept. A similar point was, in fact, made by Salvador Canals in 1896 with respect to the depiction of cultured mulattoes. In a review of Eugenio Sellés's drama, *La mujer de Loth* (1896), Canals wrote that audiences could not react positively to the character of Ascensión, a mulatta, at a time when the mulattoes surrounding Maceo were depicted as savage hordes impervious to civilization.[56]

Insurgent activity increased after Rizal's execution. By early January 1897, it seemed clear that the insurrection in Cavite province signaled the beginning of a serious conflict. But by April, Spaniards rejoiced at the province's apparent pacification. On 3 April 1897, a patriotic demonstration broke out in the Eslava theater in Madrid. During a performance of the zarzuela *Los cocineros*, the popular actor Emilio Carreras altered a song so as to include a reference to the recent victories in Cavite. He also managed to congratulate the brave army in the Philippines. The audience rose to its feet and erupted in *vivas* to Spain, to the troops, to the Queen, and to General Polavieja. The orchestra, at the public's behest, played the "Marcha de Cádiz" twice while the audience continued to raise a great clamor.

By June 1897, when *Filipinas por España* opened in Barcelona, many people thought that the insurrection in the Philippines had been quashed. The play was cast in triumphant mode, drawing as it did on very recent memories of the retaking of the city of Cavite.

The dramatist puts his characters through a series of harrowing events, but the final two scenes present first a panorama of the conquered city of Cavite and finally an actor impersonating General Lachambre, who delivers a paean of praise to Spain and to Spanish military might.

The principal theme of this play is the nobility of Spanish men and women in contrast to the savagery, deceit, and treachery of Tagalogs. Two interwoven plots illustrate the theme. One deals with the love triangle formed by the Spaniards Elena, Serafín, and Leonardo, and the other with the Tagalogs' advances in Cavite, which threaten the financial interests of Elena's family. The first plot is resolved when Serafín, whom Elena has married after a year's fruitless wait for the return of her true love (the soldier Leonardo), is ordered to blow up a fortress under attack by Tagalogs—and himself with it. The fortress dominates the stage in act three with its tower and walls from which a Spanish flag waves. Elena and Serafín were separated by the fighting before they consummated their union; therefore, with Serafín dead, Elena and Leonardo (who has reappeared) are able to marry at the end of the play, their minds and bodies unsullied by any form of betrayal.

The second plot places Spaniards in contact with the Tagalogs whom they eventually defeat. Tagalogs are represented, above all, as animal-like. Early on in the play Jaime, the Catalan assistant to Leonardo, describes a Tagalog as an orangutan, perfectly suited for the Barcelona zoo. Later, Elena's father, Sr. Durán, refers to them as the "accursed race" ("maldita raza"). Act four, entitled "The Stranglers" ("Los estranguladores")—a fanciful conflation, perhaps, of the Indian stranglers, made known to thousands of readers in Eugène Sue's *Wandering Jew* (1845), with Filipinos—opens in a jungle setting. Several *Tagalogs* of a "repugnant appearance" are stretched out on rocks and on the ground. In the ensuing action, they succeed in killing Durán, Elena's father, but the rest of the Spaniards fleeing the rebels manage to escape.

The animal imagery used to describe Tagalogs reflects similar material on Filipinos in the press. Two articles by popular columnists that appeared in *El Imparcial* during the first week of October 1896 are typical. The first, by Mariano de Cavia, is entitled "The Monkey Insurgent" ("El papión insurrecto"), and begins thus:

A respectable gentleman has complained to me—and I do not know whether he does so in the name of the Hispano-Filipino Association or as a representative of the Society for the Protection of Animals— concerning what I permitted myself to write the day before yesterday about rebel Tagalogs, Chinese mestizo traitors, and chimpanzee or mandrill quadroons.

Se me duele un buen señor, y no me dice si en nombre de la Asociación Hispano-Filipina o en representación de la Protectora de Animales, por aquello que anteayer me permití escribir de tagalos rebeldes, traidores mestizos de sangley, y cuarterones de chimpancé o de mandril.

The author proceeds to justify the remarks that had led to the complaint by explaining that Tagalog females mate with monkeys and produce mixed animal and human offspring. The proof? Accounts of expeditions made by female Tagalogs into the jungle in search of male monkeys, along with descriptions of the resulting fights between monkeys and jealous male Tagalogs—accounts purportedly found in *La antigua civilización tagalog (Apuntes)* by the Filipino writer Pedro Alexandro Molo Agustín Paterno, published in Madrid in 1887. Tongue-in-cheek as it may have been, the journalist's message was clear: Tagalogs were uncivilized and animal-like; Spaniards were needed to elevate them to a civilized state.

The second article, by the popular journalist Luis Taboada, satirizes the fatuousness of those Filipinos who believe that they are superior to monkeys:

The news from the Philippines brought to us by the steamship *Isla de Panay* reveals the state of exaltation in which some monkeys from that archipelago find themselves.

It seems that in their desire to imitate their brother simians in Cuba, they have taken up arms to the cry of "Death to men! Long live free monkeys in a free jungle!"

Las noticias de Filipinas que nos ha traído el vapor *Isla de Panay* revelan el estado de excitación en que se encuentran algunos monos de aquel Archipiélago.

Parece que en su deseo de imitar a sus congéneres de Cuba, han empuñado las armas al grito de "¡Muera el hombre! ¡Viva el mono libre en el bejuco libre!"

Taboada then describes a Filipino whose name is Silvestre, who came to Madrid to study and at first spent much of his time perched in a tree in the Retiro. Urged by his landlady to act like a man, he began to play the role of a man. Before long, he was "asking for emancipation for the champanzee, the vote for the gorilla, and the right to hold public office for orangutans over the age of twenty, provided they present certification of good conduct" ("[estaba] pidiendo la emancipación del chimpancé, y el voto electoral para el gorila, y el derecho a los cargos públicos para el orangután mayor de veinte años, con tal de que presentase certificación de buena conducta"). Eventually, he returned to the Philippines, where as a lieutenant colonel in charge of a group of insurgents at Cavite "he wears checkered trousers, oilcloth spats, polka-dotted stockings without heel or toe patches, fringed slippers, a hat with green parrot feathers and a shirt with the tail outside the pants" ("viste pantalón de cuadros, polainas de hule, calcetines de lunares, sin talón ni puntera, babuchas de orilla, sombrero apuntado con plumas de loro verde y camisa con la falda por fuera del pantalón"). Taboada ends the piece thus:

> Silvestre is one of the most illustrious heads of the Filipino rebellion, thanks to having lived amongst us as a lodger at Doña Nemesia's, but . . .
> But Silvestre remains a monkey on the inside.

> Silvestre es uno de los más ilustrados jefes de la rebelión filipina, gracias a haber vivido entre nosotros en calidad de huésped de doña Nemesia, pero . . .
> Pero Silvestre continúa siendo mono por la parte de dentro.

José Rizal spent much of his adult life attempting to refute the idea that Filipinos were an anthropoid race, an idea he considered widespread among Spaniards. Students of the Philippines such as the colonial apologist W. E. Retana, denied that he and like-minded commentators considered the *indio* "an almost irrational being" ("como ser casi irracional)," but the popular press and theater continued to exploit descriptions found in some Spanish ethnographic studies and in travelers' accounts of the *indios* as savages closer to animals than to human beings.[57] Retana claimed that he, along with many other observers, considered the indigenous Filipinos to be fully human, but situated for the present at a child's level of intelligence and capacity for good judgement and, as such, in need of the tutelage of Spaniards before they could assume responsibility for themselves. Retana, who was Rizal's first Spanish biographer, later nuanced many of his originally negative views of the nature of indigenous Filipinos.

Some of those who wrote on Filipinos at the time of the 1887 Exposition or in connection with it assumed, as a matter of course, that the Malay "race" to which all Filipinos except the *negritos* were considered to belong was inferior to whites in terms of the degree of civilization it had attained. Some others seemed to believe in their biological inferiority. Pablo Feced, for example, wrote from Manila in 1888: "It is true that here, at this horrible distance from the fatherland, confronting these inferior races, our hearts draw nearer, grow close and become as one" ("Eso sí, aquí, a esta distancia horrible de la Patria y en frente a estas razas inferiores, los corazones se acercan, estrechan y confunden").[58] Feced's book included many articles published previously in *El Liberal*, a Madrid newspaper where, according to W. E. Retana, they were very popular.[59]

Manuel Antón, the eminent Spanish anthropologist who lectured on the indigenous inhabitants of Europe, America, and Oceania at the Ateneo and the Universidad Central during the 1880s and 1890s, wrote the section on the anthropology of the Philippines for the series of articles on the exposition published by the Madrid newspaper *El Globo*. Like most of his colleagues both in Spain and elsewhere, he divided the inhabitants of the archipelago into two groups, the *negritos* and the Malays. Antón deplored the need to insist at the outset that, despite the "preoccupations" of some people that have led them to believe otherwise, all Filipinos belong to the human species.[60] Of the *negritos* he wrote: "This race, one of the lowest in the ranking of civilizations and one of the most primitive in the geological ranking is, nonetheless, worthy of respect because its customs and institutions reveal the essential characteristics of the human personality" ("Raza esta de las más inferiores en el orden de la civilización y de las más primitivas en el orden geológico, es, sin embargo, digna de respeto, porque sus costumbres e instituciones, nos muestran que poseen los caracteres esenciales de la humana personalidad").[61] As for the predominant group, the Malays, he wrote:

We find no significant differences from an intellectual and moral point of view, between the Filipino Malays whom we have had occasion to study and Europeans who occupy an analogous place in the social hierarchy: the *moro* Mandi is as intelligent and as gentlemanly in his actions as any cultivated European, and given that most of them belong to the class of artisans, we noticed—not without surprise—that before returning to us the thermometers that they had had in their mouths, they carefully dried them off first; one of several acts not always observed among European peasants.

No encontramos diferencia notable, bajo el punto de vista intelectual y moral, entre los malayos filipinos que hemos tenido ocasión de estudiar y los europeos de análoga jerarquía social: el moro Mandi es tan inteligente y tan caballeresco en sus acciones como cualquier europeo de esmerada cultura, y con ser los más de ellos individuos de clase artesana, reparamos, no sin sorpresa, que al devolvernos el termómetro que habían tenido en la boca un cierto tiempo, enjugábanlo antes cuidadosamente; y como éste otros actos no siempre observados en los campesinos europeos.[62]

Antón's work is proof that refutations—however condescending they might be—of the self-serving racial theories proffered by apologists for colonialism did exist and did receive a hearing in Spain. However, while Antón lectured before elite audiences and wrote erudite papers and books for that same component of the public, ordinary people read fiction and newspapers and attended plays that, for the most part, promulgated the views of racial theorists with political agendas.

Among those writers who reached a wider audience was the journalist and novelist referred to earlier, Antonia Rodríguez de Ureta. She pointedly approved of a marriage between a Spaniard and a mestizo in her novel *Pacita* (1885, 2d ed. 1892). The mestizo she had in mind, it must be noted, was a Spanish mestizo, of whom there were relatively few—about 75,000, according to the 1890 census figures.[63] Better a mestizo of good character for her daughter, she had the fictional mother reflect, than a pure-blooded Spaniard who would make her unhappy. The novelist's tolerance sprang less from her fervent Catholicism than from practical considerations of what marriage with the kind of low-bred Spaniard she believed to be most prevalent in the Philippines was likely to entail. Even though the novelist did not refer to indigenous Filipinos as animals, she did consider indolence a racial trait they all shared. Like Retana and other former residents of the colony, she harbored a special animus against Chinese mestizos. Of the Filipinos connected to *La Solidaridad*, she wrote: "Some Chinese mestizos founded a miserable little journal in Barcelona with the object of offending the Spanish name" ("Algunos mestizos chinos fundaron en Barcelona una miserable revistilla con objeto de ofender el nombre español").[64] Behind much of the criticism directed against them was the belief shared by many contemporaries that the Chinese and Chinese mestizos were in control of a disproportionate amount of wealth in the Philippines and that they presented a greater threat to Spanish rule than the *indios*. Edgar Wickberg writes that toward the end of the nineteenth century, Spaniards typically labelled "the *indio* a brute incapable of anything but animal's work; the [Chinese] mestizo a seditious outsider who filled him with subversive ideas."[65]

Ferdinand Blumentritt, the Austrian ethnologist, colleague, and friend of Rizal, tried, like Rizal, to reach a larger audience in his efforts to combat notions of the essential racial inferiority of Filipinos. His work, at first highly respected and lauded in Spain, was later excoriated by political enemies precisely because of his friendship with Rizal and his support of Rizal's ideas.[66]

Filipinas por España fully subscribes to popular perceptions of Tagalogs as animals. In addition, their reputed treachery and disloyalty is exemplified in the play by the Durán family servant, Malabar. Caught stealing by Durán's wife long before—old Philippine hands repeatedly informed Spaniards that *indios* were incorrigible thieves—Malabar was pardoned by that lady and allowed to continue in service. In return, years later Malabar seizes her and her young son. He tells her that she must deliver her daughter, Elena, to him or he will burn her son alive. In explanation of this ferocious demand, he tells her that he has always desired Elena and only joined the insurgents as a means of making her his. The lust of mulattoes for white women depicted in earlier plays such as *Cuba libre* and *Cuba* was presented in just this way—as sufficient motive for joining the insurrection. It was clearly meant to be perceived by Spanish audiences as an ignoble way of taking advantage of a desired woman in the midst of the reigning chaos. Malabar's desire for Elena is not, however, wholly based on lust. He admires her for her higher qualities and has done so.

from childhood, when we grew up together and saw each other often, and I was always looking at her as one contemplates God. But since I was a poor servant and she was a great lady, I a wretch and she a wealthy peninsular, it was impossible even to imagine that she would listen to my pleas . . . Yes, I robbed, I robbed . . . to make myself rich for her. I was one of the first to shout the cry of rebellion in order to become somebody . . . for her . . . It was all for her. Now do you understand? Do you see Malabar's intentions clearly?

desde nuestra infancia que nos veíamos y crecimos juntos, y yo mirándola como se contempla a Dios. Mas yo pobre criado y ella gran señora, yo un infeliz y ella una rica peninsular, no era natural poder imaginar siquiera que escuchara mis súplicas . . . Sí robé, robé . . . para hacerme rico por ella. He sido de los primeros en dar el grito de rebelión para ser algo . . . por ella . . . Todo por ella, ¿lo comprendes ahora todo? ¿Veis en claro las intenciones de Malabar?

Malabar's explanation suggests that Spanish theater audiences were receptive to the notion that the white woman symbolizes the most highly valued prize, which would forever be denied to dark-skinned men, whether blacks and mulattoes or *indios* and mestizos. By allowing Malabar to harbor an appreciation for higher qualities in a woman, the dramatist has lifted him above the animal level on which Tagalogs in this play exist. However, his destructive rage and his threat to burn Elena's brother alive, swiftly bring him down again. Elena's mother confirms his true nature when she cries out, after hearing his explanation, that he is a ferocious, blood-thirsty tiger.

It is significant that, apart from Malabar's explanation for his rebellious activity, the only explanation for the insurrection offered in the play is voiced in the opening scenes in which some Tagalogs refer to the God of Victory and Bonifacio I (Andrés Bonifacio, the insurgent leader) as their deliverers from oppression. Mention of Bonifacio I is a reference to the fact that some "tribes" in Imus proclaimed Andrés Bonifacio king toward the end of 1896.[67] The point of the reference is to emphasize the Tagalogs' willingness to make a low-born rebel leader their superior—a gesture that underscores their lack of judgment. From the first scene to the last, the landscape is represented as savage and the indigenous people who inhabit it as primitive, repugnant, and bestial. The clear message is that at stake in this conflict is the civilization brought by Spaniards pitted against the barbarism of an inferior people.

In theory, the curious theatergoer could have consulted a variety of sources for information about the causes of the insurrection. Radically contrasting viewpoints on events in the Philippines existed, although the books and articles in which they were expressed were not within the grasp of the ordinary Spaniard. Between 1889 and 1895, interested and literate Spaniards might have read the pro-independence Filipino journal *La Solidaridad* (1889-1895), published first in Barcelona and later in Madrid, along with the pro-colonialist *La política de España en Filipinas (1891-1898)*, published in Madrid. By the spring of 1897 a fair number of books (fiction and nonfiction) and pamphlets on the Philippines had appeared. Specialists in anthropology, geography, and history delivered presentations on the peoples and lands of the archipelago in *ateneos* and in other venues. These were, of course, conferences to which a very limited number of the public had access. Nonetheless, newspapers such as *El Imparcial, El Liberal, La Reforma*, or *La Armonía* often carried articles about Cuba and the Philippines, and at times other newspapers picked up and ran such articles.

The high-circulation press occasionally offered some interpretation of events in the Philippines rather than restricting coverage to battle reports. On 3 June 1897, only three days before *Filipinas por España* opened, Manuel Alhama, a correspondent for *El Imparcial* who had just returned from Manila, began a series of articles on the Philippines. In the first installment, entitled "Why Are There Filibusters" ("¿Por qué hay filibusteros?"), Alhama stated that Filipinos were not currently capable of achieving self-government, but that in a few years they would be able to mount an insurrection crueler and lengthier than the Cuban war to date. Spaniards, in his view, were to blame for the present state of affairs. Essentially, they had blundered by blurring the distinction between Filipinos and whites. Indigenous colonized people are not the intellectual equals of Europeans, he explained, yet Spaniards had inappropriately educated Filipinos in Manila to become lawyers and doctors. Freemasons swelled their heads further by preaching fraternity and equality. The result, as José Rizal showed in *El filibusterismo*, was that the students became the elite ringleaders among the insurgents.

In Alhama's opinion, Filipinos should not have been allowed to study for the clergy: "When they emerge from the seminary they consider themselves just as priestly and consecrated as the priests and friars of the white race and just as worthy as they are of respect and consideration" ("Al salir del seminario estímase tan sacerdote y tan ungido como los curas y frailes de raza blanca y tan digno como ellos de respeto y de estimación"). However, because they do not earn as much money as the clergy from the peninsula, they become dissatisfied and end up joining the insurgents. In reference to Filipinos engaged in other occupations, Alhama finds it inexplicable that *indios* and mestizos have been allowed to amass fortunes when Spaniards ought to be in control of the significant wealth in the islands.

In his second article, " The Friars" ("Los frailes"), on 5 June, Alhama blames Spanish friars for their role in inciting unrest. He charges them with being too lenient with inferiors, too greedy, and with owning too much property. On the whole, and despite attributing blame to certain elements among the colonizers, Alhama conveys the same message as *Filipinas por España*—the civilization Spaniards brought to the Philippines is in danger of annihilation at the hands of an inferior and barbarous race.[68]

At about the same time that the first two of Alhama's articles reached readers, a flurry of articles and letters appeared in the national press in response to a piece Felipe Trigo had published in *El Nacional* on 11 May. Trigo—remembered now for his novels of social criticism—was a military doctor whose hands had been mutilated in battle in the Philippines. His essay "Cuatro generales: Polavieja, Blanco, Lachambre, y Primo de Rivera," was written in order to justify General Ramón Blanco's actions at the beginning of the insurrection. (General Blanco, who held the *capitanía general* of the Philippines from 1893 to 1896, had been accused of unpardonable inaction at the beginning of the rebellion by Archbishop Nozaleda of Manila.) In the course of the controversy that followed publication of his article, Trigo, who had known Manuel Alhama in Manila, agreed with the latter's assessment of blame for the uprising.

In June, Trigo responded to an attack against him by Juan Vázquez de Mella who wrote for *El Correo Español*—an attack motivated by Trigo's criticism of the role of the friars in the Philippines. The letter Trigo sent back to Mella's paper spelled out frankly what he thought Spanish colonial policy should have been in the archipelago and why it had failed:

> You can't have it both ways. Either a nation's intentions regarding its colonies are generous, in which case that nation should aim to thoroughly civilize the indigenous colonial population and not be surprised later when the colony, *having attained its majority*, tries to emancipate itself from the tutelage of the mother country—as happened to powerful England with the United States, to us with Mexico, Santo Domingo, etc., etc., and is now happening with Cuba; or the intention of nations is egoistic, in which case, those nations ought, by all means to seek the happiness of the colonies by introducing a small degree of civilization into savage customs, but never the unlimited intellectual progress of the natives. On the contrary, nations ought to block it, as does the perspicacious and practical England in its Asian possessions. There is no middle way possible, yet the friars in the Philippines have chosen the middle way.

> Una de dos, o la intención de las naciones para con sus colonias es generosa, y entonces deben procurar la civilización perfecta de la población indígena colonial, y no extrañarse luego de que la colonia *hecha mayor de edad* trate de emanciparse de la tutela materna, como le sucedió a la poderosa Inglaterra con los Estados-Unidos, como nos sucedió a nosotros con Méjico, con Santo Domingo, etc., etc., y nos está sucediendo con Cuba; o la intención de las naciones es egoísta, y entonces deben procurar, sí la felicidad de las colonias con cierto pequeño grado de civilización en las costumbres salvajes, pero nunca el progreso intelectual indefinido de los naturales, que antes al contrario, debe estorbarse, como hace la perspicaz y práctica Inglaterra en sus posesiones del Asia. No hay término medio posible, y los frailes en Filipinas han querido el término medio.[69]

In a public presentation of the volume he coedited with Pedro Laín Entralgo, *España en 1898: las claves del desastre*, Carlos Serrano is reported to have said that "the basic problem that led to the confrontation between the United States and Spain was that our country never considered these territories [i.e., Cuba and the Philippines] as colonies, but rather as a part of the Spanish nation" ("el problema básico que enfrentó a Estados Unidos y España fue que nuestro país nunca consideró a estos territorios como colonias, sino como parte de la nación española."[70] Whatever Serrano means by *país*—the

Spanish people, or the state, or perhaps both—his statement should not obscure the fact that many Spaniards, of whom Trigo was one, viewed the two colonies quite differently. The extent of Spanish settlement in each colony (slight in the Philippines) and the use of Castilian as the language of instruction (minimal in the Philippines) and of ordinary intercourse (also minimal in the archipelago)—considerations mentioned by Trigo—were only two among many that made it possible for the latter to publicly defend egoistic colonial policy in the Philippines.[71]

The prime minister, Antonio Cánovas, expressed views similar to Trigo's in 1897 when he said that although it was difficult to resolve conflicting ideas as to how much autonomy should be granted in Cuba, the Philippines could develop "under a paternal regimen, one neither excessively severe nor excessively kindly" ("bajo un régimen paternal, ni excesivamente severo ni excesivamente bondadoso").[72] Cánovas also asserted that it was Chinese mestizos who had spearheaded the revolt against Spanish sovereignty; the Spanish mestizos and the indigenous inhabitants, he believed, were basically loyal.[73]

Trigo's point on the difference between the two colonies is further emphasized by a passage in the letter to *El Correo Español* quoted above in which he describes the consequences of the friars' policy of setting themselves up as the sole interpreters for the *indios*. He wrote that the friars' refusal to teach them Castilian meant that when successive waves of Spaniards came to Manila for their brief tours of service in commerce, government, or whatever, they might as well have been in a foreign country. As they observe the natives, speaking execrable Spanish, they are like "people filing through a museum before the same eternally ridiculous *indios* and the same eternally crafty friars" "[son] como un público desfilando por un museo, por delante de los eternos ridículos indios y de los eternos habilidosos frailes").[74] Significantly, even though several correspondents and letter writers took issue, as staunch supporters of the orders, with Trigo's condemnation of the friars, no one defended the friars' policy of providing a measure of education to selected elements of the Filipino population.

The triumphal ending of *Filipinas por España* in the last scene but one presents a panoramic view of the city of Cavite, parts of which are burning. On the right, the spectator spies the sea with ships firing upon the city. There are Spanish soldiers everywhere. Suddenly a cry is heard: "Cavite is ours!" Martial music and *vivas* follow. In the final scene an actor astride his horse and representing General Lachambre, delivers a brief speech:

"Soldiers. Comrades all! Spain is invincible . . . Spain is the fatherland of heroes. Its army and navy are the envy of the entire world. In the name of the fatherland I salute you all. We enter Cavite covered with laurels, and I enter proud to be surrounded by so many heroes. Soldiers! Long live Spain! Long live the army! To Cavite! The Philippines for Spain!"

"Soldados. ¡Camaradas todos! España es invencible . . . España es la patria de los héroes. El ejército de mar y tierra es admiración del mundo entero. Yo en nombre de la patria, os felicito a todos. Vamos a entrar en Cavite cubiertos de laurel y yo orgulloso de rodearme de tantos héroes . . . Soldados . . . ¡Viva España! ¡Viva el ejército! ¡A Cavite! ¡Filipinas por España!"

The orchestra plays the "Grand March" as the soldiers form ranks. The curtain falls.

Jaime, the Catalan youth, does not forget his fatherland, Cataluña, in the midst of *vivas* for Spain. Earlier, when he was in the fortress expecting to be blown up alongside the other remaining Spaniards, he recalled stories his father had told him about the bravery of men who defended Gerona when it was under siege by the French. When the fortress is about to blow, the others shout "Long live Spain!", but Jaime shouts "Long live Cataluña!"—to the joy, no doubt, of the Barcelona audience.

Ya se van los quintos, madre

On 15 January 1898, the theater section of *La Ilustración Española y Americana* advised readers that a new zarzuela with text by a Señor Alfaro and music by Tomás Bretón had just been delivered to the management of the Teatro de la Comedia. Nothing further appeared concerning the zarzuela, nor does it appear among Bretón's works. One year earlier, on 1 January 1897, Bretón's zarzuela *Botín de Guerra* debuted at the Teatro de la Zarzuela in Madrid. Although it took place during the War of Independence, Bretón thought that the text by Eusebio Sierra furnished him material to express his patriotic sentiments in regard to the colonial insurrections. A modest success in Madrid, the zarzuela then toured the provinces, "taking advantage of the patriotic fervor aroused by the sad events taking place in the war in Cuba" ("aprovechando el fervor patriótico, excitado por la actualidad triste de la guerra de Cuba").[75]

Muerte de Maceo

The regeneration of the slave through religious exercises has been proclaimed and prescribed in all the *codes noirs* and Regulations governing from that of Louis XIV of France to the inspired law of 1789 in the Spanish colonies. Negroes prayed—or were supposed to pray the rosary every night; negroes were to have Christian morality explained to them every week; negroes were to be baptized and married in accord with the precepts of Catholicism. Judging by all the precautions taken, the negroes of Cuba and all the Antilles should be saints. And now we are told that they cannot be freed . . . *because they are savages!*

La regeneración del esclavo por los ejercicios religiosos ha sido proclamada y preceptuada en todos los códigos negros y los Reglamentos de esclavos, desde el de Luis XIV de Francia hasta el bien inspirado de 1789 en las colonias españolas. Los negros rezaban —o debían— rezar todas las noches el rosario; a los negros se les debían explicar semanalmente la moral cristiana; los negros debían ser bautizados y casados conforme a los preceptos del catolicismo. A juzgar por las precauciones, los negros de Cuba y de todas las Antillas debían ser casi unos santos. Y ahora se nos dice que no se puede hacer la abolición . . . *¡porque son unos salvajes!*

Rafael M. de Labra, *La brutalidad de los negros* (1876)

When the notice of Antonio Maceo's death was confirmed on 10 December 1896 there were celebrations throughout Spain. In Sevilla the news spread to cafes and theaters, giving rise to great rejoicing. A patriotic demonstration was held in that city at the San Fernando theater. The audience, informed of the news by an extra edition of the local paper, interrupted the play in progress. An actor moved to the front of the stage where he read the detailed report of the mulatto general's death carried in *El Porvenir*. His reading was punctuated by shouts and *vivas* from the public. Another actor then brought out a national flag; the orchestra played the "Marcha real" and the entire audience burst out in *vivas* to Spain, to the army, and to *El Porvenir* (*El Imparcial*, 12 November 1896.) On the previous day *El Imparcial* reported that in Zaragoza not a few people related Maceo's death to the novena celebrated the Sunday before in which the Holy Christ of the Seo (cathedral) was transported to the chapel of la Virgen del Pilar.

On 21 January 1897, not long after Antonio Maceo's death, *El Imparcial* printed a piece meant to cut him down to size. He was a bogus hero, the author wrote, "a crude fellow, without any education or elevation of spirit, a man who had risen from the social scum that was his natural milieu; he was a man who belonged to an inferior race; he possessed a heart filled with ambition, pride, rancor and hatred for the white race" ("un hombre basto, sin instrucción ni elevación de alma, surgido de la espuma social, de una raza inferior, lleno su corazón de ambiciones, de soberbia, de rencores y odios contra la raza blanca"). Despite efforts to demystify him and associate him with denigratory depictions of blacks and mulattoes, the image of Maceo as a fierce and formidable warrior had captured the imaginations of people throughout Spain and proved difficult to dislodge. Pablo Picasso, who was fifteen when Maceo died, recalled in later years that as a child in Málaga he and his playmates would take the Cuban's name when they played soldier.[76]

On 25 January 1898, two years after Maceo's death, *El Imparcial* ran an ad for the sale of *The Death of Maceo*—an art work consisting of a group of eight life-size wax figures representing "with astonishing realism" ("con pasmosa realidad") the death of the famous insurgent. Described as equal to the best figures on view in foreign wax museums, the ad claimed that in the month it had been on exhibit in Barcelona 15,000 people had seen it. Maceo's presence had been so commanding that many Spaniards, including the prime minister, Antonio Cánovas, thought that his death signaled the end of the Cuban insurrection.[77]

Antonio Maceo had been an important figure in the first insurrection (1868-1878) and in the *Guerra chiquita* of 1879. In 1895 he again assumed the role of military leader—he was made lieutenant general—as well as that of charismatic leader to his largely black troops. Maceo's image was forged in the press. High-circulation papers regularly reported his military maneuvers and also carried material on his appearance, character, and habits. His fearsome prowess at the head of mounted black men wielding machetes and, above all, his African ancestry fascinated the Spanish public and furnished copious material to the press as well as a significant portion to the popular theater.

In the Spanish plays that feature Maceo, he is cast in the second of the two roles normally assigned to mulattoes in Hispanic literature—that of a marginalized figure vengefully bent upon seizing power. In *Muerte de Maceo*, he is transformed into a modern incarnation of Cain. Identification with the Biblical figure's urge to take revenge, even to destroy the world in the attempt, added a significant trait to the representation of the mulatto as a political actor, while the mulatto as a variant on a type of romantic outlaw fit into a familiar literary slot and required little elaboration to be readily comprehensible to the reading and viewing public.

The two plays that appeared when Maceo died were indebted to the press for the general view they took of his significance and for certain details picked up and fictionalized for dramatic effect. Though it is uncertain whether Dolcet's dramatic monologue, *Muerte de Maceo*, published in Barcelona in 1897, was performed, it was written for performance in the theater. Its stage directions indicate that the scene takes place in the late afternoon. Maceo and his general staff are surveying the countryside from atop a hill with woods in the background and a ravine on stage left. Weapons lie scattered about. No sooner does Maceo comment that all is going well than a volley of shots rings out and he falls to the ground. His doctor and aide-de-camp hastily examine him, then flee. After a few moments of silence, Maceo, in great pain, stands up and, machete in hand, delivers a monologue.

Dolcet's version of Maceo's death was based on contemporary newspaper reports according to which the bullets from an advancing Spanish cavalry charge struck him as he rode out from camp. The *mambises* found his body shortly afterwards next to the corpse of the young son of Máximo Gómez, the general in command of the insurgent forces. Early reports also claimed that the youth, who served as

Maceo's aide-de-camp, had committed suicide over the body of his friend and mentor. For that reason, toward the end of the monologue, Maceo, coming out of a faint occasioned by his wounds, sees Gómez lying dead with one arm stretched across his (Maceo's) breast and concludes that the youth has killed himself. But, far from showing gratitude for his friend's exemplary fidelity, he curses him for taking a coward's way out. The audience seems meant to understand that just as Maceo earlier on in the monologue has shown no generous feeling toward his women, he is similarly incapable of sharing or understanding the fraternal love meant to bind Gómez to him through death. The audience may also, of course, have placed young Gómez's suicide in the larger context of the chaos resulting from the insurrection—a context that implied a loss of moral and religious bearings.

Some later press reports attributed Gómez's death to enemy fire. Panchito Gómez's father thought that his son was still alive when he was found lying across Maceo's body and that one of the Spaniards who came upon him finished him off with a machete blow. Máximo Gómez's grief was extreme. One goes to war, he wrote in his diary, expecting to be killed, but not to have one's body profaned through mutilation: "To cut a rose off the bush is not so bad, to tear it apart scornfully leaf by leaf is exceedingly bitter to accept" ("Cortar la rosa no es tan malo, deshojarla con desprecio, es lo amargo").[78] Melchor Fernández Almagro states that Panchito killed himself with his own machete.[79] Hugh Thomas believes that Pancho Gómez died "just possibly by his own hand."[80] Even though the truth about how he died may never be known, it is worth noting here that mutilation is a recurrent theme during the insurrections. Spaniards were often reminded that the motherland (or the fatherland) was being mutilated by the separatists while Spanish soldiers were being mutilated by the (mostly) black *mambises*. When it was all over, the Treaty of Paris finished off what was for many Spaniards the "dismembering" of the Spanish empire. The horror that the act of mutilation normally inspires was evoked repeatedly.

During the fifteen minutes that precede his death, the dramatist reveals the workings of Maceo's mind as he declaims fitfully, surrounded by the bodies of his men also shot by enemy snipers. In the background occasional gunfire is audible. The monologue begins and ends with Maceo addressing the dead *mambises*. In between, it is structured by his hallucinations as he falls in and out of consciousness. In his hallucinatory state, he sees before him the destruction of the land, he spies approaching Spanish ships with reinforcements, he senses rotting corpses in the midst of a now sterile nature. Then he sees figures rising up out of the earth to condemn him—dead soldiers, widows, widowers. When the accusing faces of children whose families and homes have been destroyed in the war rise up before him, he cries out, "Have pity on me! . . . You do me greater harm than a rusted, ragged-edged machete ripping out my guts!" ("¡Compasión! . . . Me hacéis más daño que machete enmohecido y dentado rasgando mis entrañas "). That is his only plea for compassion. After that cry, he responds to these visions and apparitions by recognizing himself as a modern Cain. He is pridefully defiant of his accusers, complacent before the horrors of war, and desirous now of the complete destruction of his own cause and of his followers.

At the beginning of his harangue, Maceo inveighs against the corpses for not having killed off the enemy before dying themselves. Thus appears the theme of the will to universal destruction, which is repeated in the course of the monologue. Most tellingly, Maceo expresses his contempt for those who died unavenged, asserting with pride that germs of heroism still pulse through his veins. "You . . ."— he cries out at the corpses—"were not slaves for nothing. Impotent to cast off your chains yourselves, you owe your freedom to the generosity of Spaniards." The Spanish playwright tells us, in effect, that what is good in Maceo is his Spanish blood. As the dying man is made to say, it alone accounts for his heroism. The author has Maceo acknowledge specifically the nobility of Spaniards for their abolition of slavery ten years earlier. At the end of his monologue, Maceo again excoriates the dead black men who lie around him for their weakness in the face of the more powerful Spaniards. And, in his final assertion of an identity totally different from theirs, he cries out, "You swarm of worthless negroes! . . . I don't belong to you . . . I am of mixed blood! . . ." ("¡Negrada! . . . No os pertenezco . . . ¡Mestizo soy! . . .").

As the Spaniards advance to the place where Maceo has fallen, he calls out to them to destroy everything, to annhilate the accursed blacks who reproduce like locusts. The Spaniards arrive. Maceo takes another bullet and dies. A soldier with a smoking Mauser appears, raises his gun in triumph, and shouts, "¡Viva España!" A group of soldiers run on stage bearing the flag of the fatherland. The curtain falls.

The author of this monologue evidently meant to establish Maceo's dramatic stature, first by having him express himself in rhetorical language worthy of a romantic protagonist from the 1830s and second by relating him to a monumental figure recognizable to everyone, i.e., the biblical Cain. One can only imagine how an audience (or readers) reacted to the high-flown language with which Maceo reveals himself—even though mulattoes were typically portrayed as speaking a more correct Castilian than the blacks whose speech was parodied frequently in the press. The dramatist built upon common perceptions regarding mulattoes—their lust for power, their belief in their superiority to blacks, and their desperate nihilism—and successfully integrated them with the Cain theme. In this way, he nailed down his political message, namely, that Cuban mulattoes were rebelling and fomenting rebellion among blacks much as Cain rebelled against God. In each case, the desire for revenge against those favored by God—in Maceo's case, white Spaniards and Creoles—led to an act of treachery and fraternal bloodshed. The forceful image of one man, Maceo as Cain, assigned responsibility for the Cuban disaster is the image retained by the viewer/reader.

Marta y María o la muerte de Maceo

Muerte de Maceo strikes a somewhat precarious balance in its portrayal of a destructive, nihilistic figure. It risks undermining its message by creating an arch rebel who like other similar larger-than-life figures is capable of exerting a kind of amoral attraction. The three anonymous authors of *Marta y María o la muerte de Maceo* would surely have argued that foolish young females in the audience could easily have been dazzled by the comparison of Maceo to Cain and thus rendered less attentive to the political "truths" conveyed by the piece. In effect, the three authors consciously set out in their play to debunk the appeal of Maceo as romantic outlaw and charismatic leader.

The Marta of the title, a rich American girl, has met and fallen in love with Maceo on one of his trips to Washington in search of funds for the insurrection. Despite her father's opposition, she returns to Cuba with Maceo and soon finds herself relegated to the demeaning position occupied by his other mistreated mistresses. When her father loses his fortune, Maceo, who wanted Marta primarily for her money, unequivocally reveals himself in a key scene as he really is—a brutish, drunken bully. Meanwhile, María, an old school friend of Marta, has asked that the latter intercede with Maceo on behalf of María's Spanish fiancé who has been captured by the insurgents.

The two women are contrasted in terms of their patriotism and in terms of the nature of the love they feel for their men. The American, Marta, is devoid of patriotic sentiments. One of the American characters who has known her long, describes her attraction to Maceo in these words: "In her love for Maceo she sees something original and great that is capable of animating an existence which had become embittered by a satiety of pleasure. Maceo—savage, strong, manly—presents himself to her dreamy and sickly imagination like a hero out of a novel, clothed in that aura with which *actuality*, that voluble goddess, surrounds the idols of a day, idols whom she submerges in the deepest oblivion just as rapidly as she brought them to light" ("En el amor de Maceo ve algo original y grande que puede animar su existencia amargada por la saciedad de los placeres. Maceo salvaje, fuerte, varonil aparece a su imaginación soñadora y enfermiza como un héroe novelesco, envuelto en esa aureola con que la *actualidad*, esa voluble Diosa, rodea a los ídolos que son de un día, a quienes, con la misma rapidez que ha encumbrado, sumerge después en el olvido más profundo").

María's love for Víctor, on the other hand, is closely linked to her love of Spain and all the values it stands for: loyalty, fidelity, honor. In the end, completely disillusioned with Maceo, Marta attaches herself to Pancho—the son of Máximo Gómez. Like Marta, Pancho has finally seen Maceo for what he is. The two lovers escape from Maceo's camp in order to seek a new life together. Meanwhile, the life of María's Spanish fiancé is miraculously spared despite Maceo's order to have him shot.

In the concluding scene, Maceo, who has been in vengeful pursuit of Marta and Gómez, finds them, only to be felled by a sniper.

Pancho Gómez is also fatally wounded. A distraught Marta hands him a gun so that he can end his life before the Spanish troops arrive. María, now serving as a Sister of Charity, appears with her fiancé. They offer to take Marta away but, in despair at Pancho's death, she refuses, announcing that she will now join the insurgents as an active soldier. Offstage, men shout "Long live free Cuba!" The incorrigible Marta runs to join them, crying, "My boys, out with the machetes!" ("¡Hijos míos! ¡Al machete!"), a detail that may have been suggested by the account of Maceo's death in *El Imparcial* on 10 December 1896. According to this report, several Spanish soldiers at the scene of the battle saw, fighting with the rebels, a young, attractive woman who was heard shouting "¡Al machete!"

María and her fiancé, together with two Spanish officers who arrive on the scene, sum up the significance of Maceo's death as they stand before his corpse. With Maceo dead, they exult, peace is now in sight. A new day is dawning and a radiant future awaits Spaniards and Cubans alike who, forgetting past enmity, will now exchange a fraternal kiss thereby honoring Mother Spain. It is most doubtful that the fraternal kiss was intended to be exchanged between Cubans of color—whether blacks or mulattoes—and Spaniards.

Maceo had been denied supreme command of the 1895 Cuban insurrection so that any appearance of a race war might be avoided. He himself acquiesced in this decision, believing it to be in Cuba's best interests.[81] Nonetheless, Spanish propaganda aimed to convince the public that Maceo was spearheading a race war and further that men of color like Maceo could not discharge the civic responsibilities that would come with autonomy, much less those entailed by independence. The tactic employed by the press and by the authors of *Marta y María* to convey this message was to acknowledge Maceo's notoriety, then to reveal his "true" nature. The representation of Maceo in *Muerte de Maceo* was rendered problematical because of the author's decision to model the Cuban general throughout the play on a literary type that undoubtedly held an ambivalent appeal for some viewer/readers. The choice of this figure resulted in a less clear-cut political message. The focus on the demands of his romantic ego may have enhanced interest in Maceo, but it blurred his depiction as a brute dedicated to the overthrow of white rule in Cuba—a portrayal *Marta y María* kept uppermost before the audience.

Un alcalde en la manigua

Un alcalde en la manigua debuted on 1 January 1898 at the Teatro Circo in Cartagena. A prose drama by Pascual Martínez Moreno, the play begins with the plight of Lorenzo who is going to Cuba as a substitute. He is replacing a friend who is the sole support of his family. Lorenzo is not opposed to going—he claims that he vehemently desires to defend the fatherland; yet when he leaves the stage, the village maestro comments that Lorenzo is gone, probably never to return. Cuba is strangling Spain, he remarks, to which a neighbor replies that the government is at fault for putting off decisive action against the enemy. Thus the play begins by alluding to the regrets of those who watch the poor go off to an inexcusably drawn-out war, but it soon develops into a farce. The comedy derives largely from language. The mayor of the title finds himself shipped off to Cuba quite unexpectedly and ends up speaking stage Andalusian dialect in the *manigua* with blacks speaking the fractured Castilian that always characterizes them in these plays.

The remainder of this plotless play is devoted to exchanges between the mayor and the blacks. The content of these exchanges centers on the mayor's reluctance to believe that the creatures he meets up with are really human. The play portrays the *mambises* of color solely in terms of racial attributes meant to reduce them to the level of animals. Issues that motivated and might explain the insurgency are simply ignored. The insurgents are represented as essentially unworthy to engage in combat with Spaniards.

In the earlier plays discussed above, the Spanish soldier and his family at home are depicted as defending the race and the values it stands for. The enemy is presented in terms of traitorous ingrates who are white and hordes of savages who are black or brown. Images of white Cubans who, however ungrateful, spoke Castilian, practiced Catholicism, and were formerly occupied in pursuing commerce and developing the land, signaled racial equality between that part of the enemy forces and the Spaniards. In this view, the war might arguably be seen as an honorable contest. Some such possibility had led General Polavieja to advise his propagandists during the first insurrection: "We must remove all white characteristics from the rebellion and reduce it to the colored element, that way it will count on less support and sympathy."[82]

Reports in the press on the superior numbers of black men waging unorthodox, often successful guerrilla warfare raised a different and difficult problem for representation. People of color depicted as fierce and effective combatants would in a sense dignify those warring against them, but such a portrayal might dignify people of color as well. It was not desirable to represent them as fierce warriors, as worthy foes, when a principal propaganda objective was to depict them as infantile and subhuman and thus totally unfit to govern themselves or participate meaningfully in either an autonomous or an independent Cuba.

Clearly, one of the problems for playwrights writing about the insurrections was how to present the sacrifice of so many Spanish lives in combat with allegedly undisciplined savages. *Un alcalde en la manigua* solves this problem by representing Cuban blacks through the eyes of an Andalusian who sees them as dirty, greasy animals, unable to articulate Castilian. (One of the characters tells Spaniards back home that blacks look as if they had smeared fatback all over their faces.) This depiction of the enemy may well have suggested the unacceptable anomaly of Spaniards dying at the hands of such creatures, a perception that made it the more important to emphasize—with as little reference as possible to blacks as fighters—the superiority of the whites and the need to ensure their dominance once the war was over. The author of *Un alcalde* concentrated on blacks in situations removed from combat, representing them in a disparaging, essentially harmless and ridiculous light, dancing tangos and describing in broken Castilian their two favorite pastimes, eating and sex.

El padre Juanico

> Long ago, amidst the crowd of bandits and adventurers, the serfs went off to war, without armor to protect their chests, without lances or sharp swords. The masters, sheathed in steel, followed them, their horses prancing; the serfs, the wretched ones, entered the fray first; if they won, the triumph and the booty was for their masters; if they were conquered, they were taken away like a herd of animals to work for their new masters.
>
> They suffered and looked to heaven, hoping for redress from on high; the priest enervated them with his mysteries; the noble

robbed them; the King tyrannized over them; they loved the priest, the King and the noble. The blood of slaves ran in their veins. . . .

The same thing happens today. The people, out of atavism respond to the military spirit; the bourgeoisie, out of atavism, responds to the spirit of independence. Thus the descendants of the ancient serfs go off to swell the ranks of the Army without a sign of protest—the worker abandoning the factory, the farmer forgetting the land.

Ayer, entre la turba de bandidos y aventureros, iban a la guerra los siervos del terruño sin armaduras que protegiesen su pecho, sin prolongadas lanzas ni cortantes sables. Los señores, recubiertos de acero, les seguían caracoleando sus caballos; los siervos, los miserables, entraban los primeros en la refriega; si vencían, el triunfo y el botín eran para sus señores; si eran vencidos, los llevaban como rebaño de bestias a trabajar para sus nuevos amos.

Sufrían y miraban el cielo, esperándolo todo de arriba; el cura los enervaba con sus misterios; el noble les robaba; el Rey les tiranizaba; ellos querían al cura, al Rey y al noble. Tenían sangre de esclavo. . . .

Hoy sucede lo mismo. El pueblo siente, por atavismo de raza, el espíritu militar; la burguesía siente también por atavismo de raza, el espíritu independiente. Así van ellos a engrosar las filas del Ejército, sin protestar nunca, los herederos de los antiguos siervos, abandonando la fábrica el obrero, olvidando el terruño el labrador.

Pío Baroja, "The Spirit of Subordination" ("El espíritu de subordinación"), *El Globo*, 22 March 1903

El padre Juanico, a prose drama in three acts by the well-known playwright Angel Guimerá, was first performed at the Teatro Español in Madrid on the evening of 18 March 1898. In his *Tour du peuple*, Carlos Serrano mentions the play's author as one of the first to put the question of purchasing redemption from military service on stage—a question Serrano calls a burning issue in the spring of 1898.[83] Although the question of redemption had been dealt with one year earlier in *Los dramas de la guerra*, Guimerá did deal specifically with a further legal proviso that granted exemption from service to the individual who denounced a deserter. This proviso, abolished in 1896, opened the way for malefactors to seek personal revenge or, as is the case in this play, to get rid of someone standing between the denouncer and a source of money.[84] Guimerá's play dramatizes the plight of a young orphaned heiress whose uncle has mismanaged her legacy, and who now wants to marry her off to his son in order to block any investigation of his actions. The girl's mother had arranged that a young boy in her employ for whom she felt a special fondness should be redeemed from military service when the time came. That young boy is now the object of the heiress's affections, a circumstance that first causes the uncle to refuse to redeem him and then leads him to have his son denounce the boy as a deserter. Father Juanico of the title saves the situation by sacrificing his life in a melodramatic closing scene. Before he dies—having stopped a bullet fired by the denouncer and intended for the young boy—the priest marries the latter to the heiress and adjures the uncle's now repentant son to serve as a substitute (in the military service) for the boy he had denounced.

Juan Valera, the eminent diplomat, novelist, and critic, wrote a review of the play for a popular illustrated magazine following its debut, highlighting the idyllic love between the two youthful protagonists and the uncle's abuse of his authority. Although Valera referred to the plot against the young boy, he did not develop a discussion of the problems the play raised in regard to military recruitment.[85] In fact, the play presents the uncle's use of this provision in the regulations governing conscription as one more option open to those who know how to manipulate the legal system for their own benefit. No one in the play—once the uncle's plot is revealed—reacts significantly to the injustice of the provision itself. The focus is on the uncle's fundamental selfishness and the avarice that leads him to engage in an opportunistic and iniquitous act.

Only one week later the same magazine in which Valera had published his review featured a short story that dealt with the proviso granting exemption from service to whoever denounced a deserter. The story by Juan Lapoulide, entitled *Peace through War (Por la guerra paz)* focuses at first on how easily the proviso in the military law lends itself to manipulation. The story begins in 1893. Two young men from the town of Villalobón, Juan Parrondo and Robustiano Gil, are called up for service. Juan Parrondo's uncle, the village political boss (cacique) along with the secretary of the *ayuntamiento* think that they can keep Juan from going because the Parrondo family enjoys considerable local power and the Gil family does not. However, Robustiano Gil, as an only child of a poor, sixty-year-old father, meets the conditions for exemption. Juan does not; moreover Juan's father does not believe that he—as a person of such power and prestige—should have to pay the 1,500 pesetas required to redeem his son from service.

The secretary, in league with the uncle/cacique, makes it appear that Robustiano Gil is a deserter. In fact, the secretary had not informed Robustiano of the citations to report for service and later refuses to hear any explanations for the latter's failure to do so. The provincial commission denounces Gil as a deserter and orders him to serve abroad with extra duty as a penalty. Meanwhile, Juan is provisionally exempted.

At this point, a charitable soul advises Robustiano on how to seek justice from a provincial minister. Since the cacique and the secretary wield no clout with that individual, the alleged deserter is exonerated, though not exempted from service. Juan is subsequently ordered to serve also; his father has squandered time dealing with a redemption insurance service that ultimately cheats him as it has cheated others, with the consequence that Juan's legal period of time for buying release has expired.

Both men train together. Juan is made a corporal and uses his authority to mistreat Robustiano. When the Cuban insurrection breaks out in 1895, their batallion is destined for the island. Juan's miserly father has refused to pay the full amount it takes to send another corporal in Juan's place, so both men end up sailing for Cuba. Once there, Robustiano saves Juan's life in a skirmish. Eventually, they return to Spain and to their village where two groups await them: those who side with Juan's father and those opposed, who side with Robustiano. Juan and Robustiano, now the closest of friends, refuse to allow two separate groups to welcome them home:

> And so the group, *one* group only, followed after the coach in which Juan and Robustiano rode, accompanied by the latter's father and the mayor.
>
> The neighbors walked along contentedly, and in more than one woman's eye and in some of the men's as well, shone tears that none of them could account for.
>
> The fact is that the rivalry between the Gils and the Parrondos was over. No small contributor to their newfound union was the wedding between sergeant Juan—incapacitated for further service, but not for marriage—with one of Robustiano's sisters.

Y el grupo, sólo *un grupo*, siguió tras de la galera-tartana donde con Juan y Robustiano habían subido el padre de éste y el alcalde.

Los vecinos de Villalobón caminaban muy contentos, y en más de unos ojos de mujer y en algunos de hombre asomaban lágrimas que ninguno de ellos podía explicar.

El caso es que en el pueblo se acabó la rivalidad de Giles y de Parrondos, contribuyendo a la unión de la boda del sargento Juan, inútil para el servicio, pero no para el matrimonio, con una hermana de Robustiano.[86]

The author concludes by remarking that the reader can seek out whatever moral the story may contain as he or she pleases.

The intended moral, it appears, is that injustices and divisions at home melt away when Spaniards—even those divided by class and social status—face a common enemy. Christian solidarity and forgiveness, rather than the equal administration of justice, are also, in effect, the values extolled in Guimerá's play: the priest-blessed union of the two lovers, together with Father Juanico's injunction to the repentant son to serve in place of the new husband, unites the divided groups in the name of the sacrament of marriage and of personal remorse. Neither in the play nor in the story is there any hint of a call for changes in the laws governing military service. Instead, the authors of these patriotic fictions aimed at assuaging the pain of the victims and relatives of an unjust conscription system by assuring readers of the abiding consolations of forbearance and Christian charity.

In connection with *Por la guerra paz* and other patriotic exhortations to unity in the theater and fiction, it is useful to recall a passage from the memoirs of a conscript from Madrid's lower middle class, Tomás Álvarez Angulo. Following a graphic description of the sleeping quarters and food he himself experienced, he remarks that the repugnant conditions of the barracks in Madrid at the beginning of the Cuban insurrection in 1895 made it difficult to impose the compliance with military duty required of all patriotic Spaniards. He then described what happened when a delegation of workers approached Práxedes Sagasta on 1 May 1896 to present their findings on the injustice of permitting the well-off to purchase redemption from service. Sagasta replied that it would be impossible to accede to their petition for redress, "because you yourselves must recognize that it would be an atrocity to put young men from good

families in the awful barracks we have here" ("porque ustedes mis-
mos reconocerán que sería una atrocidad llevar a los hijos de buenas
familias a esos cuarteles tan malos que tenemos"). According to
Álvarez Angulo, the worker's representative replied harshly that no
one was asking for reform: what was wanted was simple compliance
with the law that made military service obligatory for all Spaniards
in wartime.[87] Finally, Sebastian Balfour cites the following remarks
of General Martínez Campos, made toward the end of the century.
They presented another, no doubt more compelling argument
advanced by those in power against the intermingling of the privileged classes with the poor: ". . . one cannot bring into the army a
revolutionary yeast of 20,000 to 25,000 young men educated in
advanced principles because it would cause the ignorant mass to fer-
ment and would very seriously undermine the ruling order."[88]

By the spring of 1898, fear of a social revolution, motivated in
part by opposition to the draft, prompted an article in *El Heraldo de
Madrid* by the future president and head of the Liberal Party, José
Canalejas. He warned that the government should not allow itself to
be deceived just because for years the submissive proletariat had
appeared to participate wholeheartedly in the "Marcha de Cádiz,"
the *vivas* to Spain, and so on. Now [3 March 1898] the protests in
favor of obligatory military service and the demonstrations mounted by hungry workers should wake people up to the persistence and
gravity of the underlying problem of the Cuban war—a problem of
"money and blood."[89]

Aún hay patria, Veremundo

This one-act "patriotic improvisation" ("improvisación patriótica")
with music by M. Fernández Caballero and text by the well-known
writer of political satires referred to earlier in this study, Eduardo
Navarro Gonzalvo, opened on 9 May 1898 at the Teatro de la
Zarzuela in Madrid. The setting is the courtyard of a tenement
house in Madrid. An unseen Yankee, a pork vendor, has a room on
the ground floor, outside of which hang strings of sausages.
Prominently displayed on his door is the head of a pig placed
between the letters E and U (for Estados Unidos). The neighbors
want the Yankee evicted, but the owner of the property, Patricia,

cannot afford to do it. Moreover, she is not herself of late—not the feisty *manola* of old. She recovers her spirits when her sons appear: they are Juan Soldado (Soldier) and Gallardete, a sailor. Patricia, it turns out, is Mother Spain. Her sons represent the two branches of the armed forces. The Yankee represents the United States, which, in the course of the play's telescoped time, destroys the Spanish fleet in Manila Bay. Patricia's sailor son describes how the bombs fell on the "rotting planks of our aging ships." Despite this disaster, all agree to persevere in seeking revenge, for Spain's history demands no less of them.

The play is an unabashed and simplistic call to patriotism: Spain is worth dying for because it is noble, as its history demonstrates; the United States is venal and common and cannot prevail. There is no plot, nor are any issues raised—with the exception of the fleeting reference to the age and inadequacy of the Spanish ships ("rotting planks of the aging ships") sunk in Manila Bay. This brief reminder of Spain's lack of preparedness for war is dropped and is not taken up again. The emphasis is on the need for all Spaniards to sacrifice— young and old, men and women, rich and poor.

The author attempts to move the audience through the use of the poster-like image of the mother and sons. At the end of scene fourteen, Patricia and her two sons embrace while, in the background, one of the neighbors appears holding aloft a Spanish flag. The apotheosis that immediately precedes the end of the play presents the audience with a view of Havana Bay. Various ships are bombarding the city. Morro castle is on the left. Stage front, a proud lion resting on a trophy of flags, arms, cannons, etc., is placed in such a way as to suggest that it is defying the onslaught of the ships. The last scene again features a grouping consisting of Patricia and her sons. Juan Soldado beseeches her to enlace her arms with theirs so that their arms may serve as armor for her breast. The sailor points to the lion, crying out that it lives still and is the emblem of her (Mother Spain's) race. All three embrace again on stage left as the music swells and the curtain slowly falls.

The review that appeared in *El Imparcial* on 11 May, two days after its opening, likened *Aún hay patria, Veremundo* to a play (not located for the present study) entitled *El Tío Sam*. The reviewer wrote that each play displayed the kind of *patriotería teatral*, or stage patriotism, that is always in bad taste. Navarro Gonzalvo's practiced stagecraft did attenuate the stale patriotic cliches sufficiently to win the public's applause, the critic wrote, but authors and impresarios should take note nonetheless that dragging the flag and the uniforms of soldiers and sailors across the stage at a time when so many men have sacrificed themselves heroically for the fatherland leaves a sad impression and depresses the spirits of audiences. Productions of this kind, he concluded, are not lyric-comic.

El mantón de Manila

J. de L. (José de Laserna), the critic who signed the review of *Veremundo*, voiced a similar criticism of *El mantón de Manila* in *El Imparcial* the day after its first appearance on 11 May 1898 at the Teatro de Apolo in Madrid. This *boceto lírico*, or lyric sketch, with a text by Fiacro Yrayzoz, featured a score by the much-acclaimed maestro Federico Chueca. Laserna wrote that the public was tired of patriotic displays: neither the march played when the batallion passed across the stage, nor the flag, nor the *vivas* for Spain could rouse the audience from its indifference.

The play takes place in a poor neighborhood in Madrid. Lucía has just learned that her sweetheart, Santos, has been conscripted and, as he puts it, will soon be fighting blacks in Havana. Lucía accepts a costly Manila shawl from a wealthy admirer with the pretensions of a Don Juan and then sells it in order to purchase Santos's redemption from service. Until the end of the play, Santos is unaware of Lucía's reason for accepting the shawl: he mistakenly believes that she has thrown him over for her rich suitor. This slight entertainment has Santos and Lucía expressing the usual patriotic sentiments at the beginning of the play—"The fatherland comes first and then comes our love" ("Que la patria es lo primero, / y después es nuestro amor")—only to forget them as soon as Lucía succeeds in raising the money for a substitute. The chorus approves her gesture: "That's what it is to really love a man!" ("¡Eso se llama querer a un hombre!"), and no one gives any thought to the sponger and ne'er-do-well Marcelino, the substitute paid eighty pesetas to go in Santos's place. Conscription in this play amounts to little more than a plot device used to delay the inevitable triumph of love.

Gigantes y cabezudos

Between 11 May 1898, when *Mantón de Manila* appeared, and 29 November 1898, when *Gigantes y cabezudos* received its first performance at the Teatro de la Zarzuela, Spain had lost its empire. On 1 May, the United States had sunk the Spanish fleet in Manila Bay. On 3 July, the Spanish fleet was defeated in Santiago Bay. On 25 July, about one week after the city of Santiago fell to the North Americans, U.S. forces landed in Puerto Rico. On 12 August a Preliminary Peace Protocol was signed according to which Spain recognized the loss of Cuba and Puerto Rico. Fighting had continued in the Philippines, but by 14 August, Manila surrendered. By the beginning of November Spaniards realized that the United States meant to stay in the Philippines.

The government feared the consequences of public discontent following the 1 May defeat at Cavite. Madrid was placed under military command, and on 14 July continuing fears of the possibility of social revolution led the government to suspend constitutional guarantees and impose prior-restraint orders on the press.[90] In his discussion of the aftermath of the Disaster, Fernández Almagro pinpoints the two issues that the Socialist Party raised in order to discredit the monarchy: its failure to impose obligatory military service and its failure to provide for the welfare of repatriated soldiers. Both issues directly affected large numbers of people. No less than the injustice that permitted the wealthy to evade military service through a cash redemption, the plight of the sick, hungry, and depressed soldiers, which transcended the Socialist Party program, was taken up by anarchists and republicans of all stripes and quickly became a genuinely popular issue, though not a profoundly disruptive one as the government had feared.[91] The press generally represented the mood of the Spanish people not as revolutionary but as depressed, apathetic, hopeless. Nevertheless, again according to the press, Spaniards did react strongly to several issues—among them the treatment of Spanish prisoners of war in the Philippines and the condition of the repatriated soldiers.

Gigantes y cabezudos touched upon the second of the two issues. The zarzuela's text was written by the prolific and popular Miguel Echegaray; the music was composed by M. Fernández Caballero. José de Laserna reviewed the zarzuela for *El Imparcial* the day after its opening. Even though he acknowledged its great success with the audience, Laserna did not think that it presented an authentic picture of the types and customs of Aragón as it should have done, nor in his view did it adequately depict Zaragoza and its popular fiesta of *gigantes* and *cabezudos* (oversized figures sometimes on stilts and dwarf-like figures with large heads).

The zarzuela's connection to the events of 1898 hinges on Pilar's love for Jesús, a soldier in Cuba. An unnamed sergeant who is in love with Pilar lies to her, telling her that Jesús has married another woman in Cuba. But Pilar is steadfast and, near the end of the one-act zarzuela, Jesús returns unmarried to Zaragoza, the scene of the action. Misunderstandings are resolved and the two lovers are reunited. Two moments apparently stood out for contemporary audiences: the reading aloud of a letter from Jesús in Cuba, describing how sick he was, how short of money and of clothing (he wrote that he was almost naked), and the chorus of the repatriated soldiers of whom Jesús is one. The first-night audience applauded the chorus enthusiastically. Laserna called it valiant, vigorous, and inspired: "What originality, what youthful vigor there is in this beautiful song of manly tenderness elicited by the sight of one's native soil!" ("¡Qué frescura, qué juvenil empuje el de este hermoso canto de ternura varonil a la vista de la patria natal!")

Deleito y Piñuela, historian of the *género chico*, also emphasized the great popularity of the soldiers' chorus, noting that everyone sang the verses, "At last I look upon you/ famous Ebro" ("Por fin te miro/ Ebro famoso") and "Ay, the poor mothers,/ how they have wept!" ("¡Ay, pobres madres,/ cuánto han llorado!"). He went on to remark that the zarzuela was popular even though the libretto was already outdated when it was written. Above all, it had the disadvantage of bringing up a subject that was a source of great pain: the loss of the colonies. The Cuban War, he noted, had inspired optimistic and patriotic zarzuelas since the time of *Cuba libre*, but by 1898, as this zarzuela demonstrated, writers for this genre were finally left with nothing to offer but the depiction of returning soldiers defeated not by the enemy in battle, but by tropical fevers and by the crumbling of Spain's fictitious military and naval forces.[92]

The lamentable condition of the repatriated soldiers in 1898 was then and still remains a potent image of the Disaster. The first boatload of 1,000 returning veterans docked at La Coruña on 23 August. In the course of the passage from Cuba, 60 soldiers had died. Less than a month before the premiere of *Gigantes*, the steamship *Montserrat* docked in Cádiz with 1,498 soldiers on board of whom 800 were gravely ill. Some 96 men had died on board and were cast into the sea. The editorialist in *El Imparcial* who reported the *Montserrat*'s arrival from Cuba on 2 November 1898 wrote:

> The horrors of war present this sad and moving epilogue. Every day the pitiful sight is repeated, but the heart cannot become accustomed to witnessing it. On the contrary, the most recent victims cause deeper pain than the ones who came before and, as the number of men sacrificed increases, the grief felt by the nation takes on the proportions of a horrendous tragedy.

> Los horrores de la guerra traen este epílogo conmovedor y tristísimo. Cada día se renueva el espectáculo lastimoso, pero no puede acostumbrarse el corazón a presenciarle; antes, por el contrario, las últimas víctimas causan dolor más hondo que las anteriores; porque al ir aumentando la cifra de los sacrificados, toma el sentimiento nacional proporciones de horrenda tragedia.

For many months, in cities, towns, and on country roads, Spaniards saw returning veterans dressed in rags, ill, bandaged, many on crutches, making their way home. Among other contemporaries who recorded their impressions of these grim scenes was Tomás Álvarez Angulo, who was himself ill when he returned from Cuba. In his memoirs, he wrote that he saw men, still dressed in the striped cotton uniform of the Spanish army, fall down dead in the streets of Madrid.[93] Enrique Gutiérrez Gamero also wrote a memorable description of his reactions to the sight of returning veterans in his *Mis primeros ochenta años*.[94]

Such memories persisted and resonated long afterwards with Spaniards who had witnessed such sights, as well as with those who only read about them. One of the first and most graphic of the memoirs that appeared after 1898 was Ricardo Burguete's *¡La Guerra! Cuba (Diario de un testigo)*, published in 1902. He ended his book with a description of the third-class section of the *Colón*, a ship returning sick and wounded soldiers to Spain:

> The war returns what is left: the fever-stricken, men with dysentery,, the tubercular, the mutilated. With almost no hope of salvation, all

of them return in search of the fatherland's welcoming embrace. Who knows! Perhaps the blessed kiss of the homeland and of their mothers will revive them. The impatience they feel to get back makes even the sickest of them climb repeatedly up to the deck. From the covered stern, I see them ascending the steps wrapped in blankets despite the heat and showing signs of fatigue—emaciated bodies, hands and feet the color of wax, and faces marked by the horrible lividness of death. The war returns what is left. Those young bodies are all that remains of as many other lives cut down along the mudflats, in the depth of the woods, or in the puddles on the floors of fetid blockhouses.

Some are breathing only by a miracle; and under the canvas and waterproof sheets on deck or under the lifeboats they hold a death-like posture for hours, even days.

We have lost four men whom we had to throw into the sea.

La guerra devuelve su sobrante: palúdicos, disentéricos, tuberculosos, amputados. Sin esperanza de salvación en su mayoría, todos vienen en demanda del regazo patrio. ¡Quién sabe! Tal vez revivan al beso bendito de la patria y de la madre. La impaciencia de llegar hace subir de continuo a cubierta aún a los más graves. Desde la toldilla, veo ascender por las escaleras, tapujados en mantas, a pesar del calor, y dando muestras de fatiga, cuerpos extenuados, manos y pies color de cera y semblantes descompuestas con la horrible lividez de la muerte. La guerra devuelve su sobrante. Todos aquellos cuerpos juveniles son el sobrante de otras tantas vidas segadas a lo largo de las ciénagas, en el fondo de los bosques o en el encharcado suelo de los fortines mefíticos.

Algunos alientan milagrosamente; y bajo las lonas y encerados de cubierta o al resguardo de los botes, conservan durante horas, y aun días, posturas de muerte.

Hemos perdido cuatro, que ha sido preciso lanzar al mar.[95]

A modern commentator on a performance of *Gigantes y cabezudos*, Enrique Franco, writes that despite its folkloric brilliance and patriotic veneer, the specter of the national disaster hovers over the zarzuela. Thus the soldiers who form the chorus, although they sing with apparent joy and emotive forcefulness, are transformed and distorted—as if by a fun-house mirror—into Nonell's dramatic drawings of soldiers returning to the fatherland wounded and bent with defeat and misery.[96] Franco's original Spanish refers to the distortion and transformation of the soldiers in the eyes of later viewers as somehow similar to the technique used in creating the *esperpento*. The turn-of-the-century Spanish writer Ramón del Valle Inclán used this term to describe some of his works in which reality is grotesquely distorted so as to reveal the absurdity and tragedy of life. Isidre Nonell, the Catalan painter whom Franco names here, showed his drawings of repatriated soldiers from Cuba and the Philippines, *España después de la guerra*, at the famous tavern Els Quatre Gats in Barcelona in December 1898. In 1899 they were on view at the Galeries Vollard in Paris where they were well received.[97]

Nonell was not alone in making returning soldiers the subject of his art; another painter, Alberto Pla y Rubio, had done so earlier with the second of his two canvases, *Off to War* and *Back from War* (*A la Guerra* and *De la guerra*). Joaquín Mir, a colleague of Nonell in Barcelona, drew returning veterans in 1899. All three artists helped to fix for later generations of Spaniards who did not themselves observe returning soldiers what was surely becoming a central image of the Disaster.

Alberto Pla y Rubio's first painting, *A la guerra*, depicted the departure in 1893 of Spanish soldiers for Melilla, Spain's enclave on the North African coast where a Muslim revolt had taken place. At that time, national enthusiasm for renewed combat between the cross and the crescent had created a bellicose mood convincingly captured by the painter, who won first prize for his work at the 1895 Exposición de Bellas Artes.[98] His second painting depicts a repatriate soldier back from Cuba. Francisco Alcántara described it in *El Imparcial* on 14 June 1897:

> The soldier from Cuba returns to his village blind. He arrives home unexpectedly and startles his compatriots with the terrible spectacle of his blindness. His sister, who has been drawn into the street by the villagers' shouts, comes face to face with the black bitterness of her brother's condition. She leads him home, followed by a crowd that is urged on by the curiosity which tragedy awakens.
>
> Leaning on his sister's shoulder, his eyes bandaged, his left hand anxiously reaching for the door of the house of his parents, of his infancy and youth—the artist represents him at the moment in which his mother becomes aware of his presence. She has put down her sewing, and on her feet now, lets out a terrible cry. With one hand on her forehead and another on her broken heart, from eyes that are dry of tears she hurls an angry and terrible protest.

El soldado de Cuba vuelve a su pueblo ciego. Llega de improviso y sorprende a sus paisanos con el terrible espectáculo de su ceguera. La hermana, que atraída por los gritos de las gentes se encuentra en la calle con tan negra amargura, le conduce a la casa paterna. Síguenles todos en tropel con la anhelante curiosidad que lo trágico despierta.

Apoyado en el hombro de la hermana, vendados los ojos, palpando ansioso con la mano izquierda la puerta de sus padres, de su infancia y juventud, nos le presenta el artista en el momento de sorprender a la madre que abandona su labor, y lanzando grito terrible, de pie, con una mano en la frente y otra en el pecho desgarrado, exhala por los ojos secos una protesta iracunda y terrible.

The critic goes on to praise Pla y Rubio for the "masculine power" of his palette, and for having chosen a topic with contemporary relevance—a topic realized in a "beautiful painting" that does honor to the art of the fatherland.

What did this and similar images of sick and wounded returning soldiers mean to those who saw them reproduced in newspapers and magazines? An unfocused regret at the loss of so many lives? Did the mothers' grief, and in Pla's case, her "angry and terrible protest" at her son's condition inspire antiwar or even antistate sentiments? In his commentary on Pla y Rubio's picture, Alcántara does not speculate on how viewers might have interpreted it. Except for the general observations referred to above, he mentions only the "sinister" contrast between the details of the domestic scene, i.e., the doorway, the sewing basket, etc., and the pathos of the scene in which mother and son meet again. Whatever meanings they may have suggested, powerful images of repatriated soldiers comparable to those of Pla y Rubio, Mir, and Nonell dominate the last two plays under discussion here.

¡Quince bajas!

On 3 December 1898 in *El Imparcial* José de Laserna reviewed Pascual Millán's prose drama in three acts that had been performed the previous night at the Nuevo Teatro in Madrid. Laserna began by complaining that he had clearly been preaching in the desert because despite his repeated admonitions that the topic was inappropriate, plays about the loss of the colonies were still being produced. The public, he granted, was benevolent although *¡Quince bajas!* in his view was neither moving nor interesting. Laserna ended by noting that when, at the end of the performance several army officers objected to a phrase in the play that they thought could be interpreted unfavorably, the author immediately withdrew it.

On the night of the second performance, the play was shut down by order of Madrid's civil governor. Nine days later *El Imparcial* reported that the cancellation of *¡Quince bajas!* had led to the closing of the theater, causing considerable financial loss to the impresario who had complied in every way with his obligations.

When the play was published in 1899 its author provided an explanation of these events. Because it deals directly with several of the issues raised in this study, a considerable portion of Millán's account will be inserted here. He began by observing that advance publicity for the play had aroused the curiosity of the public. Millán was well known as a novelist, but this was his first play:

> For that reason the theater was quite full, and the audience comprised all classes—from the modest worker who occupied a seat in the upper balcony to the *luminaries* of Madrid society who filled the lower floor, with theater people predominating, as is *de rigueur* . . . When the show was over and I was in a small adjoining salon accepting the congratulations of friends and colleagues, someone told me that one of my lines had displeased some young army officers who had attended the performance.

> El teatro, por esta razón, se vio muy concurrido, y el público lo componían personas de todas clases, desde el modesto operario que ocupaba su asiento en galería, hasta los *conspícuos* de la sociedad madrileña que llenaban la sala, abundando, como es de rigor, la gente del *oficio* . . . Terminada la función y cuando, en el saloncillo, recibía yo las felicitaciones de amigos y compañeros, hubo alguien de advertirme que una frase del drama había disgustado a algunos jóvenes oficiales del ejército que asistieron a la representación.[99]

Millán explained that he offered to take out the offending lines since he had not put them in intentionally. The next night, just moments before the show was to begin, the civil governor arrived and indefinitely suspended performances of the play. Why? Millán quoted the governor's letter to the impresario of the Nuevo Teatro. The letter claimed that the governor had information leading him to believe that disruptive political demonstrations were planned for the next performance of *¡Quince bajas!*, that it was his duty to prevent disorder, and that therefore, in accord with Article 25 of the Provincial Law, he was suspending further performances of the play. Millán did not believe that the order came from the office of the civil governor, but from higher up:

> Perhaps the government, aware that the play brings the issue of obligatory military service right onto the stage, that it clearly shows the galling inequality of rich and poor with respect to the Fatherland (which is defended rifle in hand only by those disinherited by fortune, while those whom fortune favors scoff at the whole thing with criminal indifference . . .); perhaps the government, having discovered that the lower classes planned to loudly express its sympathies, and that some individuals from the army (once the offending phrase had been suppressed) planned at the very same time to enthusiastically applaud a drama that exalts the Spanish soldier at a time when everyone is demanding an accounting from him that should not be his to give—perhaps—I repeat, the government, knowing of these plans, feared that those demonstrations, agreed upon by representatives of the people and of the army, would cause unease to the powers that be, and wanted to avoid that at all cost.
>
> This is the only possible way to explain the play's suspension.

> Quizás el gobierno, al ver que en el drama se lleva a la escena la cuestión del servicio militar obligatorio, que allí se pone de manifiesto la irritante desigualdad entre el pobre y el rico para con la Patria (a la cual sólo defienden con el fusil en la mano los desheredados de la suerte, mientras los favorecidos por ella, con un criminal indiferencia se burlan de todo . . .); quizá el gobierno al saber que las clases populares se proponían expresar ruidosamente sus simpatías y algunos individuos del ejército (una vez suprimida la frase que hubo de molestarles) pensaban igualmente aplaudir cuando todo el mundo trata de exigirle responsabilidades no suyas quizá, repito, el gobierno, sabedor de tales propósitos, temió que aquellas manifestaciones hechas de consuno por representantes del pueblo y del ejército trajesen alguna desazón a los Poderes públicos y quiso evitarlas a toda costa.
>
> Sólo así se explica la suspensión de la obra. (p. 2)

In response to questions put to him after the first performance, Millán explained why the play had not been produced earlier when it would have been more opportune. It was written, he wrote, in 1896 when there was much patriotic fervor in Spain, when all Europe marveled at Spain's sending 250,000 men to the colonies, at its sowing the *manigua* with Spanish corpses solely in order to preserve its legendary martial reputation; it was a time when heroes like the one at Cascorro came to public attention, and every soldier was a Caesar, every guerrilla chief a martyr. At that time, Millán wrote, he was out of the country and, although his friends tried, they failed to secure an engagement for his play. Here Millán quoted *El Día* and *El Globo*, both of which claimed that it was the impresarios and their usual machinations that delayed production. Millán then observed that despite the fact that the play would certainly have been more opportune two years earlier, several Madrid papers, including *El Liberal*, *El Heraldo de Madrid*, and *La Correspondencia de España*, had noted its exceptional success at the first night's performance.

Millán's work, like *Los dramas de la guerra*, is concerned primarily with the devastating effects of the separatist wars on the poor—in this case two rural *quintos*, their wife and sweetheart respectively, and family. His overt criticism of the injustice of the system of conscription is clearly expressed; but above all, Millán concentrated on making the plight of the victim of injustice, the poor soldier, as vivid as possible. He chose for his protagonist a strong, handsome young man, Pedro, whose sweetheart, Marcela, is also courted by Cipriano, the village school teacher. Cipriano has been able to pay the sum required to avoid service abroad. The mayor of the village, a veteran of past wars like several of the older men in plays previously discussed here, is filled with nostalgia as he discourses for the benefit of the townspeople on the glory of dying for the fatherland. Too poor to raise the 2,000 pesetas needed to escape service, Pedro and another villager, Gaspar, a married man with children, must depart for Cuba.

A mother's voice intervenes at this point. Gaspar's mother, Petra, disagrees with the mayor's dictum that the fatherland always comes before one's son. She cries: "The fatherland! What do I care about that? What's for sure is that if Gaspar does not come back, it won't be the fatherland that weeps for him, and the fatherland will not come here to sow his fields!" (¡La patria! ¿A mí qué me importa eso? ¡A fe que si no vuelve Gaspar, no será la patria la que le llore ni

la que le venga aquí a sembrar las tierras!") (15). The mayor's
response to this outburst is to remark that mothers are always egoistic. In the next scene, Petra rails against the corruption of a system
that permits single men to be exempted from service provided they
have connections, while men like Gaspar with families, but without
influential friends to help them, are called up. Finally, she bitterly
condemns the practice of evading service through a cash payment. If
everyone were treated equally, she could bear it, she says, but, "the
idea that a son should be killed, not necessarily because of the war,
not necessarily because of the government, but because he is poor
. . . You [addressing the mayor] don't understand because you don't
have sons" ("que le maten un hijo, quizás no por la guerra, ni por el
gobierno, sino por la pobreza . . . Tú no te haces cargo porque no
tiés hijos") (17). The mother in this play is as resistant to the role
assigned her—that of making sacrifices, if need be, the sacrifice of a
son—as the mother in *Familia y patria*. But unlike that mother, Petra
is poor and voices the specific complaints of a mother who knows
that she will now face even greater want. The mayor, the representative of authority in the play, simply dismisses her.

In Pedro's absence, Cipriano pursues Marcela, suggesting to her
that his position as a teacher is a better one than Pedro is ever likely
to have. Several months have elapsed when a rumor begins to circulate that Pedro has returned to the village but is in hiding. Cipriano
assumes that the young man has deserted and has returned to take
Marcela away with him: "It's possible that he wants to live with you
in some other country rather than go on fighting with negroes.
Anyone would do the same thing!" ("Puede que prefiera vivir contigo en otros países que andar batiéndose con los negros. ¡Cualquiera
haría lo mismo!") (29). In fact, Pedro has been repatriated. However,
he is no longer the strong, handsome man he once was; in fact, he is
so altered by disease and his wounds that he hesitates to show himself to Marcela. As for Gaspar, he was hacked to pieces in Cuba by
blacks wielding machetes. The press had reported at the time that
there had been *¡Quince bajas!*, that is, fifteen casualties, but since the
fallen were soldiers and not officers, their names were not recorded,
nor were their relatives notified of their deaths.

Eventually, Pedro does show himself. He appears in the doorway of Petra's house where Cipriano and Marcela are seated alone

talking. The stage directions read: "He is completely disfigured, very ill, and with his head bandaged. He wears a striped uniform and a soldier's cap. At his neck he wears a scarf and on his breast a cross. He is wet from the rain. Cipriano draws back. Marcela stares at him, frightened" ("Viene completamente desfigurado, muy enfermo y con la cabeza vendada; viste traje de rayadillo y gorra de cuartel. Trae un tapabocas puesto al cuello y una cruz en el pecho. Aparece moja-do por la lluvia. Cipriano retrocede. Marcela se queda mirándole, espantada") (32). Pedro realizes immediately that his altered appear-ance has cost him dearly: Marcela no longer loves him. At the end of the scene, Pedro observes bitterly that he would have preferred to die in battle as Gaspar did since he would be mourned sincerely. However, some die and others—like him—come back ruined men. Then, in a gesture designed to shock Cipriano and Marcela into full awareness of the war's toll on him, Pedro yanks off his bandage and reveals his head and forehead, disfigured by a large scar. Cipriano again draws back. Marcela falls down, covering her face with her hands. Pedro laughs nervously, repeating that some have died and others have come back looking like him.

In a subsequent scene, alone with Marcela, Pedro again con-trasts the wounded veteran's loss of youth and beauty and the impediment he becomes to others to the aftermath of a soldier's death on the battlefield. Millán's insistence on the despair of the returned veteran, based here upon Pedro's awareness of his body's ravaged state, is so exceptional compared to the treatment given this subject by other contemporary Spanish plays and popular literature as to warrant the following long excerpt from Pedro's speech.

Pedro begins by telling Marcela that on the long journey back from Cuba it never occurred to him to complain about his fate. But when he saw her reaction to his appearance, he abominated the campaign and all those who made him go to Cuba. Now he would like to kill everyone who is in good health. He chides Marcela for her typically female, superficial attraction to him when he was hand-some and vigorous.

> But that's all over now: there's no more youth—or at least it's as if there weren't any—no more beauty, no strength, no grace, no high spirits, nothing. Everything has changed but my heart, and since you can't see it you don't value it. You can't see anything but how repul-

sive-looking the man you were once so proud of is now. Everything, everything has changed: there's nothing left but a bundle of sickness surrounded by bottles and pills—rot outside and inside—because my blood is even more putrid than my skin. Ah, if I had thought about all this when I was there, you wouldn't have the displeasure of seeing me now! . . . *(Marcela cries.)* And you think I shouldn't envy Gaspar! Do you think it's better for a man to die between the sheets disgusting everybody, and then when he's finally done for have them gather him up like something noxious and throw him in a hole, without shedding a single tear—no, as if they were getting rid of a load that had been weighing them down? Do you think that's better than a healthy man stopping a bullet on the battlefield, in the air and the sun, and being buried along with other brave men by comrades; not like a sick man all rotted before he died, but like a man who was healthy even after death? Not a man who has left a room full of medicines, but a man who has left a body pulsing with young, vigorous blood that's still warm. Not a man who has died with the mark of suffering on his face, but with a look of enthusiasm. And instead of listening to the moans of four old women, how much better to hear the music that calls men to the attack. And instead of the priest's sad Latin gibberish, to hear the voice of the cannon that sends you off to the attack! Men who end up as I will—even after we're buried, people will avoid us and burn our clothing. But things that belonged to those who died in battle will be preserved like relics—just as I've brought back Gaspar's scapular for Aunt Petra. It's covered with blood, but it's the blood of the man they killed, not the blood of a man who died. That's why it doesn't disgust people. The fortunate ought to die like Gaspar. The damned die like me.

Pero aquello acabó: ya no hay *juventú*—o como si no lo hubiera—ya no hay hermosura, ni fuerza, ni gracia, ni bríos, ni *ná*. *Tó* ha *cambiao* menos el corazón, y como ese no se enseña, no lo estimas: tú no *pués* ver más que esa facha asquerosa adonde iba a parar aquel de quien tan orgullosa estabas. *Tó, tó* ha *mudao*: ya no hay aquí más que un depósito de enfermedades *rodeao* de botellas y píldoras; podredumbre por fuera y por dentro, porque más *podría* que la piel tengo la sangre. ¡Ah! Si yo *hubiea* allí *pensao* esto, no tendrías el disgusto de verme . . . *(Marcela llora.)* ¡Y *quiés* que no envidie a Gaspar! ¿Te *paece* mejor *pa* un hombre morir entre sábanas *repunando* a *tós* y que en cuanto acabe lo cojan como a cosa mala y lo metan en el hoyo, sin una lágrima, antes al contrario, como el que se quita un peso de encima? ¿Te *paece* mejor eso, que allí, en el campo, al aire, al sol, en plena *salú* quedar *atravesao* por una bala y que te entierren tus compañeros, entre otros valientes, no como enfermo, *podrío* antes de morir, sino como sano aun después de muerto; no dejando una procesión de medicinas, sino un reguero de sangre jóven, vigorosa, caliente *toavía*; no llevando en el semblante la marca del sufrimiento, sino del entusiasmo; y en vez de escuchar los gimoteos de cuatro viejas, oír la música que toca el paso de ataque; y en lugar de los tristes latinajos del cura, que sea la voz del cañon la que te despida? Los que acaban como acabaré yo, hasta después de *enterraos* se les huye y se queman sus ropas; mientras lo que que [*sic*] ha *sío* de los otros, se guarda como reliquia; que así traigo yo *pa* la tía Petra el escapulario que llevaba Gaspar, lleno de sangre; pero sangre del que mataron, no del que se murió; por eso no repugna. Como Gaspar deben morir los dichosos. Como yo, acaban los malditos. (pp. 39-40)

Pedro later reveals the details of Gaspar's death at the hands of blacks—a death he had witnessed and tried to prevent. This is the drama's only reference to the enemy: it is the usual identification of the insurgents as predominantly black. There is no reference to the causes of the war. The aged mayor does not refer to the causes of the wars he recalls: the soldier's life and fortunate death on the battlefield are what thrill him. No one in the play seems to think that the reasons for going to war are important or relevant. In response to Pedro's account of her son's death, a despondent Petra does not question *why* he died. Instead she remarks that if her son had been identified by name instead of merely figuring as another number in the fifteen deaths reported at the time, she might have wept for him during all these months. For the second time in these plays (the first was in *Los dramas de la guerra*) the government's practice in reporting casualties, i.e., providing the names of officers but not soldiers, emerges as a source of deep bitterness for the surviving relatives. Once the death is confirmed, the audience is assured that it is not justification for the death that Petra wants, but rather the enactment of religious ritual.

In a scene with Cipriano, Pedro urges his former rival to marry Marcela. She had, after all, been willing to keep her word and sacrifice herself to him and thus deserves to be happy. Finally, pointing to the cross on his chest, Pedro addresses Cipriano with desperate irony:

When I am dead try to take this *(pointing to the cross)*, because what put it on my chest is what will make you happy. *(Heatedly.)* Now you see! In exchange for my health, my strength! In exchange for the

family I expected to have! . . . In exchange for my whole life . . . they put this . . . insignia here! *(Sarcastically.)* Just figure out for yourself whether the wedding present I'm giving you is worth anything! *(He lets himself fall back, covering his face in desperation. Cipriano looks at him with pity.)*
    Cipriano. *(Aside.)* "God wants it so!"

Cuando me haya muerto procura recoger ésta *(señalando a la cruz)*, porque la misma causa que me la puso en el pecho es la que te hace a ti dichoso. *(Con mucho calor.)* ¡Ya ves! ¡a cambio de mi *salú*, de mi fuerza . . . ¡de la familia que esperaba hacer! . . . ¡a cambio de mi vida toda...me pusieron aquí esta . . . insignia! *(Con sarcasmo.)* ¡Imagínate tú si vale el regalo de boda que *quieo* hacerte! *(Se deja caer cubrién-dose el rostro con desesperación. Cipriano le mira con lástima.)*
    Cipriano. *(Aparte.)* ¡Dios lo quiere! (44-45).

In the final scene, Pedro's chagrin at seeing Cipriano and Marcela together with a lifetime ahead of them, leads him, in a last bid for revenge, to try to stab Cipriano, but too weak to strike the blow he falls dead to the ground. As he falls, he starts to curse the couple, but instead he curses bullets that do not kill when that is their mission—a bitter allusion to his fate on the battleground, i.e., to have been struck, but not mortally wounded. The mayor approaches Pedro's body, and as he does so, he treads on the cross awarded for military valor that has fallen from Pedro's chest. He picks it up and hands it to Cipriano who claims it as a souvenir of the valiant soldier. The mayor then ends the play with these words: "The soldier's cross is a cross of stone" ("La cruz del *soldao* es una cruz de piedra") (p. 50). Ambiguous words that to a modern viewer might suggest the ultimate futility of a soldier's acts as symbolized by the other cross that serves as headstone for his grave. In the mouth of the mayor, they may rather have conveyed to the 1898 audience the stoical realism of an old soldier.

Pedro's own words in this play are no less ambiguous. On the one hand, he appears to regret only one thing—that he did not die in battle so that he could have been mourned properly for his sacrifice. On the other hand, his despair at seeing how repulsed Marcela is by his appearance leads him, at least momentarily, to hate the war and those who sent him to it. Millán evidently succeeded in convincing the officers who attended the play on the first night of his admiration for the loyalty and fortitude of the Spanish soldier, but he also allowed Pedro to suggest that the sacrifice of his health, his happiness, and finally, his life was too great a price to pay for Spain's continued presence in Cuba.

L'Héroe

Although Santiago Rusiñol's play L'Héroe appeared after 1898 and therefore does not fall within the bounds of this study, it deserves mention specifically in connection with ¡Quince bajas!. L'Héroe debuted at the Teatre Romea in Barcelona on 17 April 1903. The large and politically mixed audience which had advance information about the play's subject matter, variously applauded and protested throughout the performance. Reportedly, the atmosphere was highly charged.[100]

On 19 April 1903, a reporter for El Globo noted that the play had produced displeasure and indignation in the military: "In it [the play] militarism is harshly attacked. It is feared that disagreeable events may take place" ("En él se ataca duramente el militarismo. Se teme que sobrevengan desagradables sucesos"). On the following day the same paper reported that the civil governor of Barcelona had prohibited further performances.

The hero of the title is a conscript (a quinto) who goes off to fight in the Philippines. Military service transforms him from the goodhearted fellow he had been into a cruel wretch. Rusiñol attributes the change directly to the exaltation of bellicosity and to militarism. In stark contrast to Pascual Millán's apparent praise for the Spanish soldier's loyalty even when called upon to make extreme sacrifices, Rusiñol presents brutalization of the ordinary conscript as the end result of military service in the insurrectionary wars, a theme no playwright had touched before. Josep María Poblet writes that the play's last lines were repeated everywhere—by some in praise, in protest by others. The lines were spoken by the man who has just killed the "hero." Sword in hand, he says: "Who says I've killed the hero! I've killed the village lout! Look at those men there: it's the men working at the looms who are the heroes!" ("I què he d'haver mort l'héroe! He mort el gandul del poble! Mireu-los: els del teler són els héroes!").[101]

Notes

[1]*Diccionario de la literatura cubana*, vol. 2 (Havana: Editorial Letras Cubanas, 1984), 1003.

[2]*Teatro/Ignacio Sarachaga*. Selección y prólogo de Rine Leal (Havana: Editorial Letras Cubanas, 1990), 19. In *Perfil histórico de las letras cubanas desde los orígenes hasta 1898* (Havana: Letras Cubanas, 1983), 299, different points of view regarding the political significance of the *teatro bufo* are presented and the conclusion reached that in the broadest sense this theater was separatist: "Todo parece indicar que en realidad se trataba entonces de una manifestación de nacionalismo." For a discussion of the internal differences that divided autonomists, see Marta Bizcarrondo, "Entre Cuba y España: el dilema del autonomismo," *Cuadernos Hispanoamericanos* 577-78 (1998): 171-98.

[3]*Diccionario de la literatura cubana*, 1003. See also Rine Leal, *Breve historia del teatro cubano* (Havana: Editorial Letras Cubanas, 1980) and Eduardo Robreño, *Historia del teatro popular cubano* (Havana: Oficina del Historiador de la Ciudad, 1961).

[4]See Helg's "Independent Cuba: A Comparative Perspective," *Ethnohistory* 44, no. 1 (winter 1997): 64.

[5]See Sebastian Balfour, *The End of the Spanish Empire 1898-1923* (Oxford: Clarendon Press, 1997), 139, for a reference to Catalan interests in Cuba in the nineteenth century. Francesc Cabana, *La burguesía catalana: una aproximación histórica* (Barcelona: Proa, 1996) has information on the Marqués de Comillas, owner of the Transatlántica shipping company which held the monopoly on transport of troops to the Antilles and to the Philippines.

[6]The photos are inventoried in the Foundation's *Catálogo de Fotografías de la Biblioteca del Teatro Español*.

[7]See Louis A. Pérez, *Cuba between Empires, 1878-1902* (Pittsburgh: University of Pittsburgh Press, 1983), 106.

[8]See Alejandro de la Fuente, "Race and Inequality in Cuba, 1899-1981," *Journal of Contemporary History* 30 (1995): 135. The figures quoted come from the War Department Office Director Census of Cuba, *Report on the Census of Cuba, 1899* (Washington, D.C.). For statements by contemporary proponents of the race war interpretation, see Ada Ferrer, "To Make a Free Nation: Race and the Struggle for Independence in Cuba, 1868-1898" (Ph.D. diss., University of Michigan 1995), 134-40.

[9]Quoted in José Deleito y Piñuela, *Origen y apogeo del "género chico"* (Madrid: Revista del Occidente, 1949), 164.

[10]Ibid.

[11]Ibid., 165.

[12]See Helg's "Independent Cuba," 64. See also Jay Kinsbruner, *Not of Pure Blood: The Free People of Color and Racial Prejudice in 19th-Century Puerto Rico* (Durham, N.C.: Duke University Press, 1996). "La Escalera" refers to events in Matanzas, Cuba, in 1844. About 4,000 people were arrested in the wake of several slave revolts and accused of conspiracy. The blacks among them were tied to ladders *(escaleras)* and whipped to force confessions. Many were whipped to death or shot. See Hugh Thomas, *Cuba: The Pursuit of Freedom* (New York: Harper Row, 1971), 205.

[13]In regard to the Philippines, there was not so great an emphasis on the possibility of racial dissension either during the insurrection or after separation from Spain—should it take place. Some of the various indigenous ethnic groups inhabiting the islands were depicted, however, as more barbarous than the Chinese mestizos who, like mulattoes, were considered to be untrustworthy, dangerous, and avid for power. Edgar Wickberg calculates that Chinese mestizos made up about 6 percent of the population in the second half of the nineteenth century— between 150,000 and 300,000 in a mean population of about 5,500,000. See Wickberg's *The Chinese in Philippine Life 1850-1898* (New Haven: Yale University Press, 1965), 134. An excellent study of the current state of research on the Chinese in the Philippines is Fe Susan Go's "Documenting the Chinese Filipinos: Archival Sources," *Kinaadman* 20 (1998): 113-39.

[14]Two recent publications present a good selection of cartoons from Spanish and non-Spanish papers and magazines from the late 1890s; Manuel Méndez Saavedra, *1898: la guerra hispanoamericana en caricatura/The Spanish-American War in Cartoons* (San Juan, P.R.: La Comisión Puertorriqueña para la Celebración del Quinto Centenario del Descubrimiento de América y Puerto Rico, 1992), and *La gráfica política del 98: Catálogo de la Exposición* (Cáceres: Centro Extremeño de Estudios y Cooperación con Iberoamérica [Cexeci], 1998).

[15]Francisco de Paulo Cañamaque y Jiménez, *Las islas filipinas (De todo un poco)* (Madrid: Fernando Fe, 1880), 58.

[16]"Razas y naciones de Europa" (speech read at the Universidad Central at the beginning of the academic year 1895-1896) (Madrid: Imprenta Colonial, 1895), 41. Count Joseph-Arthur de Gobineau (1816-1882) was the author of *Essai sur l'inégalité des races humaines* (Paris: Firmin-Didot, 1884) whose ideas influenced German racial theorists.

[17]For information on *ñáñigos* and the Abakuá, see Lydia Cabrera, *La sociedad secreta Abakuá narrada por viejos adeptos* (Miami, Fla.: Ediciones

CR, 1970); and chapter 4 of Eugenio Matibag, *Afro-Cuban Religious Experience: Cultural Reflections in Narrative* (Gainesville: University Press of Florida, 1996).

[18]The romantic elements in the make-up of Castelar's Cuban slave may also be found in the eponymous protagonist of *Sab*, an 1841 novel by the Cuban novelist and poet, Gertrudis Gómez de Avellaneda. See *Sab*, with prologue and notes by Mary Cruz (Havana: Editorial Arte y Literatura, 1976). Mary Cruz's prologue to this edition provides the historical context for the Hispanic abolitionist novel and its representations of negroes and mulattoes. See also Sharon Fivel-Démoret, "The Production and Consumption of Propaganda literature: The Cuban Anti-Slavery Novel," *Bulletin of Hispanic Studies* 66 (1989): 1-11. For a recent survey of literature in which mulattoes figure, see Werner Sollars, *Neither Black nor White yet Both: Thematic Explorations of Interracial Literature* (New York, Oxford: Oxford University Press, 1997). Although there are a number of omissions in Sollars's record of Hispanic representations of mulattoes, chapter 8 of his study, "Excursus on the 'Tragic Mulatto'; or The Fate of a Stereotype," is valuable. See also Lourdes Martínez-Echazabal, *Para una semiótica de la mulatez* (Madrid: Porrúa, 1990).

[19]In her volume of reminiscenses, *Lo que vi en Cuba* (Havana: Imprenta La Universal, 1916), Canel noted (p. 236) that her play, *La mulata*, appeared in Havana in 1893 "con éxito extraordinario" and that it subsequently triumphed all over America. She remarked (p. 288) that a Cuban mulatta approached her in 1914 and told her that women of color owed her a great deal for "fue usted la primera blanca que nos dignificó en Cuba" ("you were the first white woman to dignify us in Cuba"). Nonetheless, Canel wrote, her ideas concerning racial equality earned her considerable enmity at the time of Cuba's War of Independence. For a recent study of the mulatta in Cuban and Caribbean literature that uses cultural and feminist theories as critical tools, see Vera Kutzinski, *Sugar's Secrets: Race and the Erotics of Cuban Nationalism* (Charlottesville: University Press of Virginia, 1993).

[20]Rafael Gasset attributed the appearance of Havana to an aesthetic dictated by the Creole woman on the one hand, and the total lack of one among the negroes on the other. He mused that the presence of fine buildings in the midst of wretched huts and narrow back alleys branching out from beautiful, expansive avenues symbolized the different accomplishments of two races that lived together without really coming together: "All that is beautiful and artistic has been built to satisfy the delicate ideal of the Creole woman. All that is ugly, dark, and repugnant represents the trace left in the midst of this civilization by the passage of the negro race" ("Lo hermoso, lo artístico ha

sido construido para satisfacer el delicado ideal de la mujer criolla. Lo feo, lo oscuro, lo hediondo es la huella que deja en medio de esta civilización el paso de la raza negra") (*El Imparcial*, 7 November 1895).

[21]The passage quoted below is from p. 378 of Insúa's *Finis: últimos días de España en Cuba* (Madrid: Romero, 1901). Insúa was also the author of *El problema cubano* (Madrid: Imprenta del Asilo de Huérfanos del Sagrado Corazón de Jesús, 1897). Born in Galicia in 1858, Insúa traveled to Cuba in 1877 and only returned to Spain in 1900. His novel, *Finis*, presents a vivid picture of the upper strata of Havana society in 1898 and 1899. Though sympathetic to the Spanish cause and a believer in the theory that the Americans themselves sank the *Maine* so as to provide a pretext for their entry into the war, Insúa was not blind to all criticism of the Spanish government. The narrator (p. 132) refers to the dismay that marked public opinion in Spain by February of 1898 as thousands more men were sent to Cuba while at the same time men who had left as simple colonels only months before were returning as division and brigade commanders. Similarly, modest bureaucrats were returning from Cuba with banknotes sticking out of their pockets. Despite abuses, Insúa clearly believed that Peninsular Spaniards who allied themselves with autonomists or separatists had paved the way to a worse abuse, namely, racial mixing. As Julia—herself at one point an advocate of autonomy—laments, "Is this what it is all coming to? The liberty we all sighed for and for which we have sacrificed wealth, honor, life and peace is being won so that negroes can have white wives?" ("¿Esto es lo que nos aguardaba? La libertad por que tanto suspirábamos y por la cual sacrificamos riqueza, honor, vida y sosiego, ¿se conquista para que unos negros tengan mujeres blancas?") (97).

The following passage from Rebecca Scott's "Race, Labor and Citizenship in Cuba: A View from the Sugar District of Cienfuegos, 1886-1909," *HAHR* 78, no. 4 (1998): 704-5, documents a real, specific instance of opposition to the integration of people of color into a public place: "The colonial government had formally ruled in favor of access to public places, and on January 4, 1894, a group of men of color attempted to integrate the elegant Teatro Terry [in Cienfuegos] by attending a performance of *Los Hugonotes*. The ensuing fracas precipitated ferocious debate in the press, denunciation of the activists from various quarters, and criticism of the colonial authorities for having failed to respect the opposition of the white majority to the idea of 'decreeing social equality.' "

[22]*Final del Imperio: España, 1895-1898* (Madrid: Siglo XXI de España Editores, 1984), 97-98. Serrano cites the *Diaris i records de Pere Corominas*, vol. 1, *Els anys de joventut* (Barcelona: Curial, 1974), 32, for recollections of the demonstrations at the Novedades.

²³For Betances, see Ada Suárez Díaz, *El antillano: biografía del Dr. Ramón Emeterio Betances, 1827-1898* (San Juan, P.R.: Centro de Estudios Avanzados de Puerto Rico y el Caribe, Revista Caribe, 1988); Paul Estrade, *La colonia cubana de París, 1895-1898: el combate patriótico de Betances y la solidaridad de los revolucionarios franceses* (Havana: Editorial de Ciencias Sociales, 1984). For Betances's role in the assassination of the Spanish prime minister, Antonio Cánovas in August 1897, see M. Fernández Almagro, *Historia política de la España contemporánea 1897/1902*, vol. 3 (Madrid: Alianza, 1970), 14-15.

²⁴*La literatura en 1881* (Madrid: Alfredo de Carlos Hierro, 1882), 82-83. Nearly fifteen years later, José Yxart, in *El arte escénico en España*, vol. 1 (Barcelona: La Vanguardia, 1894-1896), 356-67, wrote (disapprovingly), as noted above, that Spanish audiences persisted in their taste for blood and violent tragedy on stage.

²⁵See Emilio Castelar, *Miscelánea de historia, de religión, de arte y de política* (Madrid: A. de San Martín/Agustín Jubera, 1874), 153-54. Castelar was so fond of this formulation that he repeated it often in his moral admonitions to the Spanish people.

²⁶C.f. Santiago Ramón y Cajal, who wrote in reference to the Sisters of Charity at the time of his tour of duty in Cuba in 1874: "out of sheer habit these worthy persons quickly acquired a disheartening insensibility to the pain of others" (" a causa del hábito, estas personas beneméritas adquirieron pronto, ante el dolor ajeno, desconsoladora insensibilidad"). From Cajal's *Obras literarias completas* (Madrid: Aguilar, 1961), 250. St. Vincent de Paul (1575-1660) founded the Order of the Sisters of Charity. They were dedicated to the teaching of the young and the care of the sick, the old and the poor.

²⁷Reverter's remarks appeared in his *Filipinas por España: narración episódica de la rebelión en el Archipiélago Filipino*, vol. 2 (Barcelona: Centro Editorial de Alberto Martín, 1897), 523. For a modern history of female fighters in the Philippine War of Independence, see Rafaelita Hilario Soriano, ed., *Women in the Philippine Revolution* (Quezon City: Printon Press, 1995), 523. Apparently, there were women who not only took part but also led in combat. Several of the Filipino women who actively participated in the struggle for independence were Masons. Nathan Green's comments appeared in *Story of Spain and Cuba* (Baltimore: International News and Book, 1896), 186. I have seen a reference to a book by Enrique Ubieta, *La mujer en la revolución cubana*, published in Havana in about 1911 that may contain material on women combatants, but I have not been able to locate a copy. Chapter 1 of Lynn K. Stoner, *From the House to the Streets: The Cuban Woman's Movement for Legal Reform, 1898-1940* (Durham: Duke

University Press, 1991), has material on women fighters. Ada Ferrer's "Rustic Men, Civilized Nation: Race, Culture, and Contention on the eve of Cuban Independence," *HAHR* 78, no. 4 (1998): 663-86, has a reference on p. 679 to *mambisas* (female rebels) who fought alongside men.

[28]See Elshtain's *Women and War* (New York: Basic Books, 1987).

[29]See *A Letter to the Young Women of Malolos* (Manila: Bureau of Printing, 1932). This letter of 1889 was written as a response to a protest on the part of the young women of Malolos whose desire to have a private school founded for the teaching of Spanish had incurred the strong objections of the Spanish religious authorities.

[30]Note 2 on p.42 of the work cited (Madrid: L. Aguado, 1891).

[31]Ada Ferrer provides two definitions of *mambí*: 1) literally the offspring of a monkey and a vulture 2) the Indian term for rebels against the first Spanish conquerors. She notes that while the term may originally have been pejorative, in time the rebels themselves used it with pride in referring to themselves. From Ferrer's "To Make a Free Nation: Race and the Struggle for Independence in Cuba, 1868-1898" (Ph.D. diss., University of Michigan, 1995), 63.

[32]*Historia Patria*. (New Haven: Yale University Press, 1997), 88.

[33]In Roland B. Tolentino, "Nation, Nationalisms, and 'Los Últimos de Filipinas': An Imperialist Desire for Colonialist Nostalgia," in *Refiguring Spain; Cinema/Media/ Representation*, edited by Marsha Kinder (Durham: Duke University Press, 1997), 141-42. For the story of Baler, see M. Leguineche, *Yo te diré . . . la verdadera historia de los últimos de Filipinas* (Madrid: El País-Ailar, 1998).

[34]The reference in this speech to "yellow" insurgents is unique in these plays: the Cuban Chinese fighting for independence are otherwise invisible. For a largely anecdotal account of their role, see Juan Jiménez Pastrana, *Los chinos en la lucha por la liberación cubana (1847-1930)* (Havana: Instituto de Historia, 1963), 94-101.

[35]Nuria Sales de Bohigas in *Sobre esclavos, reclutas y mercaderes de quintos* (Barcelona: Ariel, 1974) discusses the economic and social consequences of the *quinta* on pp. 209-19. She refers to literary works that dealt with the issue from Fernán Caballero up to the period comprising the insurrections, including an 1869 play by Gervasio Amat, *Quintas y caixas*, which showed how ruinous it was for a family of farmers to pay the amount required to exempt a son from service. See also N. Sales de Bohigas, "Some Opinions on Exemptions from Military Service in Nineteenth-Century Europe," *Comparative Studies in Society and History* 10 (1968): 261-89; Fernando Fernández Bastarreche, "The Spanish Military from the Age of Disasters to

the Civil War," in *Armed Forces in Spain Past and Present*, edited by Rafael Bañón Martínez and Thomas M. Barker (Boulder: Columbia University Press, 1988), 213-47; and Stanley Payne, *Los militares y la política en la España contemporánea* (Paris: Rueda Ibérico, 1968).

[36]For those riots see Iver Bernstein, *The New York City Draft Riots: Their Significance for American Society and Politics in the Age of the Civil War* (New York: Oxford University Press, 1990). José Ferrer de Couto, cited earlier as the author of the widely read *Los negros en sus diversos estados y condiciones: tales como son, como se supone que son y como deben ser* (1864), was in New York in 1864 editing *La Crónica* (a newspaper that defended Spain against the attacks of Cuban exiles living in the U.S.), according to Arthur Corwin, *Spain and the Abolition of Slavery in Cuba 1817-1886* (Austin: Institute of Latin American Studies, 1967), 164. Ferrer described the New York City riots of the previous year on pp. 265-67 of his book, attributing them to the eternal quarrel of the poor against the rich (the poor complain because they cannot afford to buy exemption from the draft) and to revulsion at going to war in order to win emancipation for an inferior race. For a discussion of the relative lack of organized public opposition to the draft in Spain, see pp. 373-80 of Elena Hernández Sandoica and María Fernanda Mancebo, "Higiene y sociedad en la guerra de Cuba 1895-1898): notas sobre soldados y proletarios," *Estudios de Historia Social* 5-6 (1978).

[37]See Sales de Bohigas, *Sobre esclavos*, p. 275, for statistics on deserters by region, 1861-1885. See also Carlos Serrano, "Prófugos y desertores en la guerra de Cuba," *Estudios de Historia Social* 22-23 (1982): 253-78.

[38]For military critics of the conscription, see Sebastian Balfour, *The End of the Spanish Empire*, p. 168, and Elena Hernández Sandoica and María Fernanda Mancebo, "Higiene y sociedad," 373-74.

[39]See Hernández Sandoica and Mancebo, "Higiene y sociedad," 40.

[40]Quoted from p. 12 of John David Smith's review, "The Revised Versions," *Times Literary Supplement*, 12 December 1997.

[41]For a discussion of the implications for society of the traditional, "strong" family system in Spain, see David S. Reher, *Perspectives on the Family in Spain, Past and Present* (Oxford: Oxford University Press, 1997).

[42]See Tesifonte Gallego, *La insurrección cubana* (Madrid: Imprenta Central de los Ferrocarriles, 1897), 114.

[43]See Hugh Thomas, *Cuba. The Pursuit of Freedom* (New York: Harper & Row, 1971), 276. See also Nicolás Sánchez-Albornoz, ed., *Españoles hacia América: la emigración en masa, 1830-1930* (Madrid: Alianza, 1995). Jordi Maluquer de Motes's study, *Nación e inmigración: los españoles en Cuba (ss. XIX y XX)* (Madrid: Ediciones Jucar, 1992), 48-59, reports the number of

Spanish emigrants to Cuba between 1882 and 1899 (524,658, of whom 427,185 returned to the peninsula) but does not break down the total according to sex. I am grateful to University of New Orleans graduate student Janie Zackin for bringing Maluquer's study to my attention.

[44]See Christopher Schmidt-Nowara, "The Problem of Slavery in the Age of Capital: Abolitionism, Liberalism, and Counter-Hegemony in Spain, Cuba, and Puerto Rico, 1833-1886" (Ph.D. diss., University of Michigan, 1995), 445.

[45]D. M. Walls y Merino, *Relato de un viaje de España a Filipinas*, 2d ed. (Madrid: Impresor de los Hijos de M. G. Hernández, 1895). His account appeared also in the Madrid journal *Revista Contemporánea*.

[46]See *Rizal's Correspondence with Fellow Reformists*, vol. 3, bk. 3 (Manila: National Heroes Commission, 1963), 76.

[47]See "Discurso pronunciado por D. Graciano López Jaena el 25 de febrero de 1889 en el Ateneo Barcelonés," *La Solidaridad* 1 (1889): 28-48. The word *filipino* requires explanation. As Benedict Anderson explains in his article, "Hard to Imagine: A Puzzle in the History of Philippine Nationalism," in *Cultures and Texts: Representations of Philippine Society*, edited by Raul Pertierra and Eduardo F. Ugarte (Diliman, Quezon City, 1994), 94, the word was undergoing a change in meaning at the end of the nineteenth century. Up to then, it normally meant a *criollo*, or pure-blooded Spaniard born in the archipelago, and it was spelled with a small "f." Gradually, it came to connote the inhabitants of the Philippines and was used with a capital "f." It is used in this study to refer to non-Spanish inhabitants of the islands in general—with the exception of transient Chinese. When relevant, classifications such as *mestizo* (usually connoting Chinese mestizo before 1900) or *indios* (unmixed indigenous peoples) are employed.

[48]See Benito Legarda Jr., "Philippine Participation in the St. Louis Exposition of 1904," *Kinaadman* 19 (1997): 276-79. Legarda's quote from Blount is from the latter's *The American Occupation of the Philippines 1898-1912* (New York: Putnam, 1913), 576. The Igorots in Madrid were not reported to have eaten dogs. For comments about some of those present at the exposition, see William Henry Scott, "The Igorot Who Went to Madrid," in *History on the Cordillera: Collected Writings on Mountain Province History* (Baguio City: Baguio Printing and Publishing, 1975), 12-13.

[49]See Ángel Pérez, *Igorrotes: estudio geográfico y etnográfico* (Manila: Imprenta de "El Marcantil," 1902), 159.

[50]Taga-Ilog, "Impresiones madrileñas de un filipino," *La Solidaridad* (Barcelona) 23 October 1889. For a recent biography of Luna, see Vivencio R. José, *Antonio Luna* (Manila: Tahanan, 1995).

[51]From pp. 21-22 of the *Código Penal y Ley de Enjuiciamiento Criminal para las Islas Filipinas* (Madrid: Centro Editorial de Góngora, 1896).

[52]See Gabriel Millet, Manuel Ruiz de Quevedo, and Agustín Sardá, *La raza de color en Cuba* (Madrid: Fortanet, 1894), 17-18, for a discussion of needed changes in the penal code in a letter from Rafael María de Labra to the three authors in their capacity as representatives of the Sociedades de la Raza de Color de la Isla de Cuba.

[53]The articles appeared in the issues of 13 September 1892, pp.266-67, and 14 February 1893, pp. 42-43.

[54]See *The Trial of Rizal*, W. E. Retana's transcription of the official Spanish documents. Edited and translated with notes by H. de la Costa, S.J. (Manila: Ateneo de Manila University Press, 1996). For Rizal's biography, see W. E. Retana, *Vida y escritos del Dr. Rizal* (Madrid, 1907); and Austin Coates, *Rizal: Philippine Nationalist and Martyr* (New York: Oxford University Press, 1968). Reynaldo C. Ileto discusses cultural traditions that account for Rizal's impact on the separatist movement and beyond in "Rizal and the Underside of Philippine History," in *Moral Order and the Question of Change: Essays on Southeast Asian Thought* (New Haven: Yale University Southeast Asia Studies, 1982), 274-337.

[55]Edgar Wickberg explains that Rizal's grandfather, a third-generation Chinese mestizo, had his family transferred from the mestizo *padrón*, or tax register, to that of the *indios*, so that both his father and Rizal himself, were considered *indio*. This legal procedure, known as the *dispensa de ley*, or *gracias al sacar*, was commonly used in the Spanish American Empire in the late eighteenth century. There could be financial and social advantages to changing one's status from mestizo to *indio* as well as the reverse. See Edgar Wickberg, *The Chinese in Philippine Life*, 33-34, for a discussion of Rizal's family and of the legal procedure in question.

[56]See *El año teatral* (Madrid: El Nacional, 1896), 232.

[57]See Wenceslao E. Retana, *Apuntes para la historia* (Madrid: Manuel Minuesa de los Ríos, 1890), 73.

[58]See p. 11 of Feced's *Esbozos y pinceladas por Quioquiap* (Manila: Establecimiento Tipográfico de Ramírez y Compañía, 1888), 11.

[59]See W. E. Retana, *Vida y escritos del Dr. Rizal*, 162.

[60]Manuel Antón, "Antropología," in *Exposición de Filipinas: colección de artículos publicados en* El Globo, *diario ilustrado, político, científico y literario* (Madrid: Establecimiento Tipográfico de El Globo, a cargo de J. Salgado de Trigo, 1887), 84.

[61]Ibid., 89.

[62]Ibid., 96.

[63]See *Filipinas: problema fundamental por un español de larga residencia en aquellas islas* (Madrid: Imprenta de Don Luis Aguado, 1891), 15.

[64]*Pacita*, 88.

[65]See Wickberg's *The Chinese in Philippine Life*, 145.

[66]See *El Noli me tangere de Rizal, juzgado por el profesor F. Blumentritt* (Barcelona, 1889) and his *Las razas del Archipiélago Filipino* (Madrid: Fortanet, 1890).

[67]See M. Fernández Almagro, *Historia política de la España contemporánea 1885-1897*, vol. 2 (Madrid: Alianza, 1969), 349. E. Reverter Delmas in his *Filipinas por España: narración episódica de la rebelión en el Archipiélago Filipino*, vol. 2 (Barcelona: Centro Editorial de Alberto Martín, 1897) also mocked Andrés Bonifacio, referring to him as Bonifacio I, King of the Tagalos. Reverter's narrative of the Philippine rebellion was published too late in 1897 to have furnished the title for the play under discussion, but late enough for him to have appropriated the title of the play. Curiously, p. 119 ff. recount incidents in the towns of Paz and Bataan that could have provided some of the plot elements for the play, i.e., the kidnapping of a Spanish administrator and the actions of bloodthirsty Tagalo savages in a jungle clearing. Reverter's account of the insurrection ended shortly after Cánovas's assassination in the late summer of 1897. Already viewing the war as a lost cause, Reverter wrote that the loss of the Philippines was not due solely to the Tagalog rebels but also to the lack of foresight and the obtuseness of Spanish ministers. Reverter's work of over 600 pages would not have reached many readers.

[68]C.f. M. Fernández Almagro's account of the insurrections, first published in 1959. For this modern historian, the roots of the desire for Philippine independence lay in racial conflict and in the animosity of the idolatrous Tagalog toward the Spanish Catholic clergy, which he believed legitimately engaged in teaching as an important part of its missionary role and which enjoyed unchallengeable social power. The race issue and the aversion to the Church—both ably exploited by the Masons—combined, as in Cuba, with the simple yearning for independence, writes Fernández Almagro. However, he argues, the indigenous element in the Philippines predominated in the struggle against Spain to a far greater extent than did its corresponding element—people of color—in Cuba, where the white man, whether Creole or not, intervened decisively, and where a large number of educated people joined in, as was not the case in the Philippines. Fernández Almagro's analysis largely dismisses the role educated Filipinos played in advocating autonomy or independence. It avoids assigning blame of any kind to the fri-

ars. It does not acknowledge discriminatory policies toward the indigenous clergy nor any other discriminatory laws or policies affecting Filipinos that might have elicited charges of mistreatment on racial grounds. In all these respects, his analysis differs from that of informed contemporary Spaniards— unless they were voicing the views of official Spanish colonial policy. See Fernández Almagro, *Historia política*, vol. 2, 339. For more recent perspectives on the causes and conduct of the insurrection, see Vicente L. Rafael, "Nationalism, Imagery and the Filipino Intelligentsia of the Nineteenth Century," in *Discrepant Histories: Translocal Essays in Filipino Cultures*, edited by Vicente L. Rafael (Philadelphia: Temple University Press, 1995), 133-58; María Dolores Elizalde Pérez-Grueso, "Filipinas, 1898," *Revista de Occidente* 202-3 (1998): 224-49; Susana Cuartero Escobés, "El nacionalismo indepen- dentista del Katipunan," (225-34); and María Teresa Gutiérrez Rodríguez, "Antecedentes de la independencia de Filipinas: la influencia de la masonería y de los Estados Unidos," (235-42), both essays in *Antes del "Desastre": orígenes y antecedentes de la crisis del 98*, edited by Juan Pablo Fusi and Antonio Niño (Madrid: Universidad Complutense de Madrid: 1996).

[69]From Felipe Trigo, *La campaña filipina (Impresiones de un soldado)*, vol. 1, *El General Blanco y la insurrección* (Madrid: Fernando Fe, 1897), 46. This volume contains Trigo's original article, which was reproduced in whole or in part in many Madrid papers as well as in the provinces. It lists those papers and includes articles supporting or opposing his views, together with letters from readers.

[70]Quoted in *El País Digital* (12 May 1998), 8.

[71]At the end of Spanish rule in the Philippines only 5 percent of the population spoke Spanish. About forty years later, according to the last colonial census of 1939, 2.6 percent of the 16,000,000 inhabitants of the Philippines spoke Spanish. See Benedict Anderson, "Hard to Imagine: A Puzzle in the History of Philippine Nationalism," in *Cultures and Texts: Representations of Philippine Society*, edited by Raúl Pertierra and Eduardo F. Ugarte. (Diliman, Quezon City: University of the Philippines Press, 1994), 104; 110, note 2.

[72]See M. Fernández Almagro, *Historia política*, vol. 2, 388.

[73]Gaston Routier, *L'Espagne en 1897* (Paris: Librairie H. Le Soudier, 1897), 208-9.

[74]Trigo, *La campaña filipina*, 48.

[75]See Gabriel Hernández González (Javier de Montillana), *Bretón* (Salamanca: Talleres Gráficos Núñez, 1952), 102-3.

[76]See Philip S. Foner, *Antonio Maceo: The "Bronze Titan" of Cuba's Struggle for Independence* (New York: Monthly Review Press, 1977), 221.

[77]See Gaston Routier, *L'Espagne en 1897*, 176. The interview Routier conducted with Cánovas on Maceo's death was published widely in the European and American press before its appearance in the book cited here.

[78]Quoted in Diana Iznaga, *Presencia del testimonio en la literatura sobre las guerras por la independencia nacional (1868-1898)* (Havana: Editorial Letras Cubanas, 1989), 273.

[79]See Fernández Almagro, *Historia política*, vol. 2, 317.

[80]See Thomas, *Cuba: The Pursuit of Freedom*, 339.

[81]See Leopoldo Horrego Estuch, *Juan Gualberto Gómez: un gran inconforme*, 2d ed. (Havana: La Milagrosa, 1954), 74. Gómez agreed with Maceo's analysis that although "he was as white as he was black" ("tan blanco como negro"), he could not lead the insurgents because he would be suspected of racial motivation.

[82]From Francisco Pérez Guzmán and Rodolfo Sarracino, *La guerra chiquita: una experiencia necesaria* (Havana: Editorial Letras Cubas, 1982), 166, as quoted by Ada Ferrer, "To Make a Free Nation," 137.

[83]See *Le Tour du Peuple: Crise nationale, mouvements populaires et populisme en Espagne (1890-1898)* (Madrid: Siglo XXI, 1984), 12-13.

[84]In another brief discussion of Guimerá's play, Carlos Serrano quotes the circular published in the *Diario Oficial del Ministerio de la Guerra* (Madrid) 21, 29 January 1896, that abolished the abusive proviso which had led to the denouncing of children and of men too old for military service. See Serrano's "Prófugos y desertores," 254.

[85]"Sobre la primera representación de *El Padre Juanico*," *La Ilustración Espanola y Americana*, 22 marzo de 1898, 174-75.

[86]Juan Lapoulide, "Por la guerra paz," *La Ilustración Española y Americana*, 30 March 1898, 194.

[87]Tomás Álvarez Ángulo, *Memorias de un hombre sin importancia (1878-1961)* (Madrid: Aguilar, 1962), 181.

[88]See Balfour, *The End of the Spanish Empire*, 168. The remarks (translated in Balfour) are taken from Antonio Pirala's *España y la Regencia: anales de diez y seis años (1885-1902)*, 3 vols. (Madrid/Havana: V. Suárez, 1904-07), 171.

[89]See Hernández Sandoica and Mancebo, "Higiene y sociedad," 378-79.

[90]See M. Fernández Almagro, *Historia política*, vol. 3, 104-5; 150.

[91]Ibid., 185.

[92]José Deleito y Piñuela, *Origen y apogeo*, 403-4.

[93]*Memorias de un hombre sin importancia*, 244.

[94]See *Mis primeros ochenta años* (Madrid: Aguilar, 1962), 323-33. In the United States meanwhile, Kathleen Blake Watkins of the Toronto *Mail and Express* described the appearance of a boat load of American troops returning from Santiago de Cuba:

The "boys in blue" are coming home. Not too many weeks ago, I watched a splendid army embark to go to war—bands playing, colors flying, people cheering along the mile of great ships that lay along the wharves of Tampa.

Last night, by the light of a few lanterns, I watched in shock as that army returned—wounded men in ragged uniforms, with arms, heads, and feet swathed in dirty, bloodstained bandages. They passed by me—limping or on stretchers—to waiting ambulances.

Quiet groups of people observed the procession. There were no bands or flying colors, and no cheering. Every heart was too full of pride and grief for the tongue to give expression.

At a small table on the top deck of the ship sat a couple of men, taking down names and issuing tickets to nearby hospitals. I watched the poor fellows as they descended the gangplank—the little tickets held tightly between their teeth—their arms or legs helpless and bodies limp and drooping.

Tired, broken, weary men, coming home to rest. There was not a murmur from any of them. Their record told the story—one of glorious fighting, magnificent courage, and many, many wounds.

Three hundred and fifty sick and wounded soldiers were taken off the *Iriquois* that night. A sudden shudder passed through me as I looked upon the poor, helpless forms on stretchers laid out in neat rows under the light of the moon on the lonely wharf.

Quoted from A. B. Feuer, *The Santiago Campaign of 1898: A Soldier's View of the Spanish-American War* (Westport, Connec-ticut, London: Praeger, 1993), 128.

[95]Burguete, *¡La Guerra! Cuba (Diario de un testigo)* (Barcelona: n.p., 1902), 194-95. Twelve years after the Disaster, Blásquez de Pedro wrote the "poema-monólogo" *La agonía del repatriado* whose stage directions evoke the same quiet despair as Burguete's passage: "The set represents the third-class section of a transatlantic ship. In one of the cabins sits the repatriated soldier. His face reveals extreme debility, a mortal pallor, deep sadness. His hair is long and matted, his clothing ragged" ("La escena representa el interior de un transatlántico, departamento de tercera clase. En uno de los camarotes de primer término estará incorporado el repatriado. Su rostro

mostrará suma extenuación, mortal palidez, profunda tristeza. Tendrá los cabellos largos y enmarañados y la ropa destrozada"). Cited by Lily Litvak in *Musa libertaria: arte, literatura y vida cultural del anarquismo español (1880-1913)* (Barcelona: Antoni Bosch, 1981), 242. A different and equally absorbing personal account of the Cuban War of Independence emerges from Josep Conangla's recently published *Memorias de mi juventud en Cuba: un soldado del ejército español en la guerra separatista*, with a prologue by Joaquín Roy (Barcelona: Ediciones Península, 1998). Conangla did not see combat in Cuba and did not comment extensively on the suffering of returning Spanish soldiers. However, he did comment on something most Spaniards in Cuba did not write about: the suffering of the Cuban *reconcentrados*, victims of General Weyler's plan to exterminate the guerrilla insurgents. A work included in the memoirs—his poem, "Misa roja," first published in Catalán in 1904—describes an open-air mass held for Spanish soldiers housed in barracks on the outskirts of a town inhabited by many displaced, starving people (300,000 died according to Raúl Izquierdo Canosa in *La reconcentración 1896-1897* [Havana: Ediciones Verde Olivo, 1997]) and constitutes a savage attack on the church, which he believed was complicit in the devastation of the Cuban population.

[96]See "Temporada de género chico: 'La gente seria' y 'Gigantes y cabezudos,'" *El País*, 13 July 1979.

[97]John Richardson, *A Life of Picasso*, vol. 1, 1881-1906. (New York: Random House, 1991), 135 and 494. Richardson does not hesitate to describe Nonell's series as "antistate as well as antiwar" but offers no explanation as to why he does so. Enric Jardí, in his *Nonell* (New York: Tudor Publishing, nd), 98, writes that the show in Els Quatre Gats awakened little interest on the part of the public, and refers to the article by Nonell's friend, José María Jordá, lamenting this reaction in *La Publicidad* (Barcelona) 21-XII-1898. It is understandable that a public still not inured to the sight of miserable repatriates on the streets of Barcelona may have been less eager to view Nonell's drawings than the Parisian French. See also Carolina Nonell, *Isidro Nonell. Su vida y su obra* (Madrid: Editorial Dossat, 1963).

[98]For a discussion of assumptions concerning nationalism and culture among academicians during the 1890s, see Óscar E. Vázquez, "Defining *Hispanidad*: Allegories, Geneologies and Cultural Politics in the Madrid Academy's Competition of 1893," *Art History* 20 (1997): 100-23. For the conflict in Melilla, see Agustín R. Rodríguez, "El conflicto de Melilla en 1893," *Hispania* (Madrid) 49, no. 171 (1989): 235-66; and María del Carmen González Velilla and María Berta Pacios González-Loureiro, "La crisis de Melilla de 1893-1894," *Antes del "Desastre,"* edited by Fusi and Niño, 323-36.

[99]Pascual Millán, *¡Quince bajas!* (Madrid: El Enano, 1899), 1. The page numbers for subsequent citations from this play appear in the text.

[100]See Josep María Poblet, *Vida y obra literaria de Santiago Rusiñol* (Barcelona: Editorial Bruguera, 1966), 65-66.

[101]From "L'Héroe," *Obres Completes*, vol. 1, with a prologue by Carles Soldevila (Barcelona: Editorial Selecta, 1973), 1247.

CONCLUSION

Answers to the question posed at the beginning of this study—how do the plays examined here seek to shape public opinion and form public consciousness—must be preceded by recalling once again the restraints placed on disruptive or dissenting attitudes and ideas by censorship and self-censorship. One of the plays that was potentially most forceful in raising questions about conscription, *¡Quince bajas!*, not only was produced two years after it was written and several months after the cessation of hostilities, but was closed after only one performance. Since it had little or no impact on public opinion as a play performed before a live audience, it is presented here as significant negative evidence, i.e., to show what could not be presented to the public when it might have made some difference in the way people viewed the government's conduct of the war, specifically with regard to recruitment, but potentially in connection with the broader question of the legitimacy of the government.

There were loopholes in attempts to prohibit or censor plays altogether. *¡Quince bajas!*, for example, was made available to readers when it was published shortly after its first and only performance on 2 December 1898. Playwrights whose works were prohibited for one reason or another were by no means necessarily condemned to silence. One year earlier, for example, the mayor of San Sebastián prohibited performances of Leopoldo Cano's popular drama *La Pasionaria*. The mayor of Palma, in his turn, prohibited performances of Joaquín Dicenta's extremely popular *Juan José*, his *El señor feudal*, and Ángel Guimerá's *María Rosa*. In response to the San Sebastián mayor's action, the Society of Dramatists resolved to withdraw all their works from theaters in that city until the ban was revoked. More to the point, *La Voz de Guipúzcoa* (with 7,000 readers) arranged to publish *La Pasionaria* in its columns, theoretically making the play accessible to far more people than the 700 who might have seen it in the theater.[1] The government officials and *neos* (right-wing Catholic traditionalists) who sought to block these plays undoubtedly feared the possible consequences of performances before volatile audiences more than those that might be occasioned by a solitary reading of the same work.

Censorship not only made the expression of certain ideas difficult, but also made it possible to advance others. Press censorship and lack of reliable information in regard to U.S. naval strength made it plausible to portray North Americans in some of the plays (for example, *Aún hay país*, *Veremundo*) as materially, as well as morally, weak and deficient.

In general terms, the plays presented a framework within which audiences were encouraged to think about Spanish domination in the colonies primarily in terms of race and gender. Class issues, particularly relevant with regard to military recruitment, were not entirely ignored, especially in the plays performed in 1897 and 1898, but they were shunted to the side and viewed as minor hindrances to solidarity, as social misunderstandings that religious piety, in the service of the compelling need for national unity, could resolve.

Of all the types represented in the plays the figure of the *quinto* is unquestionably the one that changes most significantly. He is depicted in the early plays of 1895 and 1896 as a boastful, somewhat comical figure eager to go off to war or as a simple *soldadito* who goes quietly because there is no alternative. With *Los dramas de la guerra* in 1897 audiences began to see a different kind of soldier on stage, one who was embittered by his inability to buy his way out and who made little attempt to conceal the suffering he and his comrades underwent in Cuba. Finally, once the war was over, the soldier-protagonists of *¡Quince bajas!* and *L'Héroe* made the figure of the *quinto* genuinely complex and problematic. The fate of these two decent and loyal men who were subjected to a corrupt recruitment system and a corrupting military environment raised a number of questions, among them, no doubt, skepticism about the motives of the government that permitted the abuses leading to their destruction.

Spanish attitudes regarding racial differences were no different from those of North Americans and other Europeans. Consequently, the emphasis in the plays was not placed exclusively on reaffirming such attitudes, although assumptions about the inferiority of people of color were stressed repeatedly in order to justify Spanish domination and to make the point that self-government was out of the question. Despite the general consensus in the West concerning the superiority of whites over people of color, Spaniards were alert to the fact that North Americans, professed believers in liberty, equality, and fraternity, occasionally faulted Spain for its treatment of Filipinos and people of color in Cuba. Therefore, the Spanish press kept readers informed about race relations in the United States, covering such news as the atrocities committed by whites against Indians, whom many Americans considered vermin to be exterminated, the lynchings and other related activities of the Ku Klux Klan, the *Plessy vs. Ferguson* decision in 1896, which effectively endorsed segregation, and, finally, the mistreatment of negro infantry troops in Florida en route to Cuba in 1898.

As for the Philippines, the Spanish press took note immediately of the tensions between Americans and Filipinos. White American troops called Filipinos "niggers" and treated them as they did negroes in the United States. In a much-remarked-upon speech before the American Senate, Senator Alfred J. Beveridge declared that Filipinos were like children: "They are not capable of self-government. How could they be? They are not of a self-governing race." They are "a race of Malay children of barbarism."[2] On 12 January 1901, H. P. Howard, a judge advocate of the Military Commission in the headquarters of the First District, Department Northern Luzon, Philippine Islands, wrote a letter to Howard Townsend from Vigan, Ilocos Sur. His letter brings together many of the stereotypes that had been in circulation in Spain regarding Filipinos. To his friend in New York, Howard wrote:

> I am sorry to say that these people do not improve on long acquaintance. We have all been in the dark about their true character, their racial traits, their instincts, capacity and disposition. On short acquaintance, during which we saw the more or less educated mixed blood (mixed with Chinese, a Spanish mixture being extremely rare), we were much surprised at the wealth, education, and intelligence displayed.
>
> Longer acquaintance has shown us much more, and we now see how thin was the veneer of imitation civilization which so easily deceived us at first, in the surprise at finding something besides unclad savages on the island, living in well-built towns.
>
> I can perhaps sum it all up by simply saying, 'they are not *men*.' Honesty, truth, justice, pity,—are either extinct among these people, or else still undevelopped [*sic*] . . . We are coming to understand

these people as they really are,—Malay savages by nature, with the gloss of European civilization.

(From "Misc. Mss Townsend, Howard, quoted by permission of the New-York Historical Society)

In order to reinforce support for continued Spanish domination in the colonies, the plays drove home the idea that whites alone could impose order on the chaotic and mutually hostile racial mixes inhabiting both colonies. In Cuba, rivalry between negroes and mulattoes would inevitably lead to race war. In the Philippines, audiences were led to believe, the degree of civilization attained up to the present by the indigenous inhabitants put them at the level of children. The more civilized mestizos, in the aftermath of much repression and bloodshed, would eventually assert their ascendancy. The plays thus clearly conveyed the idea that people of color could not be left to rule themselves. The press often pointed out that the Haitian and Dominican revolutions proved the validity of this claim: emancipation from white rule in those countries plainly demonstrated the fact that black self-rule was disastrous.

Spain, the plays suggested, could govern people of color successfully in the future provided the unmixed elements in the colonies continued to place their welfare in the hands of their superior Spanish masters and provided the mulattoes and Spanish mestizos deferred to the nobility of spirit infused in them by their Spanish blood instead of yielding to the savage instincts of their African or Malayan heritage. The press, popular literature, and the plays supplemented these ideas by evoking strong feelings of aversion, even abomination, toward the masses of people of color in the colonies, generally reserving provisional acceptance for selected individuals of mixed parentage who assimilated to Spanish ways.

The gender roles of Spaniards in the plays are unproblematical for the most part. Men and women play the parts assigned them by tradition. Men are the actors and women—except for the two who join male combatants in the field and the Sisters of Charity—are passive supporters of husbands, brothers, and sons. Only women as mothers present a potential capacity for disruption. In real life (though not on the stage), theirs were the only voices raised in disorderly public opposition to the unjust system of conscription. In 1896 when mothers held a protest march against sending more poor

soldiers to Cuba while, at the same time, the rich were avoiding service, the government's strategy was to deny the women agency in the
demonstration. The press reinforced that response by depicting
them as dupes of men with political agendas. In line with this strategy of depriving women of political agency and relevance, the
mothers on stage who complained about the conscription of their
sons were represented as emotional and egoistic creatures, concerned solely with their own sons and their own material welfare.
Depicted primarily as women deficient in patriotism, they were also
presented as being unreceptive to broader questions of social justice.
In this way, the injustice of the conscription system—an issue that
genuinely affected and divided Spaniards—was not excluded from
the stage, but its significance and potency were limited and defused
by associating criticism of its consequences almost entirely with
what were represented as the individual concerns of a few unrepre-
sentative Spanish mothers.

When the fighting was over and the men did or did not come
home, other men writing in the press accorded mothers the custom-
ary praise for having engendered the soldiers of the fatherland.
Praise, gratitude for their sacrifices, and recommendations that they
seek comfort in religious observances put an end for the time being
to the dilemma of how to minimize the complaints of mothers, which
had occasionally threatened to become genuinely inflammatory.

It is inevitable that the influence of these plays on public opinion should be discussed largely in terms of the ways in which their
texts represented certain significant ideological positions, yet the
impact of music, sets, staging, and choreographed group actions
portrayed on stage should not be overlooked or minimized.
Reviewers frequently referred to the emotional reception audiences
gave to the playing of the "Marcha de Cádiz" and in specific plays,
to the spectacle of soldiers raising the Spanish flag on stage or to the
sight of loyal negroes kneeling alongside Spanish soldiers, giving
thanks to God as a Spanish ship bringing reinforcements becomes
visible in the distance.

Such moments aroused sentiments that bound individual members of audiences together in a recognition of their *españolismo* or
hispanidad. The ideas and institutions dramatized on stage that were
intended to define the nation—the family, religion, racial pride root-

ed in memories of the glorious national past—were summed up and symbolized in specific, powerful images and, according to contemporary accounts, had a correspondingly powerful impact on the members of the theater audience. The likelihood that those shared moments of *españolismo* in the theater might have led to something as momentous as national regeneration on the German emperor's terms may be doubted. In any case, again according to reviewers, audiences in Spain did not remain susceptible to such moments after the early spring of 1898. What it meant to be Spanish had to be reexamined in light of the military defeats suffered in the spring and summer of 1898.

Notes

[1] *El Imparcial* of 30 January, 6 February, and 13 February 1897, has an account of these events.

[2] Quoted in *The Philippines Reader: A History of Colonialism, Neocolonialism, Dictatorship, and Resistance*. Edited by Daniel B. Schirmer and Stephen Rosskamm Shalom (Boston: South End Press, 1987), 26. The speech is taken from the *Congressional Record*, Senate (9 January 1900), 704-711.

¡QUINCE BAJAS!

DRAMA EN TRES ACTOS Y EN PROSA

original de

Pascual Millán

ESTRENADO EN EL NUEVO TEATRO
LA NOCHE DEL 2 DE DICIEMBRE DE 1898

PRÓLOGO

La suspensión de un drama

Mucha me repugna tener que hablar de mi propia persona, y a fe que si pudiera evitarlo lo haría rotundamente. Pero tratándose de un asunto en el cual yo soy protagonista, no me queda otro remedio que el de vencer mi repugnancia y abordar la cuestión.

Y como los malos caminos hay que pasarlos pronto, entro desde luego en materia.

En la noche del 2 de diciembre último se estrenó en el Nuevo Teatro de esta corte mi drama *¡Quince bajas!*

Era la primera obra que daba a la escena y, como ya llevo mucho tiempo emborronando cuartillas para el público, el estreno de la producción despertó alguna curiosidad.

El teatro, por esta razón, se vio muy concurrido; y el público lo componían personas de todas clases, desde el modesto operario que ocupaba su asiento en galería, hasta los *conspicuos* de la sociedad madrileña que llenaban la sala, abundando, como es de rigor, la gente del *oficio*.

Llegó el momento, se oyeron en los pasillos las llamadas de rúbrica, diose luz a la batería, sonó el timbre y arriba . . . el telón.

Aplaudió el público muchas veces durante el acto primero, y llamó a los actores a la terminación del mismo.

En el segundo se repitieron los aplausos y fue llamado el autor, quien no se presentó por guardar el incógnito hasta el final.

Entonces "reprodujéronse los aplausos (dice *El Liberal*), y se presentó seis o siete veces en escena nuestro compañero en la prensa D. Pascual Millán, a quien se debe la paternidad de la obra".

"El éxito de su primer drama (escribe *La Correspondencia de España*) ha debido dejar satisfecho al Sr. Millán. Frecuentes aplausos habían interrumpido el diálogo durante el curso de la representación en la situaciones culminantes y al escuchar las frases de más efecto."

"El Sr. Millán" estaba satisfecho ¡ya lo creo! Pues se decía: Si a pesar de todo lo ocurrido con la obra tuvo un éxito franco ¡que no hubiera sucedido a haber pasado las cosas de otro modo!

Terminada la función y cuando, en el saloncillo, recibía yo las felicitaciones de amigos y compañeros, hubo alguien de advertirme que una frase del drama había disgustado a algunos jóvenes oficiales del ejército que asistieron a la representación.

Y como la frase a que se aludía ni daba ni quitaba interés a la obra, ni fue escrita con ánimo de herir a nadie, manifesté a la persona que me explicó aquel disgusto:

—Pues diga usted a esos caballeros oficiales que desde ahora queda suprimida esa frase, pues no estando escrita con intención, ni suponiendo que nadie pudiera dársela, no paré en ella mientes. De haberla puesto deliberadamente no la quitaría, como no quito ninguna otra, moleste a quien moleste.

Al poco rato entraron a verme aquellos oficiales, agradecidos por mi conducta y conociendo la lealtad de mi proceder.

El Imparcial dio cuenta del incidente en estos términos:

"Varios señores oficiales del ejército que habían presenciado el estreno rechazaron una frase del drama que pudiera interpretarse desfavorablemente; pero el autor se apresuró con noble espontaneidad a retirarla y quedó terminado el asunto."

Dichos señores oficiales, ante la conducta del autor, expresaron su decidido propósito de acudir a la segunda representación de *¡Quince bajas!* y premiar con sus aplausos lo que ellos consideraban un acto de caballerosidad.

La cosa marchaba como sobre ruedas, porque hasta el público de galería, que ya sabía por la prensa el asunto de la obra (pues los periódicos la consagraron un espacio y un cariño que nunca olvidaré), quiso tomar su parte en aquella manifestación de simpatía.

¡Cuál no sería mi sorpresa cuando momentos antes de ir a empezar la segunda representación del drama llega al teatro el gobernador civil y suspende indefinidamente las de *¡Quince bajas!*

¿Qué había motivado esa medida?

Nadie lo sabe.

El *Heraldo de Madrid* publicaba al siguiente día estos párrafos:

"DRAMA PROHIBIDO.—El drama *¡Quince bajas!* Estrenado con un buen éxito excepcional en el Nuevo Teatro, ha desaparecido del cartel por orden del gobernador civil.

"Nuestro muy querido compañero en la prensa don Pascual Millán, autor de aquel notable drama, no podía sospechar que una obra tan benévolamente acogida por la crítica literaria y con tanto cariño recibida por un numeroso público, pudiese concitar medidas de rigor por parte del Gobierno."

Indudablemente, no cabía tal sospecha.

Pero . . . los hechos son los hechos y ahí está el oficio del gobernador que los comprueba.

Dice así:

"Sr. Empresario del Nuevo Teatro:

Teniendo fundadas noticias de que con ocasión de la representación en ese Teatro de la obra titulada "Quince bajas", se intenta producir en ese local desórdenes públicos que tengo el deber de prevenir y de evitar, he acordado, en uso de las atribuciones que me competen por el artículo 25 de la Lay Provincial vigente, suspender las representaciones de la obra mencionada. = Lo que comunico a V. para su conocimiento y efectos. = Dios guarde a V. muchos años. = Madrid 3 de Diciembre de 1898. = *Alberto Aguilera*."

Que el lector juzgue este oficio.

No, no era evidentemente el gobernador de la provincia quien dejaba en suspenso las representaciones del drama. D. Alberto Aguilera y el autor de la obra se profesan verdadero afecto, y como político y como particular el Sr. Aguilera sólo atenciones tuvo siempre para con el amigo.

El tiro, indudablemente, venía de mas alto. Quizá el gobierno, al ver que en el drama se lleva a la escena la cuestión del servicio militar obligatorio, que allí se pone de manifiesto al irritante desigualdad entre el pobre y el rico para con la Patria (a la cual sólo defienden con el fusil en la mano los desheredados de la suerte, mientras los favorecidos por ella, con una criminal indiferencia se burlan de todo . . .); quizá el gobierno al saber que las clases populares se proponían expresar ruidosamente sus simpatías, y algunos individuos del ejército (una vez suprimida la frase que hubo de molestarles) pensaban igualmente aplaudir con entusiasmo un drama que viene a ensalzar al soldado español cuando todo el mundo trata de exigirle responsabilidades no suyas, quizá, repito, el gobierno, sabedor de tales propósitos, temió que aquellas manifestaciones hechas de consuno por representantes del pueblo y del ejército trajesen alguna desazón a los Poderes públicos y quiso evitarlas a toda costa.

Sólo así se explica la suspensión de la obra.

Réstame, por último, decir algo sobre un punto que es preciso dejar bien aclarado.

Ha sido unánime la opinión de que si el drama *¡Quince bajas!* se hubiera estrenado hace algunos meses el éxito habría sido todavía mayor, porque entonces hubiese resultado más oportuno.

Verdad. Pero no es mía la culpa si eso no ha sucedido.

El drama se escribió hace más de dos años, cuando había entusiasmo por las tropas, cuando se las despedía a los acordes de la *Marcha de Cádiz*, cuando todos nos sentíamos orgullosos al gritar ¡Viva España!, cuando nos admiraba Europa entera al ver que sin aparatos de ninguna especie poníamos en nuestras colonias un ejército de 250.000 hombres u sembrábamos la manigua con cadáveres de españoles sólo por mantener la leyenda forjada acerca de nuestro país, cuando se surgían héroes como el de Cascorro y cada soldado era un César y cada jefe de guerrilla un mártir.

Entonces fue escrito el drama; pero yo me hallaba en el extranjero, contra mi voluntad, y desde allí no pude conseguir que la obra se representase.

La envié a mis amigos, a mis compañeros y nada pudieron hacer.

"Las empresas teatrales, como dice muy bien *El Día*, impidieron su representación en tiempo oportuno so pretexto de que era forzoso guardar ese turno que impone el monopolio que ejercen las jerarquías y las recomendaciones."

Y añade *El Globo*:

"No es de Millán la culpa de esa falta de oportunidad forzosa, sino de esas triquiñuelas de bastidores que se traducen en enojosos privilegios en favor de aquéllos que monopolizan determinadas preferencias."

Nada he de añadir por mi cuenta. Esos párrafos los dicen todo.

Ahora que el lector haga su composición de lugar.

Y ahí va la obra.

Pascual Millán.

PERSONAJES

LA TÍA PETRA

LA RUBIA

MARCELA

MOZA 1ª

MOZA 2ª

PEDRO

CIPRIANO

EL ALCALDE

GASPAR

MOZO 1º

MOZO 2º

La acción se desarrolla en un pueblo de Castilla.
Época actual, durante la campaña de Cuba.

Nota: Cuiden los actores que representen esta obra de no exagerar
las frases que están escritas con cursiva.

ACTO PRIMERO

La escena representa una era en un pueblo de Castilla. A la izquierda la casa de Gaspar con dos ventanas a la era, una en el piso bajo y otra encima, que da al granero. La puerta figura estar al otro lado de la casa, sin que la vea el espectador. Debajo de las ventanas un poyo que sirve de asiento y de mesa cuando los mozos beben y cantan. Una escalera de mano desde la era a la ventana del granero. Enseres de la trilla.

Durante la primera escena los mozos y mozas concluyen la recolección del trigo.

Al levantarse el telón, el Mozo 1º sube por la escalera con un saco lleno. La Moza 1ª y el Mozo 2º recogen en una sábana el grano que queda por el suelo. La Moza 2ª barre la era.

ESCENA PRIMERA

Mozos 1º y 2º, Mozas 1ª y 2ª, después, La Rubia

MOZA 2º   *(A la Moza 1ª.)* Te empeñaste en acabar hoy . . .

MOZA 1ª   Mejor sería que nos *estuviámos* de conversación mientras La Rubia se pudre la sangre.

MOZO 2º   ¿Y qué *tié* que ver lo que la sucede con la parva?

MOZA 1ª   Pues *ná* . . . que si mañana hay tormenta como barrunta aquel *nublao*, es un disgusto más *pa* ella y bastante es el que se vaya su marido.

MOZO 1º   *(Bajando.)* No le hagas caso. ¡Pues a buena hora se le ocurre gruñir! cuando ya está *tó terminao*.

MOZA 2ª   ¡Cabal! Si *paece* que no *tié* entrañas. ¿Te se figura poco lo que se le ha *venío* encima con la guerra?

MOZA 1ª   Si este zángano *estuviá* en el puesto de los que se van
               . . .

MOZO 2°   ¡Bah! no es *pa* tanto. No lo digo por Gaspar que
               al fin *tié* familia; pero el otro que es mozo y sin
               padres . . .

MOZA 2ª   *Tié* novia.

MOZO 2°   La más guapa y frescachona del lugar.

MOZA 1ª   Gracias por la lisonja. *(Con sorna.)*

MOZA 2ª   Ten *cuidao*, no te oiga Pedro, que aguanta pocas
               pulgas.

MOZO 1°   O Cipriano . . . que . . .

MOZO 2°   ¡Eso ya es muy antiguo!

MOZO 1°   Antiguo y de ahora: ¿qué te figuras tú?

MOZA 1ª   Ya veremos si la más guapa y frescachona sabe
               guardar consecuencia al que se va. *(Con retintín.)*

MOZO 2°   No te ofendas; pero a mí me *paece* que se la guardará,
               porque, mejorando lo presente, es el más *acabao* que
               hay por aquí y Marcela le estima.

MOZA 1ª   También Cipriano es el más *estruído.*

MOZO 1°   Eso . . . según y conforme: Más leído que el otro sí
               que lo es; pero no sabe más de lo que aprendió en los
               libros, y en sacándolo de *áhi* . . . vamos, que Pedro le
               da cien vueltas y calcula mejor y *tié* mejores *cáidas* y
               se le ocurren un porción de cosas que ¡ni que las
               estuviá leyendo cuando habla! ¡Si es más listo que el
               hambre! . . . Bien decía su capitán cuando se des-
               pidió: "¡Lástima de mozo! ¡Con lo *templao* que es y
               lo que vale sería cuanto le *diá* la gana!" ¡*Miá* que
               compararle con Cipriano! Por eso se aguantó lo que
               tós sabemos . . .

MOZA 2ª   Antes sí, él era aquí el amo; pero *ende* que cumplió el
               otro se acabaron sus *fantesías.*

Mozo 1º	Como que Pedro en cuanto vino se llevó de calle a *tóas* las mozas.
Moza 2ª	A *tóas* no.
Mozo 1º	¡Bah! Como él quisiera . . .
Moza 2ª	*(Con orgullo.)* Sí ¡como él quisiera! . . .
Moza 1ª	¡Lo que son los hombres! *Áhi* anda Cipriano penando por la Marcela como si no *hubiá* otra en el mundo, después de haberle *dejao* . . .
Mozo 1º	¡Será la primera mujer que ha *tenío* dos novios!
Moza 2ª	Desengáñate, lo que a ella le gusta es que la cortejen los dos. Mientras escucha al uno . . .
Mozo 1º	Vosotros siempre la estáis criticando, ni que *tuviáis* celos.
Moza 2ª	¡Celos!
Mozo 1º	*(Se dirige a la ventana y llama desde fuera.)* ¡Eh! Rubia . . . ya tenéis *tó* el trigo a la sombra. Buen día nos hemos *llevao pa* concluir y que Gaspar se vaya tranquilo.
Rubia	*(Sacando por la ventana un gran porrón de vino y unos cuantos vasos en una bandeja.)* *Áhi* va un refresco.
Mozo 2º	*(Cogiendo la guitarra que estará junto al poyo.)* Vamos a echar las penas. *(Templa el instrumento y toca perezosamente una seguidilla.)*

ESCENA II

Dichos, Marcela y Cipriano

Mozo 1º	*Miá* que triste viene la Marcela.
Marcela	¿Ya habéis concluido? *(Se sienta pensativa.)* *(El Mozo 2º toca, el 1º bebe, las mozas siguen barriendo la era.)*

CIPRIANO   *(Colocándose junto a Marcela y mirándola con intención, canta a media voz.)*
             "Dicen que allá por Cuba
                anda la guerra
             y él tendrá que marcharse
                aunque no quiera."

RUBIA   *(Sale de casa y al verla el Mozo 2º deja de tocar. Los otros beben.)* ¿No ha *venío* Gaspar?

CIPRIANO   Todavía no. Estará con Pedro despidiéndose de los amigos.

MARCELA   Vendrán enseguida: Pedro me lo ha dicho.

RUBIA   *(A los mozos que bromean mientras beben con Cipriano.)* ¡*Paece* mentira que tengáis gana de broma! *(Se pasa el pañuelo por los ojos.)*

CIPRIANO   ¡Bah! No somos de piedra; pero ¿quieres que todos nos pongamos a llorar porque los reservistas van a Cuba? Eso ya lo esperábamos.

RUBIA   *Verdá* y al que le toque que se aguante. *(Entra en la casa.)*

ESCENA III

DICHOS, menos LA RUBIA

MOZO 1º   *(A las mozas que han concluido las faenas y se acercan.)* ¡Y que no se alegra este chupatintas de que se vaya Pedro!

MOZA 2ª   Como que le pudre la envidia y no *pué* resistir que le quiten la novia.

CIPRIANO   *(A Marcela que permanece abatida.)* Pues no se da mucha prisa por venir a tu lado y aprovechar los momentos.

MARCELA	Vendrá en cuanto pueda: me lo ha *prometío.*
CIPRIANO	¡Válgame Dios! Nunca he visto aí pueblo tan triste. ¡Ni que se acabara el mundo!
MARCELA	Como que se va lo mejor.

ESCENA IV

DICHOS, PEDRO Y GASPAR

GASPAR	*(Haciendo por aparecer alegre.)* ¿Qué es eso, muchachos? ¿No se baila? ¿No se bebe?
CIPRIANO	Tu mujer nos lo ha prohibido.
GASPAR	*(Aparte.)* Mi mujer . . . ¡Pobre! . . . Y mi hijo, mi madre . . . *(Haciendo un esfuerzo.—Alto.)* ¡Bah! las mujeres siempre lloran.
PEDRO	*(A Marcela.)* No te apenes: alegra esa cara *pa* que me acuerde de cómo ríes: quiero verte como cuando volví del servicio.
MARCELA	*¡Pa* no marcharte!
PEDRO	Así lo creíamos; pero . . . la guerra es la guerra y . . .
GASPAR	*(Brindando.)* ¡Por nuestro pueblo!
MOZOS	¡Sí, sí, por Cubillas! *(Todos beben.)*
CIPRIANO	El soldado debe marchar contento al peligro.
PEDRO	Por eso fuiste tú tan deprisa . . . a dar los ochavos *pa* librarte.
CIPRIANO	*(Vuelve la espalda diciendo medio entredientes.)* ¡Si no te fueras! . . .
PEDRO	*(Dándole en el hombro y con resolución.)* Pero volveré, ¿lo oyes? . . . volveré.

GASPAR   *(Interponiéndose.)* Ea . . . haya paz. *(A Cipriano.)* ¡Hombre . . . que sabiendo lo que es *quiás* armarle camorra cuando está *pa* marcharse a la guerra!

CIPRIANO   Es él que paga la rabia conmigo.

PEDRO   ¿Rabia? Aquí no hay más que la que tú tienes. Vaya, vaya, Gaspar, echa la última, que voy a bailar con Marcela.

CIPRIANO   Ésta no tiene ganas de bailes.

PEDRO   Conmigo sí y ahora lo vas a ver. *(Se prepara a bailar con Marcela, la cual mira a Cipriano con desdén. Pedro y Marcela se quedan de pie, hablando; Cipriano se acerca al poyo y bebe mientras las mozas 1ª y 2ª bailan unas seguidillas.)*

GASPAR   *(Canta.)*

> Si una pierna te rompen
> en la batalla,
> no te apures, chiquillo,
> que eso no es nada;
> porque de palo
> el tener otra pierna
> cuesta barato. *(Todos aplauden.)*

MARCELA   *(Con tristeza.)* ¡Qué copla tan triste has *echao!*

CIPRIANO   Ya rezarás tú para que no vengan con patas de palo.

PEDRO   Y tú reza *pa* que yo vuelva manco en vez de cojo.

CIPRIANO   Lo mismo se me da.

PEDRO   A mí no, que *pa* ahogar a un hombre más falta hacen las manos que las piernas.

ESCENA V

DICHOS, LA RUBIA Y TÍA PETRA

RUBIA   *(Saliendo.)* ¡Qué! ¿No entras?

GASPAR   Voy. Estábamos despidiéndonos de nuestro baile.

PETRA   *(Enjugándose las lágrimas.)* Ya te hemos *preparao tó.*

RUBIA   Llevas el morral bien repleto *pal* camino. *(Entran en la casa la tía Petra, la Rubia y Gaspar. Los mozos se retiran. Cipriano se aleja por el fondo.)*

ESCENA VI

PEDRO Y MARCELA

PEDRO   Más duelo me hace Gaspar; y si yo pudiera ir dos veces por él . . .

MARCELA   ¡Claro! ¿Y yo? ¿No te importa el dejarme?

PEDRO   Tú . . . me esperarás . . . y nos casaremos. Unos meses bien *pués* aguardarme.

MARCELA   Aunque sea cien años. Mira *(haciendo una cruz con los dedos)* por ésta, que mientras tú vivas dispondrás de mi corazón.

PEDRO   Te creo . . . pero me da coraje salir de aquí sin haber *escarmentao* a ese lechuguino.

MARCELA   ¡Valiente *encanijao!*

PEDRO   Yo te escribiré siempre que pueda.

MARCELA   *(Triste.)* Yo no sé escribir y si no *tiés* respuesta pensarás de mí cualquier cosa.

PEDRO   La Rubia sabe, y cuando escriba a Gaspar me pondrá algo de tu parte. Con tal que digas: "Estoy buena, a Dios gracias, y me acuerdo de ti," estoy contento.

MARCELA   Pero me ha dicho Cipriano que tardarás en volver, porque aquello está muy largo . . . muy largo . . .

PEDRO   ¡Bah! De *toas* partes se vuelve ¡como salve uno la pelleja! . . .

MARCELA   *(Compungida.)* No digas eso.

PEDRO   Pues mira: pídele a Dios que vuelva y pídele también por Gaspar que más falta hace que yo. *(Triste.)* Él ya sabe que esas lágrimas de la tía Petra y de su mujer no se *habián* de secar . . . mientras que las que tú echas por mí . . . vamos, que me da mucha pena . . . y le tengo envidia.

MARCELA   Veo que no *tiés* confianza en mí . . .

PEDRO   Sí, pero me acuerdo de que antes has *querío* a Cipriano.

MARCELA   Cuando tú servías al rey; pero *ende* que te vi . . .

PEDRO   *Tiés* razón; sin embargo estas cavilaciones no me las puedo quitar de la cabeza. Si *estuviámos* ya *casaos*, como sé que eres *honrá* me iría más tranquilo.

MARCELA   *¡Paece* imposible! ¡Tú compararte con el chupatintas que es un mico a tu *lao!*

PEDRO   Sí; pero ricachón y medio señorito . . . míralo, míralo . . . *(Señalando a Cipriano que viene con el Alcalde.)*

MARCELA   *(Enjugándose una lágrima.)* ¿*Quiés* ponerme más triste *toavía?*

PEDRO   *(Abrazándola.) Tiés* razón. *(Haciendo por disimular.)* Perdóname . . . no seas tonta; lo que te digo es *pa* probarte y ver qué me respondías. ¡Yo pensar en ese mono! Vamos a ver qué hacen ésos. *(Entran medio abrazados en casa de Gaspar.)*

ESCENA VII

CIPRIANO, EL ALCALDE

CIPRIANO Y used, señor Alcalde ¿cree que volverán pronto?

ALCALDE Claro que sí: antes de que tú vengas de maestro al lugar.

CIPRIANO Pues eso será dentro de muy pocos meses.

ALCALDE Allí no hay más que unas partidillas . . . mucho ruido y pocas nueces . . . al gobierno le conviene *esagerar;* es como los médicos que dicen que *tó* es grave *pa* luego darse pisto de lo que han *curao.*

CIPRIANO Sí, sí; antes también en Madrid decían lo mismo; pero ahora se va poniendo aquello muy turbio.

ALCALDE No lo creas. A mí no me la dan.

Yo he *servío* durante la guerra civil y tengo mucha ley al uniforme. Mira: cuando llegábamos a un pueblo, entraba allí la alegría. *Tós* los chicos corriendo delante del batallón y mirándonos con la boca abierta . . . ; las mozas . . . no *queaba* una en la cocina; *toas* a las puertas, con unas caras de cielo ¡que nos dejaban! . . . Las *agüelas* gruñían un poco por mor de los alojamientos; pero en cuanto íbamos con la boleta gritando: "Salú, patrona" y tan contentos como *destrozaos* después de una buena *jorná,* nos abrazaban las madres llorando, y mandaban a sus hijas que nos preparasen la cena, en tanto que ellas con *medecinas* de su invención nos curaban los pies que llevábamos deshechos. Los mozos nos miraban al principio así . . . un poco de *lao;* pero al minuto cundía el buen humor y en *cá* alojamiento se armaba un baile y vengan jotas y vayan tragos, y allí salía lo mejorcillo de la despensa que ¡así son las hembras españolas! En fin, muchacho, que al dejar el pueblo aunque no llevásemos más que cuarenta y ocho horas, nos despedían como al hijo de la casa y salíamos entre aplausos, y lágrimas, y vivas, con el estómago caliente, el morral bien repleto y *(enternecido)* un escapulario más, junto al que nos prendió nuestra madre.

CIPRIANO   *(Que no ha puesto mucha atención. Aparte y mirando a la casa.)*—Esos llantos por él me exasperan.

ALCALDE   Así, desde aquel instante, teníamos una familia más y con el entusiasmo en el corazón y queriendo que nuestras victorias llegasen a aquellos sitios donde habíamos *estao* ¡entrábamos en la pelea con un coraje! y al grito de "¡Viva España!" se nos representaban *tós* aquellos lugares y no había empuje que resistiera nuestra acometida, porque *pa* batirse con hambre, con sed, con fatiga, no hay más que un *soldao:* el *soldao* español: sí; a pesar de *tó*, el *soldao* español . . .

CIPRIANO   ¡Recuerdos!

ALCALDE   Los más alegres de mi vida; y si cien veces naciera, cien veces querría ir *soldao*.

CIPRIANO   ¿Y a la guerra?

ALCALDE   Y a la guerra, que es la muerte más hermosa la del campo de batalla.

ESCENA VIII

DICHOS, PEDRO Y MARCELA

PEDRO   *(A Marcela.)*—Aquí está *toavía*.

MARCELA   *(Encogiéndose de hombros.)*—¿Y qué?

ALCALDE   Vaya, chicos; ánimo. Yo soy perro viejo y me da el corazón que volveréis muy pronto.

PEDRO   *(Mirando a Cipriano con intención.)*—Más pronto de lo que alguno quisiera.

CIPRIANO   *(Con sorna.)*—No lo dirás por ésta. *(Señalando a Marcela.)*

ESCENA IX

DICHOS, GASPAR, TÍA PETRA, después, LA RUBIA

(Gaspar sale abrazando a su madre que llora.)

PEDRO   *(Con tristeza.)*—Ni por ésta.

PETRA   ¡Hijo mío, ya no te veré más!

ALCALDE   Vaya, vaya; no entristecer a los muchachos. Tú le verás volver. ¡Y poco que nos vamos a divertir este *ivierno* cuando arrimaditos a la lumbre celebremos las Pascuas, mientras ellos nos cuentan sus aventuras! Porque, ya se sabe, los hijos de este pueblo como *haiga* donde dar . . . nunca se vienen sin adornos. *(Señalando al ojal.)*

                (Pedro habla con Marcela.)

PETRA   Que venga sano y bueno y no pido más.

RUBIA   *(Acercándose.)*—Él no *nesecita* cintajos, que sin ellos le quise y sin ellos le querré.

CIPRIANO   *(Mirando a Pedro y Marcela.)*—Sin embargo, eso halaga mucho. *(Con sarcasmo.)*

PETRA   Mira, hijo: tú no hagas caso de esas cosas y no te metas . . .

RUBIA   ¡Pues claro! *Labraor* eres, *labraor* serás y *pa* revolver la tierra no hacen falta adornos.

ALCALDE   *(A Pedro.)*—Conque, sobrino ¡a portarse! *(A Marcela.)* Y tú no llores. A los hombres les sientan bien los trabajos. Ya verás como *aluego* le encuentras más *leido* y más . . . persona. ¡Y que no aprovechará el chico lo que vea!

CIPRIANO   *(A Marcela con ironía.)*—¡Y hasta puede que vuelva de oficial! *(Pedro le mira como desafiándole.)*

ALCALDE   ¡Ea! . . . a prepararse. *(Todos entran menos Marcela y Cipriano.)*

ESCENA X

MARCELA, CIPRIANO

MARCELA   Lo que *paece* mentira es que tengas tan mala saña.

CIPRIANO   Como la tuya conmigo.

MARCELA   No dirás que te engañé. Mientras creí que te quería te lo dije; y cuando . . .

CIPRIANO   *(Interrumpiéndola.)*—Y tú te piensas que basta decirle a uno: "Mira, hasta hoy te he querido; pero ha venido al lugar un *(con sorna)* buen mozo que me gusta más que tú y puedes retirarte." ¿Te parece a ti que esto se le hace a ningún hombre? *(Marcela llora sin responder.)* Y para más escarnio, venga Pedro por aquí, Pedro por allí, que no bailo más que con él . . .

MARCELA   Di lo que te se antoje: ahora no estoy *pa na*. Me gustó Pedro; yo a él, y si no por esta maldita guerra, muy pronto estaríamos *casaos*. En cuanto a ti . . . ya te lo he dicho: te aprecio como si *fuás* mi hermano.

CIPRIANO   ¡Bien se ve! Por eso bailas hasta con el Verbo; pero conmigo . . .

MARCELA   Lo hago por no tener cuestiones con Pedro, y porque como siempre os estáis buscando camorra . . . pues, no *quió* que por mi causa *armís* un belén.

CIPRIANO   ¿Y qué te importa? Él es mucho más fuerte y saldría ganando.

MARCELA   Ya te he dicho que te quiero.

CIPRIANO   Sí, como a un hermano; y me compadeces porque
              comprendes que te has portado mal; tú no has tenido
              mucha pena al darme la despedida y ¡quieres que yo
              la tenga para dársela a él! *(Con rabia.)* Sólo al verte
              llorar . . . como sé por lo que lloras, me pongo tan
              fuera de mí que ¡me dan ganas de matarle! Así no
              pensarías más en el *buen mozo (acentuándolo).*

ESCENA XI

DICHOS, TÍA PETRA, ALCALDE

ALCALDE   *(Hablando con la tía Petra y saliendo.)* Yo también soy
              viejo; más que tú y pienso salir al camino cuando
              vuelva mi Pedro.

PETRA   Tú estás fuerte: además, un sobrino no es un hijo.

ALCALDE   Pero antes que el hijo está la patria.

PETRA   ¡La patria! ¿A mí qué me importa eso? ¡A fe que si no
              vuelve Gaspar, no será la patria la que le llore ni la
              que le venga aquí a sembrar las tierras!

ALCALDE   La patria llora a sus hijos, si mueren en el campo del
              honor. Yo presencié escenas bien tristes cuando
              enterrábamos algún valiente, con el redoble de los
              tambores que *paece* como que mandan llorar.

PETRA   ¡Oye! ¿Y era algún *soldao* el que enterraban con
              música? *(Con intención.)*

CIPRIANO   *(Al Alcalde.)* Hay que respetar su dolor.

ALCALDE   Sí, las madres siempre son egoístas.

ESCENA XII

DICHOS, GASPAR, PEDRO Y RUBIA

GASPAR   Vamos, madre. Esto no es más que un paseo por el agua. *Pa* año nuevo ya estamos de vuelta. *(A Rubia.)* Antes de embarcar escribiré. Cuida del chico y cuídate tú *pa* él, *pa* la madre y *pa* abrazar a tu marido cuando se acabe la guerra. *(La Rubia llora.)* No llores mujer.

RUBIA   ¡Que no llore! ¿Pues qué me *quea* en el mundo si tú faltas?

GASPAR   *(Haciendo por aparecer tranquilo.)* *Tiés* a tu hijo y a mi madre que te recomiendo. Toma un *criao* hasta que yo vuelva *pa* que no perdamos la labor; sigue con ella y ¿quién sabe? *Pué* que luego te alegres cuando veas que no me ha *pasao ná* y traigo unos cuartejos.

PETRA   No hables más que de venir. ¿Qué nos importan los ochavos?

ALCALDE   Esta escena será la misma en *tós* los pueblos.

PEDRO   *(Triste.)* Cuando no se deja madre . . . ni mujer . . . ni hijo . . . ¿*pa* qué *quié* uno volver?

ALCALDE   La madre no *tié* sustituta . . . mujer, ya la encontrarás a tu regreso. Éste *(por Gaspar)* volverá *pa* la familia que deja y tú *pa* la que harás. Ya sabes que te esperan. *(Mirando a Marcela, Cipriano hace un gesto de disgusto. Pedro lo ve.)*

PEDRO   Que me esperan . . . *(Con resolución.)* Tiene usted razón: yo también necesito volver. *(Mirando a Cipriano.)*

PETRA   Si cuando mandan ir tantos hombres a la guerra *tuvián* los que lo dicen el corazón de una madre ya se compadecerían un poco más y . . . *(Pedro y Gaspar arreglan las provisiones en los morrales.)*

ALCALDE   Tú no entiendes. ¿Te figuras que por gusto manda el gobierno estas cosas?

PETRA   Lo que yo sé es, que *tós semos* unos cuando los conviene; pero mi hijo va a la guerra habiendo *cumplío*, mientras el de la Casiana, pongo por caso, está sirviendo y se *quea* aquí.

RUBIA   Lleva razón. ¿Por qué no van los que no *tién* familia? Yo siempre he oído que *pa* ir a la guerra, primero están los mozos y *aluego* los *casaos*; pero aquí lo arreglaron de otro modo.

CIPRIANO   Cuestión de gobierno. Irán después.

PETRA   Y si *fuán* igual los que *tién* dinero . . . aún se conformaría una; pero *(desesperada)* que le maten un hijo, quizás no por la guerra, ni por el gobierno, sino por la pobreza . . . Tú no te haces cargo porque no *tiés* hijos. Yo, sin haber *salío* del lugar ni entender esas cosas que *icen* los papeles, sé cómo podía quedarse mi Gaspar. Que yo *tuviá* aquí *(dándose en el bolsillo)* las pesetas que me piden por librarlo, y ya verías tú lo que se me daba a mí de la guerra.

RUBIA   Lo mismo que se les da de nosotros a los que mandan.

CIPRIANO   Eso no: el gobierno socorre a las familias con media peseta diaria.

PEDRO   *(Aparte a Gaspar.)* Acabemos pronto. *(Alto.)* Vaya, que no perdamos el tren.

ALCALDE   Os acompaño.

            (Marcela se abraza a Pedro, la Rubia y Tía Petra a Gaspar. Todas lloran.)

PETRA   *(Poniendo a su hijo un escapulario.)* Rézala *tós* los días: es nuestra Patrona. *(A Pedro.)* Toma tú otro igual. *(Le entrega otro escapulario.)*

PEDRO	Gracias, tía Petra. *(Los dos amigos abrazados despiden con la mano a las mujeres.)* Si alguno de los dos *tié* una desgracia, el otro traerá la noticia.
GASPAR	Siempre procuraremos luchar juntos.
MARCELA	*(Mirando al cielo.)* ¡Dios mío! ¡que vuelvan!
PETRA	*(Abrazando a la Rubia.)* Virgen del Amparo a ti lo encomiendo *(Cipriano se adelanta para sostener a Marcela que vacila; Pedro que lo ve, desprendiéndose de Gaspar, va a cortarle el paso. Cipriano se detiene.)*
PEDRO	*(Agarrando a Cipriano por las solapas de la chaqueta con gran energía.)* Volveré, no lo olvides, volveré *(Sale mirando a Cipriano. Éste, cuando Pedro no le ve, se vuelve haciendo un gesto desdeñoso.)*

Telón lento.

Casa de la tía Petra

Una cocina de aldea con fogón en el suelo rodeado de vasijas. Sillas de madera y una mesa de lo mismo. Puerta en el fondo que da al portal. A la derecha de esta puerta una estampa de la Virgen y debajo una mesa con una lamparilla. Al otro lado una alacena. Otra puerta a la izquierda que comunica con un dormitorio. Ventana a la izquierda. Cerca del hogar una cuna con un niño. Un mantón encima de una silla.

Al levantarse el telón la Rubia prepara la cena y la tía Petra, sentada junto a la lumbre, hila en una rueca. Las dos mujeres están tristes.

ESCENA PRIMERA

LA RUBIA Y TÍA PETRA

RUBIA	Hoy no ha comido usted, madre . . . es preciso que cene.
PETRA	Bien: cierra antes la ventana ¡que entra un cierzo! . . .
RUBIA	(*Obedeciendo y encendiendo un candil.*) La Nicasia ha *tráido* una miaja de su matapuerco; si *usté* quiere pondré algo *pa* cenar.
PETRA	No; guárdalo.
RUBIA	(*Enjugándose los ojos.*) ¡Sí, lo guardaré como lo demás, y como *tó*, se pudrirá!
PETRA	*Tiés* razón; ponlo, nos lo comeremos.
RUBIA	(*Después de un instante de vacilación.*) No, madre, no; ¿*pa* qué mentir? Si no hemos de probarlo *usté* ni yo . . .
PETRA	Como nos dijo que vendría *pa* año nuevo y . . .

RUBIA   Veneno se me volvería si probase un *bocao* de mata-
             puerco no estando Gaspar; ¡después de haber creído
             que vendría ahora! . . . *(cogiendo el plato).* Allí lo
             dejaré. *(Lo mete en la alacena.)*

PETRA   Este día, ¡quién se lo había de figurar el año *pasao!*
             ¡Qué contentos estábamos!

RUBIA   Y qué distintas fueron aquellas navidades. ¡Cuántas
             coplas inventó Pedro *pa* la Marcela!

PETRA   ¡Pobre Pedro! ¡Tan bueno como es!

RUBIA   ¡Bueno! Ya lo creo. Y me se figura a mí que no se lo
             merecía la Marcela. Vamos, que me encorajina la
             conversación que se trae con el maestro. *(Poniendo
             una servilleta y dos vasos sobre la mesa.)* Vamos a cenar.

PETRA   No; no podría tomar *ná.* Hoy . . .

RUBIA   Hoy cumple los veinticinco.

PETRA   ¡Dios quiera que los cumpla! *(Suenan fuera pandere-
             tas, hierros y zambobas. La tía Petra escucha.)*

RUBIA   Son los mozos que van a esperar a los Reyes des-
             pidiéndose de las pascuas. *(Prestando atención.)* El
             maestro ronda a la Marcela.

PETRA   ¡Qué alegres están! Vamos a rezar hoy más que
             nunca *pa* que Dios le dé *salú.* ¿Dónde pasará esta
             noche de Reyes? ¡También él estará pensando en
             nosotras! *(Se arrodillan delante de la estampa de la
             Virgen y rezan en silencio mientras suenan más cerca los
             instrumentos. Cipriano, dentro, canta.)*

             Ya se marcharon las pascuas
             y otras pascuas volverán;
             pero algunos que se han ido
             puede que no vuelvan más.

PETRA   *(Levantándose.)* ¡Dios mío, qué copla! *(Suenan golpes
             en la puerta de la calle.)* Abre; yo me voy a mi cuarto.

Esa música me hace daño . . . *paece* que entre ella va a salir la voz de Gaspar y luego . . . *(Vase.) (La Rubia va a abrir.)*

ESCENA II

LA RUBIA, CIPRIANO, MARCELA

MARCELA   *(Entrando con la Rubia y Cipriano.)* Como ya me imagino que hoy estaréis muy tristes, no he *querío* que alboroten a la puerta.

CIPRIANO   Eran para ésta las coplas.

RUBIA   No nos hagáis caso y divertiros, que a *tós* les llega su San Martín . . . y otro día *pué* que tú llores cuando yo cante.

MARCELA   ¿Y la tía Petra?

RUBIA   Se ha *metío* en su cuarto . . . *pa* llorar: como hoy es el santo de . . . ya te figurarás el día que pasaremos.

CIPRIANO   Verdad; hoy es su santo y la pobre abuela, naturalmente, estará más triste.

MARCELA   ¿Le habéis escrito?

RUBIA   ¡Ya lo creo! . . . pero . . . como las otras; ni esto. *(Haciendo sonar la uña del pulgar entre los dientes.)*

MARCELA   Hace cinco meses que se marcharon; ¡cómo se pasa el tiempo!

RUBIA   A ti muy deprisa por lo que *icen.* ¡Si Pedro oyera!

MARCELA   Me *paece* que él no se acuerda mucho de mí. ¡Una carta en cinco meses!

RUBIA   Ya sabes que tampoco Gaspar ha escrito más que dos veces. Y según decía, Pedro andaba algo malucho.

CIPRIANO   *(Sentándose a la lumbre.)* ¡Hace un frío por ahí fuera! ...

MARCELA   ¡La *verdá* es que estar siempre aguardando noticias! ...

RUBIA   Sí, te cansas; pero me se figura que tan buen mozo no lo has de encontrar.

CIPRIANO   Si con la facha se comiese ...

RUBIA   Mira; yo no *quieo* meterme en lo que no me importa; pero eso de que *haiga* quien le quite la novia mientras él, vamos al decir, pelea por España, no me *paece* regular. Quitársela aquí, cara a cara, pase; pero ...

CIPRIANO   Si lo dices por mí, acuérdate que antes fue mi novia.

MARCELA   *(Medio llorando.)* Lo mismo se me da de lo que digan: tú no *tiés* motivo *pa* criticarme. Yo he *prometío* a Pedro que seré su mujer, y le aguardo *pa* cumplir mi palabra, porque le quiero; y si traigo conversación con éste, es delante de *tó* el mundo, que nadie podrá *icir* otra cosa; Cipriano es mi amigo, casi un hermano, y más le escucho por distraerme que *pa* tomar en serio lo que habla.

CIPRIANO   Muchas gracias. Mejor es que sigas esperando al buen mozo, a ver con qué te mantiene.

RUBIA   Es *trabajaor* y no ha de faltarle el pan.

CIPRIANO   Allá veremos. *(A Marcela.)* Y tú hazla caso a ésta y no a mí, que debo ser el mismo demonio según se me pone en contra.

RUBIA   No digo eso: ya sé que eres buena *comenencia:* mejor que el otro en cuanto a dinero y saber; pero ... vamos, que en estas *cercustancias* ...

PETRA   *(Dentro y llamando.)* ¡Muchacha!

RUBIA   Voy, madre ... *(Coge la cuna y se va al dormitorio.)*

ESCENA III

CIPRIANO, MARCELA.

MARCELA   ¿Ves lo que andan diciendo por *áhi?*

CIPRIANO   Envidias; no parece sino que te quiero hacer mi
               manceba para que todos te aconsejen que no me
               hagas caso. Di: ¿te he faltado yo nunca? ¿no quiero
               que seas mi mujer? ¿no te ofrezco la mejor casa del
               lugar, las mejores yuntas? ¿no te digo que estoy de-
               seando verte aviada como las señoritas y que te
               llevaré a ver Madrid y que serás la reina del pueblo?
               ¿Crees que no encontraría yo . . .

MARCELA   Sí, sí; yo te lo estimo; pero . . . ¡quiá! mientras Pedro
               viva . . .

CIPRIANO   No contestando a tus cartas, no sé cómo vas a saber
               que vive; medio año ya es bastante esperar.

MARCELA   ¡No hables así! Mira: hasta que yo no tenga la *seguriá*
               de que me ha *olvidao* o le pasó alguna desgracia, suya
               soy; y de aquí no me has de sacar.

CIPRIANO   *(Con mal humor y levantándose.)* Como quieras.
               Cuando te hayas puesto fea de llorar, y envejecida,
               y nadie te haga caso, y . . . Pedro no vuelva . . . *(Con
               intención.)*

MARCELA   *(Asustada.)* ¿Qué dices? Tú sabes algo.

CIPRIANO   Yo no sé más de lo que todo el pueblo comenta: que
               desde la batalla que dio su regimiento no se tienen
               noticias, y allí hubo muertos . . . y heridos . . . No
               sería ninguna cosa del otro jueves que . . . en fin,
               todo puede suceder y . . . *(Marcela llora. Cipriano
               impaciente.)* ¡Bah! Te dejo, que estás insufrible. ¡Dios
               quiera que no te arrepientas! Ya sabes que mi madre
               está muy delicada y quiere verme casado. No aguar-
               do más: te dejo con tus lloros. Ya sé dónde me
               pondrán buena cara. Con que espera a tu Pedro; yo
               me caso con la que tú sabes y tan amigos.

MARCELA   *(Cerrándole el paso.)* Tú no la quieres.

CIPRIANO   ¡Pchist! Querer a una chica guapa, no es difícil, y más cuando tiene la cara alegre y fresca como las rosas.

             (Se aleja. Marcela hace ademán de seguirle. Repentinamente se detiene y se sienta con mal humor. Cipriano la contempla un instante desde el fondo; después sale.)

ESCENA IV

ALCALDE, TÍA PETRA, RUBIA, MARCELA

ALCALDE   *(Entrando.)* ¿Por dónde anda esta gente?

RUBIA   *(Saliendo del dormitorio.)* Ya voy. ¡Hola, señor Alcalde!

ALCALDE   ¿Y la madre?

RUBIA   Está rezando; hoy es un día muy triste, el santo de Gaspar. ¡Y pensábamos que lo pasaría con nosotras!

ALCALDE   Lo principal es que esté bueno.

PETRA   *(Saliendo del dormitorio.)* ¿Qué te trae por aquí? Te he *sentío* y salgo . . .

ALCALDE   ¡*Ná!* Venía a ver si sabíais alguna cosa. Según mis cuentas, hoy pudo haber carta, porque el vapor estaba en Cádiz el lunes con la correspondencia; así es que ayer, *u* lo más hoy, debe llegar alguna noticia.

PETRA   ¿Y los papeles no dicen nada?

ALCALDE   No he leído más que lo que te traje; después de aquella *ación* no ha vuelto a decirse *ná* de su regimiento.

MARCELA   Por eso me figuro que deben estar buenos; allí no hablaban de más muertos que un sargento y un médico; por lo tanto, ni Gaspar ni Pedro habrán *tenío noveá*.

PETRA	No: *Áhi* tengo el periódico. *(Va por un periódico a su cuarto y sale en seguida con él, muy doblado y sucio.)*
ALCALDE	Ya sé lo que dice.
RUBIA	Lo habrá oído treinta veces: a *tó* el que viene se lo hace leer.
PETRA	*(Desdoblando el periódico y señalando.)* Aquí está.
ALCALDE	¡Anda! ¿Has aprendido a leer?
PETRA	¡Ojalá!
ALCALDE	*(Mirando el periódico.)* Bueno: esto ya es muy antiguo; las primeras noticias que llegaron.
RUBIA	Y las últimas.
MARCELA	¿Y *usté* supone que Pedro andaba también en esa *ación?* porque Gaspar decía en la carta: "Pedro, no sé si vendrá con nosotros."
ALCALDE	*Pué* que le *hubiean mandao* quedarse.
PETRA	Lo que es Gaspar allí estaba: tengo la *seguriá.* Lee, lee. *(Se prepara a oír la lectura con gran atención y con la misma la sigue.)*
ALCALDE	Es lo regular. *(Leyendo.)* "Noticias satisfactorias de la guerra. Partida deshecha. —300 enemigos muertos. —Quince bajas nuestras. —La columna del coronel Domínguez, compuesta de un batallón de Castilla y tres compañías de Cuenca, batió ayer al grueso de las fuerzas enemigas mandadas por el cabecilla Moreno. El combate fue reñidísimo: nuestros soldados portáronse valerosamente." *(Hablando.)* ¡Como siempre! *(Leyendo.)* "Después de cinco horas de ruda pelea que terminó cuerpo a cuerpo . . ."
PETRA	*Áhi, áhi* está Gaspar: sigue, sigue.

ALCALDE	*(Leyendo.)* . . . "ocurrió un hecho que no por lo común en nuestros valientes soldados deja de ser heroico."
PETRA	Eso, eso.
ALCALDE	*(Leyendo.)* "En lo más encarnizado de la lucha, y por lo resabaldizo . . ."
PETRA	"Del terreno" ¡Si me lo sé de memoria! . . . *(El Alcalde hace como que sigue leyendo. Tía Petra escucha. Marcela y Rubia estarán al otro lado de la escena.)*
RUBIA	*Ice* que no hablan de más muertos que esos dos: pero ¿y las quince bajas?
MARCELA	Serán . . .
PETRA	Veo su genio, su fuerza . . . sigue, sigue . . . *(escucha).*
MARCELA	Desde ese día *ná* sabemos.
RUBIA	¡*Ná!* Y ya ves que el señor Alcalde escribió a *Madrí* a uno que fue su capitán *pa* que averiguase; pero ¡quiá! ¡Siempre pensando y haciendo cavilaciones!
PETRA	¿Eh?
ALCALDE	*(Leyendo.)* "El enemigo . . ."
	(Entra Cipriano muy agitado.)

ESCENA V

DICHOS Y CIPRIANO

CIPRIANO	¡Ah! ¿Están ustedes leyendo?
ALCALDE	No: es el periódico antiguo: noticias de hace dos meses.
CIPRIANO	Creí . . .
RUBIA	Lo de siempre: la madre no se cansa de oírlas.
PETRA	Mientras no tenga otras, ésas serán las más frescas.

ALCALDE	Eso sí.
CIPRIANO	De manera que . . . ¿nada nuevo saben ustedes?
RUBIA	Nada.
CIPRIANO	*(A Marcela con temor.)* ¿Ni tú?
MARCELA	Ni yo.
PETRA	*(Acercándose a Cipriano.)* ¡Oye! *(Con zozobra.)* Tú algo te traes.
CIPRIANO	Yo . . . no . . . Dicen por el lugar . . .
RUBIA	¿Tiemblas? ¡Dios Santo!
PETRA	¡Mi hijo!
CIPRIANO	¡No, no, no! Lo que se cuenta, nada tiene que ver con Gaspar.
MARCELA	*(Aterrada.)* ¡Pedro! ¿Lo han *matao?*
CIPRIANO	*(Con ira y calma.)* No, tranquilízate; no ha muerto . . . Ha venido en el último vapor.
TODOS	¡Pedro ha *venío!* *(Marcela da un grito.)*
PETRA	¿Pero ha *venío* solo?
ALCALDE	No comprendo . . .
CIPRIANO	Ha venido . . . *(Con mal humor)* y no sé más.
RUBIA	¿Y cómo lo sabes? ¿A quién escribió?
CIPRIANO	No ha escrito a nadie: él mismo trae la noticia. Se presentó esta tarde en casa de la tía Ruperta.
ALCALDE	¿Mi hermana? Pues no me lo ha dicho. *Verdá* que no he *pasao* por allí.
MARCELA	*(A Cipriano.)* Di tú lo que sepas.
CIPRIANO	Cuando salí antes, oí hablar de Pedro y . . . nadie sabe gran cosa, por lo que he podido averiguar. Al hacer de noche entró en el pueblo en compañía de su tío

Beltrán que ya estaba avisado y salió con la mula a la estación. No quiere que sepan su venida hasta que él disponga ... por eso *(al Alcalde)* no se lo habrá dicho a usted su hermana.

ALCALDE   ¡Vaya una ocurrencia! ¿Por qué no *quié* presentarse? ¿No sabe que *tós* desean verle? ¿A quién *tié* miedo *pa* esconderse así?

PETRA   Pues yo me voy corriendo a buscarle, que él me traerá noticias de mi Gaspar. *(Coge el mantón, y se dispone a salir.)*

ALCALDE   *(Viendo que la tía Petra, ya lista para salir se dirige a la puerta. —A la Rubia.)* No dejes ir a la madre, no sea que Pedro traiga alguna noticia que ...

RUBIA   ¡Jesús! ¿*Usté* cree? ...

ALCALDE   No; pero ...

RUBIA   Madre; yo iré, que hace mucho frío *pa* que *usté* salga. Cuando vea que ya sabemos su *llegá*, no tendrá inconveniente en venirse conmigo y aquí nos dirá *tó* lo que sepa. Y si no se deja ver, *usté* no habrá *perdío* el viaje que *pué* costarle una *enfermedá*.

ALCALDE   Lleva razón la Rubia.

PETRA   Es que a mí no me se negará, porque me respeta.

RUBIA   Ya le diré yo que *usté* no ha *podío* salir porque está mala y ... que venga.

ALCALDE   Sí, sí, anda; yo te acompaño.

MARCELA   Yo me quedo con la tía Petra.

RUBIA   *(Se pone el mantón y sale diciendo a Marcela.)* Cuida del chico; si llora, *áhi tiés* las sopas; dáselas.

MARCELA   Vete *descuidá*. *(Vánse la Rubia y el Alcalde.)*

ESCENA VI

DICHOS, MENOS RUBIA Y ALCALDE

PETRA   *(A los que se marchan. Desde la puerta.)* No *tardís,* que
               yo no estoy *pa* esperar mucho.

CIPRIANO   Tenga usted calma, y prepárese a recibir buenas noti-
               cias de Gaspar.

PETRA   *(Muy intranquila.)* ¡Dios te oiga! Voy a ver si puedo
               aguardar rezando. *(Entra en su cuarto.)*

ESCENA VII

MARCELA, CIPRIANO

CIPRIANO   *(Con intención.)* ¿Y no sospechas la causa de su escon-
               dite?

MARCELA   ¿Yo? No.

CIPRIANO   Pues me la estoy figurando.

MARCELA   Habrá *venío* con licencia.

CIPRIANO   *(Pensativo.)* No lo creo: antes me imagino que habrá
               desertado.

MARCELA   ¡Desertar de la guerra! Tú no conoces a Pedro.

CIPRIANO   Porque le conozco y me acuerdo de la manera que se
               fue, no me extrañaría nada que hubiese hecho una
               barbaridad por presentarse aquí, donde tenía su pen-
               samiento constantemente.

MARCELA   ¿Pero qué *conseguía* con venir así . . . *perseguío* y tener
               que esconderse?

CIPRIANO   *(Con ironía.)* Quizá te proponga que huyas con él.
               Cuando lo ha hecho, bien pensado lo tendrá. Puede

que prefiera vivir contigo en otros países que andar batiéndose con los negros. ¡Cualquiera haría lo mismo!

MARCELA   *(Con orgullo.)* No dices lo que sientes: la inquina que le guardas te ciega. ¡Él huir del combate! Vaya . . . que no; no viene *escapao;* lo juraría.

CIPRIANO   Puede que tengas razón, pero si le quiero mal, no es mía la culpa, sino tuya.

(Permanecen un momento silenciosos. Se oye fuera el ruido del aire y del agua.)

MARCELA   *(Asustada.)* ¿Qué ruido es ése?

CIPRIANO   *(Muy preocupado.)* El aire y el aguacero.

MARCELA   ¡Qué noche! No sé por qué tengo miedo.

CIPRIANO   *(Con ironía.)* ¿Miedo? ¿De quién?

MARCELA   ¡Me *paece* tan raro *tó* lo que ocurre! . . . Venir Pedro, solo, precisamente el santo de Gaspar, venir sin avisar a nadie . . . de noche . . . escondiéndose; no correr aquí *pa* dar noticias del otro . . . en fin . . . no sé; pero tengo como *encogío* el corazón y . . .

CIPRIANO   Pronto saldremos de dudas. *(Aparte.)* ¡Yo que le creí muerto! *(Alto.)* ¿Y cómo estando con vida, no te ha escrito en tanto tiempo?

MARCELA   ¿Pero tú *tiés* la *seguridá* de que está en el pueblo? ¿Le has visto, o será una burla que te hacían porque saben que no le quieres?

CIPRIANO   Eso pensé yo, cuando me dieron la noticia; pero enseguida me despedí de los mozos que me lo habían dicho y dando la vuelta al pueblo me fui a casa de su tía y me puse a escuchar debajo de la ventana. No le he visto; eso no: *(con amargura)* le he oído. ¡Ah! ¡conozco muy bien su voz!

ESCENA VIII

DICHOS, Y TÍA PETRA

PETRA   *(Saliendo.)* Yo no *pueo* más. Voy a buscarlos.

MARCELA   ¡Con esta noche! Espere *usté* un poco: ya no tardarán.

CIPRIANO   Lo que hará usted es retrasar las noticias, porque es muy posible que se cruce con ellos en el camino.

PETRA   Si acaso nos encontraremos, que no van a venir por las eras con el piso que está. *(Vase.)* Adiós, no tengo calma *pa* esperar.

CIPRIANO   Voy con usted, aunque no han podido llegar y vamos a perder el viaje.

MARCELA   Yo no me *queo* sola: ya te he dicho que tengo miedo.

PETRA   *(A Cipriano.)* Quédate tú con ésa: yo ya voy bastante *acompañá* con mi desasosiego.

ESCENA IX

MARCELA, CIPRIANO

MARCELA   Podía haberme ido con ella.

CIPRIANO   Sí, y dejar solo al chico.

MARCELA   ¡Cuándo será mañana! ¡Vaya una noche de Reyes!

CIPRIANO   ¡Claro! Mañana . . . le verás.

MARCELA   ¿Y no *pués* sospechar lo que le trae?

CIPRIANO   *(Con mal humor.)* ¡Qué sé yo! Oí que hablaba; pero no pude entender lo que decía.

(Cipriano se pasea impaciente. Marcela se sienta pensativa. Silencio. Fuera se oye el ruido del agua y del aire. De

*pronto suena el golpe que produce la puerta de la calle al
ser abierta violentamente. Marcela da un grito.)*

CIPRIANO   *(Siempre con mal humor.)* Es el cierzo.

MARCELA   *(Con miedo.)* Es la puerta, que acaban de abrir.

CIPRIANO   Será que vuelven. *(Se oyen pasos.)* Ya están ahí.

*(Marcela y Cipriano se adelantan a tiempo que entra
Pedro. Éste, apoyándose en el umbral, se queda un
momento silencioso y mirándoles. Viene completamente
desfigurado, muy enfermo y con la cabeza vendada; viste
traje de rayadillo y gorra de cuartel. Trae un tapabocas
puesto al cuello y una cruz en el pecho. Aparece mojado por
la lluvia. Cipriano retrocede. Marcela se queda mirándole
espantada.)*

MARCELA   ¡Él . . . él! ¡¡Dios Santo!! *(Déjase caer en la silla; tapándose la cara con las manos.)*

ESCENA X

PEDRO, CIPRIANO, MARCELA

PEDRO   *(Aparte.)* ¡Los dos solos! *(Alto a Marcela.)* ¡Qué! ¿te
tapas los ojos por no verme?

MARCELA   *(Sin acercarse.)* Como no te esperaba y casi te he
conocío . . .

CIPRIANO   No aguardábamos . . .

PEDRO   *(Acercándose a Marcela y con amargura.)* ¿Y es así
como me recibes? ¿Es esto lo que me *jurastes?* ¡Ah!
He venido *(mirando a los dos)* en muy mala hora. ¡Por
algo no quise avisar!

CIPRIANO   Ya sabíamos que estabas en el pueblo, y a buscarte
han ido hace un rato las mujeres de esta casa para
que las dieras noticias de Gaspar.

(Pedro, que apenas puede tenerse en pie, llega con trabajo hasta una silla y se deja caer en ella pasándose la mano por la frente.)

CIPRIANO ¿Estás malo?

MARCELA ¡Virgen Santísima! ¡Viene *herío!*

PEDRO *(A Cipriano con ironía.)* ¡Gracias! No estoy malo: la prisa por venir al pueblo me hizo tomar el tren apenas salí del vapor. *(Con mucha fatiga.)* Esto me ha cansado; pero . . . ya pasará. *(Marcela y Cipriano se miran asustados de la transformación de Pedro.)* ¡Acércate *(a Marcela)*: he venido, como ves, con mucho trabajo! ¡mucho! *pa* que me cumplas tu palabra.

MARCELA *(Con resignación.)* Y te la cumpliré.

PEDRO *(A Cipriano, con ironía.)* ¿De eso hablábais cuando yo llegué?

CIPRIANO Hablábamos de ti, y nada tienes que criticar a ésta. Todo el pueblo te dirá que te guardó su palabra.

PEDRO Sí, me lo han dicho; pero os encuentro solos . . . y luego *paece* que mi presencia no os ha *gustao. (A Marcela que baja los ojos.)* ¿Por qué bajas la vista? ¡Ah! ¿Tan *cambiao* estoy que te asusto? ¡Acércate, acércate! y dime lo que has sufrido con mi ausencia.

MARCELA *(Acercándose penosamente.)* Me dan miedo tus palabras.

PEDRO No, mis palabras, no; es tu conciencia, tu proceder . . .

MARCELA *(Cogiéndole de la mano.)* Te juro que sólo he *pensao* en ti, que sólo deseé que volvieras; pero . . . como te vi . . . así . . . como has *venío* ¡tan! . . .

PEDRO *(Levantándose lentamente. Con amargura.)* Comprendo . . . Como he venido . . . *(Acercándose más y cogiéndola por un brazo.)* Como he venido . . . ¿qué te choca? Eso es lo más corriente. Se va a la guerra . . . como nosotros fuimos, jóvenes, fuertes, dichosos; ¡y luego! . . . unos no vuelven *(con pena)* como Gaspar.

CIPRIANO   ¡Gaspar!

MARCELA   ¡¡Ha muerto!!

PEDRO   *(Sin contestar continúa.)* Y otros vienen como yo; *(con mucha rabia.)* ¡Así! (Se arranca la venda y aparece con la cabeza y la frente desfiguradas por una gran cicatriz. Cipriano retrocede y Marcela se deja caer tapándose la cara. Pedro sigue, riendo nerviosamente.)* ¡Así!

Telón lento.

La escena representa el portal de una casa de pueblo (la de la tía Petra). En el fondo una puerta que da al campo. A la derecha entrada a una habitación. A la izquierda entrada a la cocina. Sillas, bancos y mesa de madera. Algunos aperos de labranza. Al levantarse el telón, la Rubia y Marcela doblan unas sábanas que sacarán de un cesto donde está la colada.

ESCENA PRIMERA

LA RUBIA Y MARCELA

(Las dos con aire triste.)

RUBIA — *Pa* mí que a Pedro le trastorna la *enfermedá.* ¡Vaya una manía! Ya lleva dos días en el pueblo y *naide* ha *lograo* verle.

MARCELA — ¡Figúrate! *Tó* cuanto he hecho por hablarle . . . como si no. Si a mí no me *quié* ver porque se imagine . . . aún lo comprendo; pero a la tía Petra que sabe que está loca por su hijo . . . y a ti . . .

RUBIA — Pues *na;* lo único que hemos *podío* averiguar por su tío que le vio ayer, y le ha *preguntao,* es que Gaspar estaba con una *hería* leve y que así que *puea* vendrá.

MARCELA — *(Aparte.)* ¡Pobre tía Petra! si supiese . . . *(Alto.)* No querrá veros hasta tener otras noticias. Aguardará alguna carta de Cuba.

RUBIA — Sí; eso ha dicho. *(Suspirando.)* ¡En qué manos estará el pobre! porque cuando sabe una que andan buenos, malo es tenerlos *alejaos;* pero en fin, se *pué* una conformar. En cambio no hay *resinación* si piensas que está enfermo y mal *atendío*, pues habiendo muchos no les *puén* cuidar bien aunque tengan *voluntá.*

(Han concluido de doblar la ropa. La Rubia coge el cesto de la colada, entrando con él en la habitación de la derecha. Después pasa a la cocina.)

ESCENA II

MARCELA

MARCELA   *(Se sienta pensativa. Hablando como para sí.)* ¡Paece mentira que se *puea* cambiar tanto! ¡Me asusta! Quiero tenerle compasión y me da miedo; le miro a la cara *pa* encontrar aquella alegría, aquellos ojos que brillaban más que el sol y veo otro de *caráter* más serio, más enjuto ¡tan amarillo! . . . Y sus ojos . . . *(Llora.)* ¡Oh! No, no *(con desesperación)* no podré cumplirle mi palabra.

ESCENA III

MARCELA, ALCALDE

ALCALDE   ¡Hola muchacha! ¿Y éstas? *(Señalando a la cocina.)*

MARCELA   La tía Petra se fue a llevar unas velas al *Santísmo, pa* que las noticias que traiga Pedro sean buenas.

ALCALDE   ¡Pobres mujeres! Yo no sé cómo decírselo. Ya, a fin de prepararlas, las conté . . .

MARCELA   Sí; lo de la *hería.* No saben tampoco que yo he visto a Pedro. Como él nos mandó a Cipriano y a mí que nos callásemos . . .

ALCALDE   Justo; *pa* darles la noticia poco a poco; aunque yo creo que ahora la encerrona de mi sobrino es por otra causa; y hasta que no esté un poco más sobre sí, no *quié* hablar con *naide.*

MARCELA   ¿Y cómo sigue?

ALCALDE   El infeliz no se conforma: *ca* vez está más *desesperao.* Me *paece* que tendrás *marío pa* poco tiempo. ¡Quiá! No se cura. ¡Si *tié* una tos! . . . ¡Pobrecillo! ¡Cualquiera le conoce! El mozo más *acabao* del pueblo cuando se fue ¡y ahora! . . . *(Marcela enjugándose los ojos se acerca a la puerta.)* ¡Qué! ¿viene alguien?

MARCELA   No . . . pensé . . . ¿Y qué *ice* Pedro de mí?

ALCALDE   Ni esto. *(Haciendo sonar con los dientes la uña del dedo pulgar.)*

MARCELA   *(Siempre mirando a fuera. Aparte.)* Ahí va Cipriano con ésa . . . Como es tan señorito *tóas* le quieren.

ALCALDE   Voy a ver a la Rubia.

MARCELA   *(Aparte.)* Y desde que Pedro ha *venío* no se acerca a hablarme.

ALCALDE   ¿Y qué le voy a decir? *(Pausa. Tomando una resolución.)* La diré que la *hería* es un poco más grave, que . . . no sé cómo diablos . . . *(Entra en la cocina. Marcela le sigue, siempre mirando a la calle. Entornan la puerta.)*

ESCENA IV

PEDRO

PEDRO   *(Entra con la venda en la cabeza y se sienta muy cansado enjugándose el sudor. Pausa.)* ¡Maldita suerte! ¿Por qué no había yo de ser el muerto? Así no tendría Marcela que pensar tanto. *(Levantándose.)* Me han dicho que aquí la encontraré. *(Llama con los nudillos en la puerta de la cocina.)*

ESCENA V

MARCELA, PEDRO

MARCELA   *(Saliendo. Sorprendida.)* ¡Ah! ¿eres tú?

PEDRO   Sí: ¡qué! ¿te disgusta hallarme? Ya sabes que tengo
               necesidá de ver a la tía Petra y decirla cómo murió
               Gaspar.

MARCELA   Aún no ha vuelto: si *quiés* entrar, *áhi tiés* a la Rubia y
               a tu tío Roque.

PEDRO   No: *¡Pa* qué empezar tan pronto! La aguardaré aquí.
               (Se sienta. Marcela se queda de pie apoyada en una silla.)
               ¡Qué felices son los muertos!

MARCELA   ¿Felices? ¡Pobre Gaspar!

PEDRO   Pues qué ¿te figuras que no me cambiaría por él?
               ¿Qué más *pué* pedir un hombre si no morir en el
               campo, batiéndose, y que luego le lloren de *verdá?*
               ¿Crees por si acaso que es mejor venir *pa* que le
               reciban a uno como a la misma peste? *(Exaltándose.)*
               ¿Te figuras que yo peno por el cacho de cabeza que
               me falta? No: lo que me duele ahora es que la bala
               no se me *hubiea llevao* los dos ojos, porque así no
               hubiese visto la cara que has puesto al encontrarme
               tan *cambiao*. Y mira: en *tó* el camino se me ocurrió
               quejarme de mi suerte; pero cuando vi lo que pen-
               sabas—porque lo sé como si lo viera—entonces he
               renegao de la campaña y de los que allí me hicieron
               ir; y me he vuelto tan malo, tan malo, que aplastaría
               a *tós* los que tienen *salú*.

MARCELA   No hables así. ¿*Quiés* que yo esté como antes, y siem-
               pre que te oigo *paece* que me echas una maldición?

PEDRO   No; a ti, no, que no *tiés* la culpa. Eres mujer, y basta.
               Como *tóas*. Yo creí que me querías y lo que te gusta-
               ba era mi *juventú*, mi fuerza—que no la había igual
               en el pueblo;—y . . .—ahora ya puedo decirlo—que

te halagaba ser la novia del buen mozo, como *tós* me llamaban. Pero aquello acabó: ya no hay *juventú*—o como si no la hubiera—ya no hay hermosura, ni fuerza, ni gracia, ni bríos, ni *ná*. *Tó* ha *cambiao* menos el corazón, y como ése no se enseña, no lo estimas: tú no *pués* ver más que esta facha asquerosa adonde vino a parar aquél de quien tan orgullosa estabas. *Tó, tó* ha *mudao:* ya no hay aquí más que un depósito de enfermedades *rodeao* de botellas y píldoras; podredumbre por fuera y por dentro, porque más *podría* que la piel tengo la sangre. ¡Ah! Si yo *hubiea* allí *pensao* esto, no tendrías el disgusto de verme . . . *(Marcela llora.)* ¡Y *quiés* que no envidie a Gaspar! ¿Te *paece* mejor *pa* un hombre morir entre sábanas *repunando* a *tós* y que en cuanto acabe lo cojan como a cosa mala y lo metan en el hoyo, sin una lágrima, antes al contrario, como el que se quita un peso de encima? ¿Te *paece* mejor eso, que allí en el campo, al aire, al sol, en plena *salú* quedar *atravesao* por una bala y que te entierren tus compañeros, entre otros valientes, no como enfermo, *podrío* antes de morir, sino como sano aun después de muerto; no dejando una procesión de medicinas, sino un reguero de sangre joven, vigorosa, caliente *toavía*; no llevando en el semblante la marca del sufrimiento, sino del entusiasmo: y en vez de escuchar los gimoteos de cuatro viejas, oír la música que toca el paso de ataque; y en lugar de los tristes latinajos del cura, que sea la voz del cañón la que te despida? Los que acaban como acabaré yo, hasta después de *enterraos* se les huye y se queman sus ropas; mientras lo que ha *sío* de los otros, se guarda como reliquia; que así traigo yo *pa* la tía Petra el escapulario que llevaba Gaspar, lleno de sangre; pero sangre del que mataron, no del que se murió; por eso no repugna. Como Gaspar deben morir los dichosos. Como yo, acaban los malditos. *(Se cubre el rostro con las manos. Marcela cae a sus pies.)*

MARCELA   Perdóname, perdóname: ¡yo no sé lo que *ices*, pero te oigo como a Dios!

PEDRO   *(Sin oírla.)* ¡Y me cuentan entre los vivos! ¡Y no merezco la gloria de haber muerto por la patria! Porque a esto no le llaman morir.

MARCELA   Tú te curarás, te curarás y nos casaremos.

PEDRO   *(Levantándose. Con dulzura.)* No; no me curaré, ni nos casaremos: me moriré; ya sé que voy a morir, y ¡Dios haga que sea pronto! ¡Pero hasta entonces . . . qué días! *(Con energía.)* No, no; ¿qué *necesidá* tengo de sufrir?

MARCELA   *(Asustada.)* Pedro ¡por Dios! Yo te cuidaré.

PEDRO   *(Rechazándola.)* ¡Qué culpa *tiés* tú *pa* que vengas a pagarlo! No llevaba razón al quejarme de ti. *(Riendo nerviosamente.)* ¡Quería que me amaras cuando debo asustarte!

ESCENA VI

DICHOS, ALCALDE

ALCALDE   Ya se lo he dicho a la Rubia: cuando venga la madre tendremos otra escena. *(A Marcela.)* Entra a consolarla. *(Marcela obedece. Pedro queda indiferente.)*

ESCENA VII

ALCALDE, PEDRO, CIPRIANO

ALCALDE   ¿Cómo te encuentras? Yo se lo he dicho *pa* evitarte un mal rato: al fin, siempre se apura uno . . .

PEDRO   *¡Verdá!* Luego daré a la tía Petra lo que a Gaspar recogí, y mañana me marcho.

CIPRIANO	*(Que ha entrado hace un momento.)* ¿Que te marchas?
ALCALDE	¡Muchacho!
PEDRO	Sí, sí; desde que llegué estoy mucho peor: ya lo ve *usté*.
ALCALDE	¿A dónde vas a ir . . . enfermo?
PEDRO	*(Con triste sonrisa.)* ¿A dónde va un enfermo? Al hospital.
ALCALDE	No lo consentiremos tus tíos: ¡pues hombre, no *paece* sino que eres de la Inclusa!
PEDRO	No lo digo por eso, sino que allí hay más médicos y . . .
ALCALDE	Bien, bien; ya hablaremos de eso.
CIPRIANO	¿Qué? ¿Piensas irte al hospital.
PEDRO	*(Mirándole.)* Allí estaré hasta que . . . me cure. *(Riendo.)*
CIPRIANO	¿Y? . . .
PEDRO	¿Marcela? Ya lo sabe. *(Se sienta.)*

ESCENA VIII

DICHOS, TÍA PETRA

PETRA	*(Entrando.)* ¡Dios oiga mis rezos! *(Al ver a Pedro le mira un instante asustada.)* ¡Jesús! ¿qué es esto? *(Pedro se levanta.)* ¿Tú? ¿Eres Pedro . . . tú?
PEDRO	*(Con siniestra sonrisa.)* Sí; yo soy Pedro, yo. *(Aparte.)* ¡Lo mismo que los otros!
PETRA	Dispensa . . . pero al pronto no te había *conocío* . . . como . . .
PEDRO	Como los demás.

ALCALDE	*(A la tía Petra.)* Vamos, vamos a dentro. *Ahi* está la Rubia y hablaremos: éste se fatiga . . . Ya me ha *contao tó* lo que sabe de Gaspar; luego entrará él.
	(La va llevando hacia la cocina. Entran allí, ella siempre mirando a Pedro, como interrogándole con la vista. Al Alcalde hace signos como para persuadirla de que él le contará todo lo que sabe.)

ESCENA IX

PEDRO, CIPRIANO

(Pedro se deja caer anonadado. Cipriano le contempla con lástima.—Silencio.)

CIPRIANO	¿Te encuentras peor?
PEDRO	Sí, desde que vine; por eso me marcho.
CIPRIANO	¿Al hospital?
PEDRO	¡Claro! ¿Tengo yo madre que me cuide?
CIPRIANO	Tienes parientes, amigos . . .
PEDRO	*(Con sorna.)* ¿Tú?
CIPRIANO	*(Con energía.)* Yo.
	(Pedro le mira. Cipriano sostiene la mirada.)
PEDRO	Puede que tengas razón.
CIPRIANO	No lo dudes. Es verdad que antes te aborrecía. Ya ves . . . a un hombre no se le quita la novia así . . . impunemente. Además, eras . . . , en fin, que te tenía rabia; pero ahora que te veo enfermo y desgraciado, antes me dejaré matar que decir a Marcela buenos ojos tienes.

PEDRO	*(Con amargura.)* ¡Comprendo; ya no soy temible! ¡Quién lo habría de pensar! ¿Tú tenerme lástima? ¡Ja, ja! ¡Eso más!
CIPRIANO	*(Con sinceridad.)* Si pudiera volverte a como estabas antes, aunque no lo creas . . .
PEDRO	*(Alargándole la mano.)* Te creo; pero me hice tan malo, que me da tirria creerte. *(Con rabia.)* Quisiera matar a alguno, a muchos, a *tós* los que son felices. *(Llora cubriéndose la cara con las manos.)*
CIPRIANO	*(Acercándose y dándole cariñosamente en el hombro.)* No tengas esos pensamientos: eres joven, te curarás . . .
PEDRO	No *quieo* curarme. ¿Crees que puedo sufrir que me *tratís* con lástima? Me gustaba más cuando tú me aborrecías. ¿Ya no valgo ni *pa* tu enemigo? *(Cada vez más excitado y levantándose.)* Ya sé lo que pensáis: que estoy muy malo, que acabaré pronto, y mientras tanto, tú y Marcela me fingís compasión y cariño, *pa* que no digan . . . Después . . . *(cambiando de tono)* perdóname; ¡no sé lo que me pasa! La desgracia me ha vuelto malo. ¡Ah! Tú no sabes lo que yo sufro. Hay ratos en que os mataría a *tós*, y otras veces os quiero, lloro como un chico y sólo pienso en desaparecer *pa* que seáis felices.
CIPRIANO	¡Cálmate: todo eso lo hace la enfermedad: estás excitado!
PEDRO	*(Conteniéndose.)* *Tiés* razón: eso debe de ser por la *enfermedá*. Sin duda la bala me ha hecho aquí *(señalando a la cabeza)* mucho trastorno.
CIPRIANO	Y tú te pones peor con tomar así las cosas.
PEDRO	*(Estrechándole las manos.)* Te había *juzgao* mal. Después de *tó*, razones tenías *pa* no quererme. *(Rechazándole.)* Pero no, no puedo creerte; tu cariño me *paece* una burla, y el suyo no *esiste*; la doy miedo y asco.

CIPRIANO   ¿Otra vez? No hablemos de eso.

PEDRO   Sí; de eso tenemos que hablar: ¿de qué quieres que
            hable? ¿Me juras que Marcela no te ha *dao* oídos?

CIPRIANO   *(Vivamente.)* Te juro que Marcela te fue consecuente
            y se piensa casar contigo.

PEDRO   *(Con amargura.)* ¡Buen marido la destinas!

CIPRIANO   El que ella ha elegido.

PEDRO   ¿Qué? ¿Ya no la *quiés* tú? *(Cipriano baja la cabeza sin
            responder. Pedro, después de contemplarle un momento y
            como queriendo adivinar lo que aquél piensa.)* Mira:
            ella es *honrá;* tú eres bueno; os *tenís* afición . . . *quieo*
            casaros.

CIPRIANO   ¡Bah!

PEDRO   *(Con intención.)* Escucha: si yo me muero en . . . el
            hospital, en cualquier parte, y *quiés* dejarme tranqui-
            lo *pa* ir al otro barrio, prométeme que te casarás con
            Marcela. Es generosa y estaba dispuesta a sacrificarse
            por mí. *(Cipriano vuelve la cabeza.)* Pues yo la quiero
            dar un buen marido. *(Se enjuga el sudor de la frente.
            Aparte y con desesperación.)* ¡No protesta! Así será, y yo
            no puedo impedirlo. *(Alto y con ironía.)* Cuando me
            haya muerto procura recoger ésta *(señalando a la
            cruz)*, porque la misma causa que me la puso en el
            pecho es la que te hace a ti dichoso. *(Con mucho calor.)*
            ¡Ya ves! ¡a cambio de mi *salú*, de mi fuerza! . . . ¡de la
            familia que esperaba hacer! . . . ¡a cambio de mi vida
            toda . . . me pusieron aquí esta . . . insignia! *(Con sar-
            casmo.)* ¡Imagina tú si vale el regalo de boda que *quieo*
            hacerte!

            *(Se deja caer cubriéndose el rostro con desesperación.
            Cipriano le mira con lástima.)*

CIPRIANO   *(Aparte.)* ¡Dios lo quiere!

ESCENA X

DICHOS. MARCELA, PETRA, RUBIA Y ALCALDE.

MARCELA   *(Muy triste.)* Ya lo saben.

CIPRIANO   ¿Qué han hecho?

MARCELA   Ya te *pués* figurar: a la tía Petra le dio una congoja.
            ¡Mucho será que no le cueste la vida! La Rubia se ha
            quedao como *alelá.*

PETRA   *(Saliendo.)* ¡Pedro! ¿Dónde está Pedro?

PEDRO   *(Adelantándose.)* ¡Aquí, tía Petra, aquí!

PETRA   *(Se le echa al cuello llorando.)* ¡Hijo mío!

RUBIA   *(Cogiendo a Pedro las manos.)* Tú ¿le viste morir?

PEDRO   No; le vi muerto, con pena, y ahora le tengo envidia.
            *(Cipriano y Marcela cambian una mirada de lástima a
            Pedro; éste la sorprende. Aparte.)* ¡Se miran!

PETRA   Cuéntame *tó* lo que sepas . . . Di, ¿sufrió mucho?

PEDRO   *Ná* de sufrimiento. Murió como tantos otros en
            medio de la pelea. Un balazo aquí *(señalando al pecho)*
            y *pax christi. (Hablando como para sí.)* Se llevó sano el
            cuerpo y *partío* el corazón: otros *(mirando a Marcela)*
            llevan *destrozao* el cuerpo y sano el corazón.
            ¡Cuestión de suerte!

PETRA   Pero ¿cuándo le viste?

PEDRO   Apenas cayó, y fue por una *casualidá*, porque a mí
            me tocó en seguida. Gaspar estaba guardando un
            ingenio con un teniente de la compañía. Aquella
            mañana nuestro coronel supo que andaba cerca el
            enemigo, y sospechándose que iban a quemar la
            finca, nos mandó formar (sin tiempo ni aun de
            comer) y al ingenio nos encaminamos. *(Entusiasmán-
            dose.) Efetivamente*; pronto vimos unas llamaradas
            que no *paecía* sino que *tó* Cuba estaba ardiendo. ¡A

ellos! gritaron los jefes; y forzando la marcha, en un santiamén nos pusimos a tiro de fusil cuando los insurrectos casi acababan con los que defendían la posesión. Al ver aquello, y más cuando supimos que eran del regimiento los que íbamos a socorrer— porque aunque *paezca* mentira, los del regimiento son como una familia, y se *tién* más ley, y se baten más contentos estando todos a una—pues, como iba diciendo . . . *(Se pasa la mano por la frente.)*

ALCALDE   No te fatigues. *(Aparte a la Rubia.)* ¡Está muy malo!

RUBIA   Peor está el otro.

PEDRO   Acabó la pelea cuerpo a cuerpo; ya no veíamos; la cuestión era matar; el caído servía de estorbo a los demás; pero no teníamos tiempo de retirarlos. En esto vi a mi capitán que estaba en el suelo, y unos cuantos negros, con los ojos y los dientes más blancos que el papel, que iban a machetearle. Aquello fue cosa de un minuto. Yo no sé cómo me las compuse; empecé ciego, con *toa* la sangre que me sonaba en la cabeza y ¡zas! . . . a derecha, ¡zas! a izquierda . . . cada golpe daba en duro. Por fin aquello acabó y vimos lo que había *resultao* . . . ¡Pa qué cansar¡ que me batí bien, salvé a mi capitán, me abrazó llorando . . .

ALCALDE   ¿Eras tú ese valiente que dice el periódico? ¿Fue la *ación* del 10 de *Otubre?*

PEDRO   La misma.

PETRA   Pero ¿y Gaspar? *(Pedro hace señas de que le dejen respirar.)*

MARCELA   *(A Cipriano.)* ¡Era él!

CIPRIANO   ¿Y esa cruz?

PEDRO   Por esa *ación* me la dieron. El enemigo deshecho, seguía batiéndose de huída; algunas balas silbaban aún. Yo busqué entre los heridos a Gaspar, después de haberle *buscao* entre los sanos. No estaba. ¡Entonces fui a los muertos!

PETRA   ¡Hijo de mi alma!

PEDRO   Allí lo encontré. Según me dijo el médico, debió morir sin penar, como si un rayo le *hubiá cogío.* Yo le registré *pa* traerme un recuerdo. Aquí está lo que llevaba. *(Va sacando lo que dice.)* Este dinero, una petaca y el escapulario de la Patrona que *usté* le puso. Está con manchas de sangre.

PETRA   *(Como loca.)* Si yo *hubiea estao* en tu lugar . . . *(al escapulario)* no le llegarían las balas. *(Lo cubre de besos.)*

RUBIA   *(Con desesperación.)* ¡Sí, béselo usted!

PETRA   *(Con desdén.)* ¡Beso las manchas! *(Tía Petra y Rubia lloran abrazadas sin hacer ya caso a lo que dice Pedro.)*

MARCELA   *(A Pedro.)* ¿Pero . . . tú?

PEDRO   Yo caí también cuando ya casi no se oía un tiro y creía haber salvado el pellejo. No sé lo que pasó . . . Al darme cuenta estaba en el hospital . . . *¿Pa* qué voy a contar esto? A nadie le importa. *(Con indiferencia.)* Mi capitán me regaló la cruz; cuando pude venir me acompañó al vapor; hice el viaje entre otros inválidos, llegué a Cádiz, y sin descansar—que la impaciencia no me dejaba—me fui al tren . . . y llegué al pueblo *(con amargura)* como *ustés* han visto.

RUBIA   ¡Qué ajenas estábamos, cuando leíamos el papel, de que traía la noticia!

PEDRO   ¡Cómo! ¿Sabíais?

ALCALDE   No; teníamos un periódico que cuenta la *ación,* y como era vuestro regimiento, nos supusimos que estaríais en ella.

PETRA   ¡Hijo de mi corazón! *(Al Alcalde.)* ¿Y por qué no ponen en los papeles los nombres de los que mueren *pa* que lo sepan sus madres?

CIPRIANO   *(A Marcela.)* Esto es muy triste. Tiene razón.

PEDRO   *(Mirando a Marcela y Cipriano.)* ¡Se hablan bajo! ¡*Toa*
                la sangre se me sube a la cabeza!

ALCALDE   *Tó* aquello que leíamos lo hizo éste. *(Señalando a
                Pedro.)* Ya presumía yo que sería alguno del pueblo.

PETRA   ¡Tres meses que me lo mataron y yo sin saberlo!

CIPRIANO   Y si no es por Pedro, ¡sabe Dios cuándo hubiéramos
                tenido la noticia!

MARCELA   Las malas no corren prisa.

PETRA   *(Encarándose con Marcela.)* ¡Que no corren prisa!
                Pues sábete que las entrañas en que lo he *tenío* se me
                hacen fuego de pensar que en estos tres meses no lo
                he *llorao.*

ALCALDE   En aquellas quince bajas estaba; no nos figurábamos
                la satisfactoria noticia. (Subrayado.)

PETRA   ¡Quince bajas! Como si no *tuvían* nombres. ¡Pues a
                fe que cuando vinieron a llevárselo al *mataero* bien
                sabían cómo se llamaba! *(La da una congoja. Marcela
                y la Rubia, sosteniéndola, entran en la cocina. Después la
                siguen Cipriano y el Alcalde. Éste hace señas a Pedro para
                que entre también.)*

ESCENA XI

PEDRO *(solo)*

PEDRO   *(Mirando hacia dentro y con amargura.)* ¡Entrar! ¡*Pa*
                verlos juntos, tan jóvenes, tan sanos y siempre
                hablándose a media voz! No saben ellos lo que sien-
                to aquí *(dándose en la frente)* ni aquí *(golpeando el
                pecho).* Si lo supieran, temblarían. *(Un golpe de tos le
                interrumpe. Cambiando bruscamente de tono y hablán-*

dose a sí.) ¡Ja, ja! ¿Quieres que tengan miedo de ti, cacho de guiñapo? ¡Miedo . . . ! Será de contagiarse . . . *(Pausa.)* ¡Oh, no *pueo* sufrir más! *(Llora en silencio. Óyese dentro la voz de Marcela.—Encogiéndose de hombros, con ironía.)* Ni siquiera me echan de menos. ¡Como ya está allí el otro . . . ! *(Vuelve a acercarse a la puerta y vuelve a detenerse.)* No: he dicho que no quiero verlos *(con energía)* y no los veré . . . ¡Adiós! ¡Adiós! *(Va a salir.)*

ESCENA XII

PEDRO Y CIPRIANO

CIPRIANO   *(Desde la puerta de la cocina.)* ¿Pedro?

PEDRO   *(Deteniéndose, pero sin volver la cabeza.)* ¿Qué?

CIPRIANO   ¿A dónde vas?

PEDRO   A . . . a . . . *(con intención)* a descansar.

CIPRIANO   Te acompañaré hasta tu casa *(mirando a la puerta de la cocina.)* No entres ahí; pasarás un mal rato . . .

PEDRO   No; ¡no entraré! *Pués* estar tranquilo. *(Se sienta.)*

CIPRIANO   ¿No te marchabas?

PEDRO   *(Con ironía.)* Sí; pero no tengas tanta prisa . . . *(Una tos seca le interrumpe.)*

ESCENA XIII

DICHOS, MARCELA, despúes TODOS

MARCELA   *(Acercándose a Cipriano y mirando a Pedro, que está desencajado y apenas puede respirar.)* ¿Qué ha *pasao* aquí?

CIPRIANO   *(Acercándose a ella le dice por lo bajo.)* Esto se acaba por
                    momentos.

MARCELA   *¡Desgraciao . . . ! (Para sí.) ¡Paece* mentira que éste sea
                    aquél . . . !

PEDRO   *(Levanta la cabeza, los ve juntos, y haciendo un esfuerzo*
                    supremo, saca una navaja de las que usan en los pueblos y
                    se acerca con sigilo hacia donde ellos están hablando bajo.)
                    ¡No; no te casarás! *(Cuando va a herir a Cipriano, le*
                    repite la tos. Marcela y Cipriano se vuelven. Marcela da
                    un grito. Cipriano procura desarmarle sin hacerle daño.
                    Hay un momento de lucha. Pedro vacila; luego cae.
                    Cipriano y Marcela se arrodillan para levantarle. Pedro
                    se incorpora, extiende la mano hacia ellos y en las ansias
                    de los últimos momentos exclama:) ¡Maldit . . . !
                    (Marcela da un grito y se tapa la cara con las manos.
                    Pedro se interrumpe, la mira un instante y dice:)
                    ¡No! . . . ¡no! . . . ¡malditas . . . las balas que no saben
                    cumplir cuando las mandan matar! *(Cae muerto y al*
                    caer, la cruz se le desprende del pecho y queda en el suelo.
                    Marcela retrocede horrorizada.)

CIPRIANO   *(Levantándose.)* ¡Dios lo ha hecho!

ALCALDE   *(Entrando seguido de la Rubia y la tía Petra.)* ¿Qué es
                    esto? . . . ¡Pedro!

CIPRIANO   ¡Sí! ¡Sí! ¡Todo ha concluido! *(Las mujeres asustadas se*
                    quedan en la puerta. El Alcalde, al acercarse a Pedro,
                    pisa sin querer la cruz que está en el suelo, y la recoge.)
                    ¡Démela usted! ¡Él me la dejó! . . . ¡Quiero guardar
                    yo la cruz del soldado valiente.

ALCALDE   *(Dándosela.)* La cruz del *soldao* es una cruz de piedra.

                    Telón

BIBLIOGRAPHY

Journals

Blanco y negro (Madrid)
La Ilustración Española y Americana (Madrid)
Madrid Cómico (Madrid)
La Política de España en Filipinas (Madrid)
La Solidaridad (Barcelona) 15 February 1889-November 1889; (Madrid) November 1889-1895.

Periodicals

La Armonía (Madrid)
El Archivo Católico (Barcelona)
La Conciencia Libre (Valencia)
El Globo (Madrid)
El Heraldo de Madrid
El Imparcial (Madrid)
El Liberal (Madrid)
El Nuevo Régimen (Madrid)
El País (Madrid)
El Progreso (Madrid)
La Reforma (Madrid)
El Resumen (Madrid)
La Semana Católica de Barcelona
El Socialista (Madrid)
El Tiempo (Madrid)

Books and Articles

Alas, Leopoldo. *Pipá*. Madrid: Fernando Fe, 1886.
_____. "El Rana." *El Imparcial*, 24 February 1896.

_____. *Teresa, Avecilla, El hombre de los estrenos*. Introduction by Leonardo Romero. Madrid: Castalia, 1975.

Altamira, Rafael. "Elogio del fanatismo." *El Imparcial*, 29 March 1897.

Álvarez Ángulo, Tomás. *Memorias de un hombre sin importancia (1878-1961)*. Madrid: Aguilar, 1962.

Anderson, Benedict. "Hard to Imagine: A Puzzle in the History of Philippine Nationalism." In *Cultures and Texts: Representations of Philippine Society*, edited by Raul Pertierra and Eduardo F. Ugarte, 81-118. Diliman, Quezon City: University of the Philippines Press (distributed outside the Philippines by the University of Hawaii Press), 1994,

_____. *Imagined Communities: Reflections on the Origin and Spead of Nationalism*. 2d ed. London: Verso, 1991.

Antón y Ferrándiz, Manuel. "Antropología." In *Exposición de Filipinas: Colección de artículos publicados en* El Globo, *diario ilustrado, político, científico y literario*, 83-103. Madrid: Establecimiento Tipográfico de *El Globo*, 1887.

_____. "Razas y naciones de Europa." Speech read at the Universidad Central at the beginning of the academic year 1895-1896. Madrid: Imprenta Colonial, 1895.

Arimón, Santiago, and Alejo García Góngora. *El código del teatro*. Madrid: Centro de Publicaciones Jurídicas, 1912.

Balfour, Sebastian. *The End of the Spanish Empire 1898-1923*. Oxford: Clarendon Press, 1997.

_____. *El fin del Imperio español*. Barcelona: Crítica, 1997.

Barrantes, Vicente. *El teatro tagalo*. Madrid: M. G. Hernández, 1889.

Becerro de Bengoa, Ricardo. "Por ambos mundos: terapéutica social del Emperador de Alemania." *La Ilustración Española y Americana* (30 May 1898): 386.

Benavides Gómez, Domingo. *Democracia y cristianismo en la España de la Restauración (1875-1931)*. Madrid: Editora Nacional, 1978.

Bernstein, Iver. *The New York City Draft Riots: Their Significance for American Society and Politics in the Age of the Civil War*. New York: Oxford University Press, 1990.

Bizcarrondo, Marta. "Entre Cuba y España: el dilema del autonomismo, 1878-1898." *Cuadernos Hispanoamericanos* 577-78 (1998): 171-98.

Blount, James H. *The American Occupation of the Philippines 1898-1912*. New York: Putnam, 1913.

Blumentritt, Ferdinand. *El "Noli me tangere" de Rizal juzgado por el Pr. F. Blumentritt*. Barcelona: Imprenta Ibérica de Francisco Fossas, 1889.

_____. *Las razas del archpiélago filipino*. Madrid: Fortanet, 1890.

Boyd, Carolyn P. *Historia Patria*. New Haven: Yale University Press, 1997.

Brau, Salvador. *Historia de Puerto Rico*. Río Piedras: Editorial Edil, 1983.

Burguete, Ricardo. *¡La guerra! Cuba (Diario de un testigo)*. Barcelona, Buenos Aires, México: Editorial Maucci, 1902.

_____. *¡La guerra! Filipinas (Memorias de un herido)*. Barcelona: Editorial Maucci, 1902.

Caballero, y Martínez, Ricardo. *España en Cuba*. Ferrol: Pita, 1896.

Cabana, Francesc. *La burguesía catalana: una aproximación histórica*. Barcelona: Proa, 1996.

Cabrera, Lydia. *La sociedad secreta Abakuá narrada por viejos adeptos*. Miami: Ediciones CR, 1970.

Canals, Salvador. *El año teatral: crónicas y documentos, 1895-1896*. Madrid: Establecimiento Tipográfico *El Nacional*, 1896.

Cañamaque y Jiménez, Francisco de Paulo. *Las islas Filipinas (De todo un poco)*. Madrid: Fernando Fe, 1880.

Canel, Eva. *Lo que vi en Cuba*. Habana: Imprenta *La Universal*, 1916.

_____. *La mulata*. Barcelona: Tipografía *La Ilustración*, 1891.

Carr, Raymond. *Spain 1808-1939*. Oxford: Clarendon, 1966.

Castelar, Emilio. *Historia de un corazón* and *Ricardo*. 2 vols. Madrid: Librería de Locadio López, 1871 [?].

_____. *Miscelánea de historia, de religión, de arte y de política*. Madrid: A. de San Martín/Agustín Jubera, 1874.

Cayuela Fernández, José G. "El desastre colonial en la prensa madrileña." *Cuadernos Hispanoamericanos* 445 (1987): 18-38.

Chápuli Navarro, Antón. *Siluetas y matices: galería filipina*. Prologue by Javier Gómez de la Serna. Madrid: La Viuda de Minuesa de los Ríos, 1894.

Coates, Austin. *Rizal. Philippine Nationalist and Martyr*. New York: Oxford University Press, 1968.

Código Penal y Ley de Enjuiciamiento Criminal para las Islas Filipinas. Madrid: Centro Editorial de Góngora, 1896.

Conangla, Josep. *Memorias de mi juventud en Cuba: un soldado en la guerra separatista (1895-1898)*, edited and introduction by Joaquín Roy. Barcelona: Ediciones Península, 1998.

Corominas, Pere. *Diaris i records de Pere Corominas*. Vol. 1. *Els anys de joventut*. Barcelona: Curial, 1974.

Corwin, Arthur F. *Spain and the Abolition of Slavery in Cuba 1817-1886*. Austin, Tex.: Institute of Latin American Studies, 1967.

Cortés, Rufino. *¡A Cuba y viva España!* Sevilla: C. del Valle, 1895.

Costa, Joaquín. *Oligarquía y casticismo como la forma actual de gobierno en España.* Vol. 2. *Informes o testimonios.* Madrid: Ediciones de la Revista de Trabajo, 1975.

Costa S.J., Horacio de la, ed. and trans. *The Trial of Rizal* (W. E. Retana's transcription of the official Spanish documents). Manila: Ateneo de Manila University Press, 1996.

Cruz, Isagani R. *A Short History of Theatre in the Philippines.* Manila: De La Salle University Press, 1971.

Cuartero Escobés, Susana. "El nacionalismo independentista del Katipunan." In *Antes del Desastre: Orígenes y antecedentes de la crisis del 98,* edited by Juan Pablo Fusi and Antonio Niño, 225–34. Madrid: Universidad Complutense de Madrid, 1996.

Dardé, Carlos. "La vida política: elecciones y partidos." In *Vísperas del 98: Orígenes y antecedentes de la crisis del 98,* edited by Juan Pablo Fusi and Antonio Niño, 65-74. Madrid: Biblioteca Nueva, 1997.

Deleito y Piñuela, José. *Estampas del Madrid teatral fin de siglo.* Vol. 1. Madrid: Editorial *Saturnino Calleja,* 1946 [?].

_____. *Origen y apogeo del "género chico."* Madrid: Revista del Occidente, 1949.

Diamond, Catherine. "Quest for the Elusive Self: The Role of Contemporary Philippine Theatre in the Formation of Cultural Identity." *The Drama Review* 40, no. 1 (T149), (spring 1996): 141-69.

Díaz de la Quintana, Alberto. *Siluetas filipinas,* por Ximeno Ximénez [pseud.] ex-periodista de Filipinas. Madrid: Robles y compañía, 1887.

Diccionario de la literatura cubana. Vol. 2. Havana: Editorial Letras Cubanas, 1984.

Dirks, Nicholas, B., ed. *Colonialism and Culture.* Ann Arbor: University of Michigan Press, 1992.

Dolcet, M. *Muerte de Maceo.* Barcelona: Tipografía de F. Badía, 1897.

Durnerin, James. *Maura et Cuba. Politique coloniale d'un ministre libéral.* Besançon: Les Belles Lettres, 1978.

Ebersole, Alva. *La obra teatral de Luciano Francisco Comella.* Valencia: Albatros, 1985.

Echegaray, Miguel. *Gigantes y Cabezudos.* 7th ed. Madrid: R. Velasco, 1898.

Elizalde Pérez-Grueso, María Dolores. "Filipinas, 1898." *Revista de Occidente* 202-3 (1998): 224-49.

Elshtain, Jean Bethke. *Women and War.* New York: Basic Books, 1987.

Estrade, Paul. *La colonia cubana de París, 1895-1898: el combate patriótico de Betances y la solidaridad de los revolucionarios franceses.* Havana: Editorial de Ciencias Sociales, 1984.

Exposición de Filipinas: colección de artículos publicados en El Globo, *diario ilustrado, político, científico y literario.* Madrid: Establecimiento tipográfico de *El Globo,* a cargo de J. Salgado de Trigo, 1887.

Feced, Pablo. *Filipinas. Esbozos y pinceladas por Quioquiap.* Manila: Establecimiento Tipográfico de Ramírez y Compañía, 1888.

Fernández Almagro, M. *Historia política de la España contemporánea.* Vols. 1-3. Madrid: Alianza, 1968-1970.

_____. *En torno al 98: política y literatura.* Madrid: Ediciones Jordan, 1948.

Fernández Bastarreche, Fernando. "The Spanish Military from the Age of Disasters to the Civil War." In *Armed Forces in Spain Past and Present,* edited by Rafael Bañón Martínez and Thomas M. Barker, 213–47. Boulder: Columbia University Press, 1988.

Ferrer, Ada. "Rustic Men Civilized Nation: Race, Culture, and Contention on the Eve of Cuban Independence." *HAHR* 78, no. 4 (1998): 663-86.

_____. "To Make a Free Nation: Race and the Struggle for Independence in Cuba, 1868-1898." Ph.D. diss., University of Michigan, 1995.

Ferrer Benimeli, J. A. *Masonería española contemporánea.* Vol. 2. *Desde 1868 hasta nuestros días.* Madrid: Siglo Veintiuno, 1980.

_____, ed. *La masonería en la España del siglo XIX.* Vol. 2. Valladolid: Consejería de Educación y Cultura, 1987.

Ferrer de Couto, José. *Los negros en sus diversos estados y condiciones: tales como son, como se supone que son, y como deben ser.* New York: Imprenta de Hallet, 1864.

Feuer, A. B. *The Santiago Campaign of 1898: A Soldier's View of the Spanish-American War.* Westport, Conn.: Praeger, 1993.

Fialka, John J. *Hotel Warriors: Covering the Gulf War.* Washington, D.C.: Woodrow Wilson Center Press, 1991.

Figuero, Javier, and Carlos G. Santa Cecilia. *La España del desastre.* Barcelona: Plaza y Janés, 1997.

Filipinas: problema fundamental por un español de larga residencia en aquellas islas. Madrid: L. Aguado, 1891.

Fivel-Démoret, Sharon Romeo. "The Production and Consumption of Propaganda Literature: The Cuban Anti-Slavery Novel." *Bulletin of Hispanic Studies* 66 (1989): 1-12.

Foner, Eric. Review of *The Amistad Revolt and American Abolition* by Karen Zeinert. *New York Times Book Review,* 31 August 1997, 13.

Foner, Philip S. *Antonio Maceo: The "Bronze Titan" of Cuba's Struggle for Independence*. New York: Monthly Review Press, 1977.

Fox, Inman. *La invención de España: nacionalismo liberal e identidad nacional*. Madrid: Cátedra, 1997.

Fuente, Alejandro de la. "Race and Inequality in Cuba, 1899-1981." *Journal of Contemporary History* 30 (1995): 131-68.

Fusi, Juan Pablo, and Antonio Niño, eds. *Antes del Desastre: orígenes y antecedentes del 98*. Madrid: Universidad Complutense de Madrid, 1997.

_____. *Vísperas del 98*. Madrid: Biblioteca Nueva, 1997.

Gallego, Tesifonte. *La insurrección cubana*. Madrid: Imprenta Central de los Ferrocarriles, 1897.

García-Barzanallana, Manuel. *La masonización de Filipinas*. Barcelona: Librería y Tipógrafía Católica, 1897. Reprinted in W. E. Retana, *Archivo del bibliófilo filipino*. Vol. 4. Madrid: Imprenta de la Viuda de M. Minuesa de los Ríos, 1897.

Gasset, Rafael. "Claros en el horizonte." *El Imparcial*, 24 November 1895.

_____. "Desde La Habana: primeras impresiones." *El Imparcial*, 7 November 1895.

Go, Fe Susan. "Documenting the Chinese Filipinos. Archival Sources." *Kinaadman* 20 (1998): 113-39.

Gómez, Juan Gualberto. *Preparando la revolución*. La Habana: Secretaría de Educación, Dirección de Cultura, 1936.

Gómez, Valentín. "El Teatro y el poder público." *El Imparcial*, 11 July 1898.

Gómez de Avellaneda, Gertrudis. *Sab*. Prologue and notes by Mary Cruz. Havana: Editorial Arte y Literatura, 1976.

González, José Luis. *El país de cuatro pisos y otros ensayos*. Princeton: M. Wiener Publishing, 1993.

_____. *Puerto Rico: The Four Storeyed Country*. Maplewood, N.J.: Waterfront Press, 1990.

González Calleja, Eduardo. "Las 'tormentas del 98': viejas y nuevas formas de conflictividad en el cambio de siglo." *Revista de Occidente* (March 1998): 90-111.

González Velilla, María del Carmen, and María Berta Pacios González-Loureiro. "La crisis de Melilla de 1893-1894." In *Antes del "Desastre": orígenes y antecedentes de la crisis del 98*, edited by Juan Pablo Fusi and Antonio Niño, 323-36. Madrid: Universidad Complutense de Madrid, 1996.

Graff, Harvey J. *The Legacies of Literacy: Continuities and Contradictions in Western Culture and Society*. Bloomington: Indiana University Press, 1987.

Gráfica política del 98: Catálogo de la Exposición. Cáceres: Centro Extremeño de Estudios y Cooperación con Iberoamérica. [Cexeci], 1998.

Green, Nathan C. *Story of Spain and Cuba.* Baltimore: International News and Book, 1896.

Groizard, Pedro. *Hojas de mi cartera: episodios de la guerra de Filipinas.* Manila: Establecimiento Tipo-litográfico de *Diario de Manila,* 1897.

Guimerá, Ángel. *El Padre Juanico.* Madrid: R. Velasco, 1898.

Gutiérrez Gamero, Emilio. *Mis primeros ochenta años.* Madrid: Aguilar, 1962.

Gutiérrez Rodríguez, María Teresa. "Antecedentes de la independencia de Filipinas: la influencia de la Masonería y de los Estados Unidos." In *Antes del "Desastre": orígenes y antecedentes de la crisis del 98,* edited by Juan Pablo Fusi and Antonio Niño, 235–42. Madrid: Universidad Complutense de Madrid, 1996.

Haro Tecglen, Eduardo. "Internacionalización de la zarzuela." *El País* (international edition), 17 October 1985.

Hause, Steven C. "The Evolution of Social History." *French Historical Studies* 19 (1996): 1191-214.

Helg, Aline. "Independent Cuba: A Comparative Perspective." *Ethnohistory* 44, no. 1 (winter 1997): 59-74.

_____.*Our Rightful Share: The Afro-Cuban Struggle for Equality, 1886-1912.* Chapel Hill: University of North Carolina Press, 1995.

Heras, Dionisio de las. *Madrid en la escena: crítica teatral.* Madrid: Samper, 1897.

Hernández, Thomas C. "The Emergence of Modern Drama in the Philippines (1898-1912) and Its Social, Political, Cultural, Dramatic, and Theatrical Background." Ph.D. diss., University of Hawaii, 1975.

Hernández González, Gabriel (Javier de Montillana). *Bretón.* Salamanca: Talleres Gráficos Núñez, 1952.

Hernández Sandoica, Elena, and María Fernanda Mancebo. "Higiene y sociedad en la guerra de Cuba (1895-1898): notas sobre soldados y proletarios." *Estudios de Historia Social* 5-6 (1978): 361-84.

Horrego Estuch, Leopoldo. *Juan Gualberto Gómez: un gran inconforme.* 2d ed. Havana: La Milagrosa, 1954.

Ileto, Reynaldo Clemeña. *Pasyon and Revolution: Popular Movements in the Philippines, 1840-1910.* Quezón City: Ateneo de Manila Press, 1980.

_____. "Rizal and the Underside of Philippine History." In *Moral Order and the Question of Change: Essays on Southeast Asian Thought,* edited by

David Wyatt and Alexander Woodside, 274-337. New Haven: Yale University Southeast Asia Program Series, 1982.

_____. "Tagalog Poetry and the Perception of the Past in the War against Spain." In *Perceptions of the Past in Southeast Asia*, edited by David Marr and Anthony Reid. Singapore: Heinemann, 1979.

Instituto de Literatura y Lingüística de la Academia de Ciencias de Cuba. *Perfil histórico de las letras cubanas desde los orígenes hasta 1898*. Havana: Letras Cubanas, 1983.

Insúa, Waldo. *Finis: últimos días de España en Cuba*. Madrid: Romero, 1901.

Iznaga, Diana. *Presencia del testimonio en la literatura sobre las guerras por la independencia nacional, 1868-1898*. La Habana: Editorial Letras Cubanas, 1989.

Izquierdo, Raúl. *La reconcentración 1896-1897*. Havana: Ediciones Verde Olivo, 1997.

Jackson, Donald Dale. "Mutiny on the Amistad." *Smithsonian* (December 1997): 115-24.

JanMohamed, Abdul R. "The Economy of Manichean Allegory: The Function of Racial Difference in Colonialist Literature." *Critical Inquiry* 12 (1985): 59-87.

Jaques y Aguado, Federico, and Manuel Fernández Caballero. *Cuba Libre*. Madrid: Imprenta de José Rodríguez, 1887.

Jardí, Enric. *Nonell*. New York: Tudor, nd.

Jiménez Pastrana, Juan. *Los chinos en la lucha por la liberación cubana (1847-1930)*. Havana: Instituto de Historia, 1963.

José, Vivencio R. *Antonio Luna*. Manila: Tahanen, 1995.

Kenmogne, Jean. "Una escritora asturiana en América: Eva Canel." *Cuadernos-Hispanoamericanos* 546 (1995): 45-61.

Kinsbruner, Jay. *Not of Pure Blood: The Free People of Color and Racial Prejudice in 19th-Century Puerto Rico*. Durham, N.C.: Duke University Press, 1996.

Kohut, Thomas A. *Wilhelm II and the Germans: A Study in Leadership*. New York: Oxford University Press, 1991.

Kutzinski, Vera. *Sugar's Secrets: Race and the Erotics of Cuban Nationalism*. Charlottesville: University Press of Virginia, 1993.

Labra, Rafael M. de. *La brutalidad de los negros*. 1st ed. 1876. Havana: n.p., 1950.

Lannon, Frances. *Privilege, Persecution, and Prophecy: The Catholic Church in Spain, 1875-1975*. Oxford: Clarendon Press, 1987.

Lapena-Bonifacio, Amelia. *The "Seditious" Tagalog Playwrights: Early American Occupation.* Manila: Zarzuela Foundation of the Philippines, 1972.

Lapoulide, Juan. "Por la guerra paz." *La Ilustración Española y Americana* (30 March 1898): 194.

Leal, Rine. *Breve historia del teatro cubano.* Havana: Editorial Letras Cubanas, 1980.

_____. ed. *Teatro/Ignacio Sarachaga.* Havana: Editorial Letras Cubanas, 1990.

Legarda, Benito, Jr. "Philippine Participation in the St. Louis Exposition of 1904." *Kinaadman* 19 (1997): 276-79.

Leguineche, Manuel. *Yo te diré . . . La verdadera historia de los últimos de Filipinas.* Madrid: El País-Ailar, 1998.

Leonard, Thomas C. "The Uncensored War." *Culturefront* (spring 1998): 59-62.

Lissorgues, Yvan. "España ante la guerra colonial de 1895 a 1898: Leopoldo Alas (Clarín), periodista, y el problema cubano." In *Cuba: les étapes d'une libération. Hommage à Juan Marinello et Noël Salomon. Actes du Colloque International des 22, 23 et 24 Novembre 1978,* 47-76. Toulouse: University of Toulouse-Le Mirail, Centre d'Études Cubaines, 1979.

Litvak, Lily. *Musa libertaria: arte, literatura y vida cultural del anarquismo español (1880-1913).* Barcelona: Antoni Bosch, 1981.

_____. "Naturalismo y teatro social en Cataluña." *Comparative Literature Studies* 5 (1968): 279-302.

López Gómez, Jesús. *Cuba.* Madrid: R. Velasco, 1896.

López Jaena, Graciano. "Discurso pronunciado por D. Graciano López Jaena el 25 de febrero de 1889 en el Ateneo Barcelonés." *La Solidaridad* 1 (1889): 28-48.

M. Valls, J. *Filipinas por España.* Barcelona: Imprenta de Pujol y Compañía, 1897.

Macías Picavea, Ricardo. *El problema nacional.* Introduction by Antonio Ramos Gascón. Madrid: Biblioteca Nueva, 1997.

Maeztú, Ramiro de. *Artículos desconocidos, 1897-1904.* Edited by E. Inman Fox. Madrid: Castalia, 1977.

Mainer, Juan Carlos. "1998 [sic] en la literatura: las huellas españolas del desastre." *Casa de las Américas* 211 (April-June 1998): 46-55.

Maluquer de Motes, Jordi. *Nación e inmigración: los españoles en Cuba (ss. XIX y XX).* Madrid: Ediciones Jucar, 1992.

Mar-Molinero, Claire, and Angel Smith, eds. *Nationalism and the Nation in the Iberian Peninsula: Competing and Conflicting Identities.* Oxford: Berg, 1997.

Marta y María o la muerte de Maceo. Barcelona: Imprenta de Francisco J. Altés, 1898.

Martí Gilabert, Francisco. *Política religiosa de la Restauración 1875-1931.* Madrid: Rialp, 1991.

Martínez, Rafael, and Thomas M. Barker, eds. *Armed Forces and Society in Spain Past and Present.* Boulder: Columbia University Press, 1988.

Martínez-Echazabal, Lourdes. *Para una semiótica de la mulatez.* Madrid: Porrúa, 1990.

Martínez Moreno, Pascual. *Un alcalde en la manigua.* Murcia: El Magisterio, 1898.

Martínez Sanz, Isidro. *Familia y Patria.* 2d. ed. Madrid: Imprenta de Evaristo Odriózola, 1896.

Matibag, Eugenio. *Afro-Cuban Religious Experience: Cultural Reflections in Writing.* Gainsville: University Press of Florida, 1996.

Membrez, Nancy, J. "Eduardo Navarro Gonzalvo and the *revista política.*" *Letras Peninsulares* 1, no. 3 (1988): 321-30.

_____. "The 'Teatro por Hora': History, Dynamics and Comprehensive Bibliography of a Madrid Industry, 1867-1922 ('Género Chico' 'Género Ínfimo' and Early Cinema)." Ph.D. diss., University of Santa Barbara, 1987.

_____. "Yanquis, filibusteros y patriotas: prensa y teatro en la España del 98." *Cincinnati Romance Review* 10 (1991): 123-45.

Méndez Saavedra, Manuel. *1898. La guerra hispanoamericana en caricaturas/The Spanish-American War in Cartoons.* San Juan, P.R.: La Comisión Puertorriqueña para la Celebración del Quinto Centenario del Descubrimiento de América y Puerto Rico, 1992.

Millán, Pascual. *¡Quince bajas!* Madrid: Imprenta de El Enano, 1899.

Miller, Tom. "Remember the *Maine.*" *Smithsonian* (February 1998): 46-57.

Millet, Gabriel, Manuel Ruiz de Quevedo, and Agustín Sardá. *La raza de color de Cuba.* Madrid: Fortanet, 1894.

Monleón, José. *El teatro del 98 frente a la sociedad española.* Madrid: Cátedra, 1975.

Montero y Vidal, José. *Cuentos filipinos.* 2d ed. Madrid: Tipografía del Asilo de Huérfanos del Sagrado Corazón de Jesús, 1883.

Morayta y Sagrario, M. *La libertad de la cátedra.* Madrid: Editorial Español-Americana, [1911].

_____. "Discurso leído en la Universidad Central en la solemne inauguración del curso académico 1884-1884." In *La Reforma Burocrática.* Madrid: Tipografía de Diego Pacheco, 1884.

Moreno de la Tejera, Vicente. *Los dramas de la guerra*. Madrid: Celestino Apaolaza, 1897.

Morón Arroyo, Ciriaco. *El alma de España: cien años de inseguridad*. Oviedo: Nobel, 1996.

Múñiz de Quevedo, José. "Piña americana." *El Imparcial*, 29 March 1897.

Muñoz, Matilde. *Historia de la zarzuela y el género chico*. Madrid: Editorial Tesoro, 1946.

Navarro Gonzalvo, Eduardo. *Aún hay patria, Veremundo*. Madrid: R. Velasco, 1898.

Noreña, María Teresa. "La prensa obrera madrileña ante la crisis del 98." In *El siglo XIX en España: doce estudios*, 571–611. Barcelona: Planeta, 1974.

Núñez de Matute, Manuel. *¡Sacrificios heroicos!* Madrid: Administración Lírico-Dramática, 1897.

Núñez Florencio, Rafael. *Militarismo y antimilitarismo en España (1888-1906)*. Madrid: Consejo Superior de Investigaciones Científicas, 1990.

_____. "Las raíces de la Ley de Jurisdicciones: los conflictos de competencia entre los tribunales civiles y militares en los años 90." In *Antes del "Desastre": orígenes y antecedentes de la crisis del 98*, 185-98. Madrid: Universidad Complutense de Madrid, 1996.

O'Connor, D. J. *Crime at El Escorial: The 1892 Child Murder, the Press, and the Jury*. San Francisco: International Scholars Press, 1995.

Ossorio y Gallardo, Ángel. "Crónica de Tribunales." *Revista de los Tribunales y de Legislación Universal* 30 (8 February 1896): 88-90; (29 August 1896): 551; (10 October 1896): 656.

Otero Mariñas, Luis. *La literatura filipina en castellano*. Madrid: Editora Nacional, 1974.

Palacio Valdés, Armando. *La literatura en 1881*. Madrid: Alfredo de Carlos Hierro, 1882.

Pardo Bazán, Emilia. "Poema humilde." *El Socialista*, 15 October 1897.

Paterno, Pedro Alexandro Molo Agustín. *La antigua civilización tagalog (Apuntes)*. Madrid, 1887.

Payne, Stanley. *Los militares y la política en la España contemporánea*. Paris: Rueda Ibérico, 1968.

Peña y Goñi, Antonio. *España desde la ópera a la zarzuela*. Madrid: Alianza, 1967.

Pérez, Ángel. *Igorrotes: estudio geográfico y etnográfico*. Manila: Imprenta de *El Mercantil*, 1902.

Pérez, Louis A., Jr. *Cuba between Empires 1878-1902*. Pittsburgh: University of Pittsburgh Press, 1982.

_____. "The Meaning of the *Maine*: Causation and the Historiography of the Spanish-American War." *Pacific Historical Review* 58 (1989): 293-322.

_____. *The War of 1898. The United States and Cuba in History and Historiography.* Chapel Hill: University of North Carolina Press, 1998.

The Philippines Reader: A History of Colonialism, Neocolonialism, Dictatorship, and Resistances. Boston: South End Press, 1987.

Pico, Fernando. *Historia general de Puerto Rico.* Río Piedras: Ediciones Huracán, 1990.

Pieterse, Jan Nederveen. *White on Black: Images of Africa and Blacks in Western Popular Culture.* New Haven: Yale University Press, 1992.

Pirala, Antonio. *Anales de la Guerra de Cuba.* 3 vols. Madrid: F. González Rojas, 1895-1898.

Pi y Margall, Francisco. *Cuba y Pi y Margall.* Havana: Editorial Lex, 1947.

_____. *Las luchas de nuestros días.* Madrid: El Progreso, 1890.

Pluvier, Jan M. *Historical Atlas of South-East Asia.* Leiden: E. J. Brill, 1995.

Poblet, Josep María. *Vida y obra literaria de Santiago Rusiñol.* Barcelona: Bruguera, 1966.

Rafael, Vicente L. *Contracting Colonialism: Translation and Christian Conversion in Tagalog Society Under Early Spanish Rule.* Durham: Duke University Press, 1993.

_____. "Nationalism, Imagery and the Filipino Intelligentsia of the Nineteenth Century." *Critical Inquiry* 16 (spring 1990): 591-611.

Ramón y Cajal, Santiago. *Obras literarias completas.* Madrid: Aguilar, 1961.

Ramos Carrión, Miguel. "El prójimo negro." *El Imparcial,* 4 January 1897).

Reher, David S. *Perspectives on the Family in Spain, Past and Present.* Oxford: Oxford University Press, 1997.

Retana y Gamboa, Wenceslao Emilio. *Apuntes para la historia (Añiterías y solidaridades).* Madrid: Manuel Minuesa de los Ríos, 1890.

_____. *Vida y escritos del Dr. Rizal.* Madrid: Librería General de Victoriano Suárez, 1907.

Reverter Delmas, Emilio. *Filipinas por España: narración episódica de la rebelión en el Archipiélago Filipino.* Vol. 2 Barcelona: Centro Editorial de Alberto Martín, 1897.

La revolución cubana y la raza de color (Apuntes y datos), por un cubano sin odios. Key West: Imprenta *La Propaganda,* 1895. (Available at www.ucm.es/info/cecal/encuentr/areas/historia/3h)

Ría-Baja, Carlos. *El desastre filipino: memorias de un prisionero.* Barcelona: Tipografía la Académica de Serra Hermanos y Russell, 1899.

Richardson, John. *A Life of Picasso*. Vol. 1. 1881-1906. New York: Random House, 1991.

Riggs, Arthur Stanley. *The Filipino Drama, 1905/Arthur Stanley Riggs*. Introduction by Doreen G. Fernández. Preface by Jaime C. Laya. Manila: Ministry of Human Settlements, Intramuros Administration, 1981.

Rizal, José. *El filibusterismo*. Manila: Instituto Nacional de Historia, 1990.

_____. *A Letter to the Young Women of Malolos*. (Tagalog, Spanish, and English). Manila: Bureau of Printing, 1932.

_____. *Noli me tangere*. Manila: Instituto Nacional de Historia, 1978.

_____. *Rizal's Correspondence with Fellow Reformists*. Vol. 3, book 3. Manila: National Heroes Commission, 1963.

Robles Múñoz, Cristóbal. "1898: la batalla por la paz: la mediación de León XIII entre España y Estados Unidos." *Revista de Indias* 46, no. 177 (1986): 247-89.

Rodríguez, Agustín R. "El conflicto de Melilla en 1893." *Hispania* (Madrid) 49, no. 171 (1989): 235-66.

Robreño, Eduardo. *Historia del teatro popular cubano*. Havana: Oficina del Historiador de la Ciudad, 1961.

Rodríguez de Ureta, Antonia. *Pacita, o la virtuosa filipina: novela recreativa de costumbres orientales*. 1st ed. Barcelona: Imprenta de J. Jepús, 1885; Barcelona: Herederos de la Viuda Pla, 1892.

Routier, Gaston. *L'Espagne en 1897*. Paris: Librairie H. Le Soudier, 1897.

Rudat, Eva M. Kahiluoto. "The View from Spain: Rococo Finesse and Esprit Versus Plebeian Manners." In *French Women and the Age of Enlightenment*, edited by Samia I. Spencer, 395-406. Bloomington: Indiana University Press, 1984.

Ruiz, José María, and Francisco Sánchez. *Memoria complementaria de la sección 2a del programa. Pobladores aborígenes, razas existentes y sus variedades. Religión, usos y costumbres de los habitantes de Filipinas*. Manila: Imprenta del Colegio de Santo Tomás, 1887.

Russinyol, Santiago. *L'Heroe*. In *Obres Completes*. Vol. 1. Prologue by Carles Soldevila. Barcelona: Editorial Selecta, 1903, 1209-48.

Salaün, Serge. "El 'Género Chico' o los mecanismos de un pacto cultural." In *El teatro menor en España a partir del siglo XVI*, 251-61. Madrid: Consejo Superior de Investigaciones Científicas, 1983.

Salazar, Adolfo. *La música de España: desde el siglo XVI a Manuel de Falla*. Madrid: Espasa Calpe, 1953.

Sales de Bohigas, Nuria. *Sobre esclavos, reclutas y mercaderes de quintos.* Barcelona: Ariel, 1974.

———. "Some Opinions on Exemptions from Military Service in Nineteenth-Century Europe." *Comparative Studies in Society and History* 10 (1968): 261-89.

Sánchez Albornoz, Nicolás, ed. *Españoles hacia América: la emigración en masa, 1830-1930.* Madrid: Alianza, 1995.

Sánchez Ferré, Pere. "La masonería española y el conflicto colonial filipino." In *La masonería en la España del siglo XIX.* Vol. 2, edited by J. A. Ferrer Benimeli, 481-96. Valladolid: Consejería de Educación y Cultura, 1987.

Sarachaga, Ignacio. *Teatro/Ignacio Sarachaga.* Selection and prologue by Rine Leal. Havana: Editorial Letras Cubanas, [1990].

Sardá y Salvany, Félix. *El liberalismo es pecado.* 3d ed. Barcelona: Librería y Tipografía Católica, 1885.

Schmidt-Nowara, Christopher. "The Problem of Slavery in the Age of Capital: Abolitionism, Liberalism, and Counter-hegemony in Spain, Cuba, and Puerto Rico, 1833-1886." Ph.D. diss., University of Michigan, 1995.

———. " 'Spanish' Cuba: Race and Class in Spanish and Cuban Antislavery Ideology, 1861-1868." *Cuban Studies* 25 (1995): 101-22.

Scott, Rebecca. "Race, Labor and Citizenship in Cuba: A View from the Sugar District of Cienfuegos." *HAHR* 78, no. 4 (1998): 687-728.

Scott, William Henry. "The Igorots Who Went to Madrid." In *History on the Cordillera: Collected Writings on Mountain Province History,* 12-13. Baguio City: Baguio Printing and Publishing, 1975.

Scribner, Bob. "Is a History of Popular Culture Possible?" *History of European Ideas* 10 (1989): 175-91.

Serrano, Carlos. *Final del Imperio: España 1895-1898.* Madrid: Siglo XXI, 1984.

———. "Notas sobre teatro obrero a finales del siglo XIX." In *El teatro menor en España a partir del siglo XVI,* 263-77. Madrid: Consejo Superior de Investigaciones Superiores, 1983.

———. "Prófugos y desertores en la guerra de Cuba." *Estudios de Historia Social* 22-23 (1982): 253-78.

———. *Le Tour du Peuple: Crise nationale, mouvements populaires et populisme en Espagne (1890-1910).* Madrid: Casa de Velázquez, 1987.

Simón Palmer, María del Carmen. "Biografía de Eva Canel (1857-1932)." In *Estudios sobre escritoras hispánicas en honor a Georgina Sabat-Rivers,* 294-304. Madrid: Castalia, 1992.

Smith, John David. "The Revised Versions." *Times Literary Supplement*, 12 December 1997, 12.

Sollors, Werner. *Neither Black nor White yet Both: Thematic Explorations of Interracial Literature*. Oxford: Oxford University Press, 1997.

Soriano, Rafaelita Hilario, ed. *Women in the Philippine Revolution*. Quezon City: Printon Press, 1995.

Stoner, Lynn K. *From the House to the Streets: The Cuban Woman's Movement for Legal Reform, 1898-1940*. Durham, N.C.: Duke University Press, 1991.

Suárez Díaz, Ada. *El antillano: biografía del Dr. Ramón Emeterio Betances, 1827-1898*. 2d ed. San Juan, P.R.: Centro de Estudios Avanzados de Puerto Rico y el Caribe, Revista Caribe, 1988.

Suppan, Steven. "Managing Culture: *Manolo* and the Majo's Good Taste." In *The Institutionalization of Literature in Spain*, edited by Wlad Godzich and Nicholas Spaddacini, 125-68. Minneapolis: The Prisma Institute, 1987.

Taga-Ilog. "Impresiones madrileñas de un filipino." *La Solidaridad* 1 (1889): 683-84.

Thomas, Hugh. *Cuba: The Pursuit of Freedom*. New York: Harper and Row, 1971.

———. "Remember the *Maine*?" *New York Review of Books*, 23 April 1998, 10-12.

———. *The Slave Trade: The History of the Atlantic Slave Trade, 1440-1870*. New York: Macmillan, 1997.

Thompson, Lawrence S. *A Bibliography of Spanish Plays on Microcards*. Hamden, Conn.: Shoestring Press, 1968.

Tolentino, Roland B. "Nation, Nationalisms, and 'Los últimos de Filipinas': An Imperialist Desire for Colonialist Nostalgia." In *Refiguring Spain: Cinema/Media/Representation*, edited by Marsha Kinder, 133-53. Durham, N.C.: Duke University Press, 1997.

Toral, Juan y José. *El sitio de Manila: memorias de un voluntario*. Madrid: Editora Nacional, 1942.

Trigo, Felipe. *La campaña filipina (Impresiones de un soldado)*. Vol. 1. *El General Blanco y la insurrección*. Madrid: Fernando Fe, 1897.

Tusell, Javier. *Antonio Maura: una biografía política*. Madrid: 1994.

Valera, Juan. "Sobre la primera representación de 'El Padre Juanico.' " *La Ilustración Española y Americana*, 22 March 1898, 174-75.

Vázquez, Óscar E. "Defining *Hispanidad*: Allegories, Geneologies and Cultural Politics in the Madrid Academy's Competition of 1893." *Art History* 20 (1997): 100-23.

Vilanova Riba, Mercedes, and Xavier Moreno Juliá. *Atlas de la evolución del analfabetismo en España de 1887 a 1981*. Madrid: Centro de Publicaciones del Ministerio de Educación y Ciencia, CIDE, 1992.

Villegas, Francisco F. "Desde la batería." *El Imparcial*, 27 December 1897.

Walls y Merino, D. M. *Relato de un viaje de España a Filipinas*. Madrid: Imprenta de los Hijos de M. G. Hernández, 1895.

Weyler y Nicolau, Valeriano. *Mi mando en Cuba*. Madrid: F. González Rojas, 1910-11.

Wickberg, Edgar. *The Chinese in Philippine Life, 1850-1898*. New Haven: Yale University Press, 1965.

Wilkerson, Marcus M. *Public Opinion and the Spanish-American War*. Baton Rouge: Louisiana State University Press, 1932.

Wisan, Joseph E. *The Cuban Crisis as Reflected in the New York Press (1895-1898)*. New York: Octagon Books, 1965.

Wolfe, Patrick. "History and Imperialism: A Century of Theory from Marx to Post-colonialism." *American Historical Review* 102 (1997): 388-420.

Wyatt, David, and Alexander Woodside, eds. *Moral Order and the Question of Change: Essays on Southeast Asian Thought*. New Haven: Yale University Southeast Asia Program Series, 1982.

Yrayzoz, Fiacro. *El Mantón de Manila*. Madrid: R. Velasco, 1898.

Yxart, José. *El arte escénico en España*. Vol. 1. Barcelona: La Vanguardia, 1894-1896.

Zurita, Marciano. *Historia del género chico*. Madrid: Prensa Popular, 1920.

INDEX